17.50
J

THE UPLAND SHOOTING LIFE

THE UPLAND

SHOOTING LIFE

George Bird Evans

ALFRED·A·KNOPF

NEW YORK / 1971

THIS IS A BORZOI BOOK
PUBLISHED BY ALFRED A. KNOPF, INC.

Copyright © 1964, 1967, 1968, 1969, 1970, 1971 by George Bird Evans
All rights reserved under International and Pan-American Copyright Conventions. Published in the United States by Alfred A. Knopf, Inc., New York, and simultaneously in Canada by Random House of Canada Limited, Toronto. Distributed by Random House, Inc., New York.

ISBN: 0–394–47295–0
Library of Congress Catalog Card Number: 72–161404

Acknowledgment is extended to the following for permission to reprint copyrighted material:

Dodd, Mead & Company, Inc.: Lines from "The Land God Forgot" and from "Law of the Yukon" from *The Collected Poems of Robert Service*.

E. P. Dutton & Co., Inc.: Excerpt from *Faraway and Long Ago*, by W. H. Hudson. Copyright 1918 by E. P. Dutton & Co., Inc. Renewal, 1946, by the Royal Society for the Protection of Birds.

The Golden Quill Press: Lines from "Old Game Dog in November" from *Poems Selected and New*, by Nancy Byrd Turner.

The Macmillan Company: Lines from "Reynard the Fox" and from "On Growing Old" from *Poems*, by John Masefield. Copyright 1919, 1920 by John Masefield, renewed 1947, 1948 by John Masefield.

Manufactured in the United States of America

ACKNOWLEDGMENTS

Portions of this book have appeared, or will appear, either as excerpts or in somewhat different form in the following publications: "Strange Ways of Grouse" and "Leaves of a Gunner's Diary" in the winter 1970 and summer 1970 issues of *The American Sportsman*; "Design for Setters," "Blackwater Paradise," "Scent Pointing Without Birds," "Test Your Hunting Know-How," "Scent and the Gun Dog," and "The Grouse and Woodcock Dog" in the December 1956, November 1964, April 1965, May 1967, February 1968, and July 1971 issues of *Field & Stream*; "Empty Shells," "The Christmas Grouse," "Daddy Miss Bird?," "Bird in Hand," "When You Inherit a Purdey," "Passing of a Pennsylvania Sportsman," "Twilight Astronaut," and "Man With a Gun" in the October 1960, November 1960, January 1961, December 1962, February 1963, March 1963, July 1967, March 1968, February 1969, April 1969, and July 1969 issues of *Pennsylvania Game News*; "The Shootingest Gentleman" in *Sports Afield*.

To Kay and Ruff and Bliss—

MORE WONDERFUL THAN I DREAMED

CONTENTS

PART ONE / *A Way of Life*

By an Evening's Fire	3
An Attitude Toward Game	7

PART TWO / *The Coverts*

The Uplands	13
Woodcock Coverts	15
Pheasant Country	18
Grouse Coverts I Have Known	23

PART THREE / *The Birds*

Woodcock Shooting	47
Grouse Shooting	73
Quail Shooting	135
Pheasant Shooting	144
Preserve Shooting	152

PART FOUR / *The Men Who Shoot*

Profiles	175
The Smell of Powder	194
Passing of a Sportsman	205

CONTENTS

PART FIVE / *The Dogs*

Gentlemen and Ladies in My Life	213
Scent and the Gun Dog	225
Education of a Grouse and Woodcock Dog	230

PART SIX / *Mixed Bag*

Shooting Flying	247
The Pleasures of a Shooting Diary	263
Bird and Bottle	270
A Gun to Remember	277
A Box of Shells	285

Index   *follows page* 301

ILLUSTRATIONS

Pen and ink drawings by George Evans.

Photographs (following page 112) by Jack Gates and Kay and George Evans.

Early symptoms. The author with his first setter.

Perfect beltons. Shadows and Feathers flanked by their parents Ruff and Wilda.

Old Hemlock Blue on his thirteenth birthday with his son Ruff.

A full hearth that has seen Christmases since 1782.

Dixie, second from right, and her brothers when life was very new.

Postprandial. Dixie cleans the kettle.

The same litter at nine weeks.

Bliss scent-points the wing hidden in typical cover situations.

Dixie holding steady as bobwhite hen runs out from point.

Dixie pointing training quail at Old Hemlock.

A triple point on pheasants; young Shadows being taught to back-point.

Bliss playing the indoors retrieving game.

A mock-up grouse made with wings and tail fan and wrapped with heavy wire.

Dr. Charles C. Norris in 1930, with Lad and Sadie.

Dr. Norris at eighty, with Nellie and Charm at Fairhill.

Illustrations

An old-time Pennsylvania grouse hunter, Cliff Springer, with his Parker.

A good overhead chance in an old clearing.

Shadows's points were always a production.

With his own dog the gunner can make pheasant preserve shooting as sporting as he cares to.

A nice selection of upland bird guns.

Bliss loved the Purdey . . .

. . . for as long as she lived.

Bliss proved what can be achieved by line breeding.

Mother and daughter, two snow beltons like lightly ticked gyrfalcons.

A finished retriever delivers the bird from a sitting position.

Grouse and woodcock provide the loveliest mixed shooting and dog work.

Difference in marking on grouse breast and throat as sex determination.

A stylish point on 'cock.

A gun diary makes those precious moments last.

Upland shooting is at its highest level when the bird-dog-gun triad is balanced by a gun and a dog worthy of the bird.

PART ONE

A Way of Life

❦ / THERE IS SOMETHING IN THE AUTUMN

THAT IS NATIVE TO MY BLOOD—

—BLISS CARMAN, *A Vagabond Song*

By an Evening's Fire

TONIGHT LIFE IS AS I WOULD HAVE IT. There is a Hunter's Moon, and a grouse and a brace of woodcock hang on the hewn-log wall of the porch in the sherry smell of leaves. Here on the sofa in front of the fire Briar lies the way Bliss used to lie with her long head in my lap, and I feel his staggered heartbeat still pounding from the day's exertion. On the other sofa Dixie twitches in her dreams beside Kay, and the fire is reflected in the row of photographs of Old Hemlock setters on the knotty pine behind them. My lids droop and embers become grapevines etched against sky where that last grouse went out high from Briar's point. This is the mellow moment when I lick the wounds of my day's misses, which don't seem nearly so important now.

If I could ask for anything beyond this, it would be to have those other setters here instead of sleeping under the hemlocks. I have them in memories of hundreds of days together with the gun and, with each, ordeals that hover like ghosts at my shoulder. Orange belton Ruff, who has been gone since '62; his sire Blue, ten years before; orange belton Feathers since '61; blue Shadows since '67; and Bliss so recently gone that it is hard to believe. But I am fortunate, for they are in the living blood of Dixie and, now, fifth-generation Briar. And I have Kay, who loves every nuance of this upland life as I do.

When asked what he did, a character in a Scott Fitzgerald novel replied, "I shoot." It seemed an inane way to sum up a life until I realized that I might say the same thing about myself. In its richest sense, gunning involves the entire year, for there is that contradiction in a gunner's character by which the birds take on as much significance as the actual shooting; and there is the dog work.

When starting a new Old Hemlock puppy, we raise the litter,

one of the most rewarding experiences I know. In summer there is yard training; when asters bloom in September we work all the dogs on our training quail; and while grouse coverts are still too thick we travel to the woodcock coverts to work on native 'cock. The peak of intensity begins in mid-October with woodcock shooting through November, grouse shooting from mid-October through February, and in between and as late as March, pheasant shooting, wild and on preserves. There are friends to share this, here and on trips. But mostly it is just Kay with her movie camera and I with my gun and the setters, saturating ourselves with experiences that feed the soul. There is postseason dog work on grouse and training quail and on spring woodcock when they come north. Writing about it gets crowded in somewhere, usually in bad weather and in spring and summer, with the setters being horribly patient, lying near me with chins on paws.

Why have so many men loved shooting and guns and dogs? Fascination with shooting has been a part of every generation of men since gunpowder. I suspect it stirred in me on those early mornings when I was got out of my crib to watch my father leave for a day's shooting, and in the evenings on his return, seeing and touching the quail he brought home. There was a setter named Ted whose dark, soft eyes peered into mine and whose pink tongue washed my hands. It is things like these that mark us as shooting men years before we are men. If I had grown to maturity without ever having killed a bird I probably could not have brought myself to do it. But how much poorer I would have been.

The nonshooter can't know bobwhites or woodcock or pheasants like the man who shoots. And who can comprehend a grouse who knows it only as the "large red-brown or gray-brown chicken-like bird" of field guides, who has never in recurrent dreams tried to swing a muzzle past a sailing grouse only to tug helplessly on a flabby trigger that won't discharge the gun?

There is tradition behind gunning, enriched by a line from a poem, an old shooting print, a painting. There is excitement in discovery, as on that rainy afternoon in the little town of Davis, West Virginia, when I was shown a life-size portrait of Victor Okaw, son of Lady's Count Gladstone, painted by Edmund Osthaus, and on a table beneath it a copy of *Eastern Upland Shooting* by my friend Dr. Charles Norris. Gunning and dogs and the pursuit of game birds link us with the past. The lines of an old gun have character that can't be approached by the automatic plumbing that passes for a gun today. Names like Parker and Fox and Ithaca evoke images of locks engraved with old-fashioned setters and pointers that look as dated as the birds. We cherish blood in our gun dogs going back beyond what many of us know of our own. And we cling to old-time hunters and what they can tell us of another age; it seems that to have hunted in those days would have been ecstasy.

There has always been this looking back—perhaps this is what seduces us—together with a tendency to worry. George Bird Grinnell (I keep hoping to learn that we are related) expressed doubts about the future of our native game birds in his *American Game Bird Shooting* in 1910 at a time when I have been told game was abundant. He had reason to worry, as I worry when I consider the wildfire spread of population and what it does to coverts.

I like to picture what grouse shooting was like here in the Alleghenies on our 241 acres when this house was hewn from white oaks in 1782. The spring-house oak was only about two hundred years old then and there were chestnut trees everywhere, and virgin woods. There were many more turkeys and probably fewer grouse. If I had walked in the lane with a dog and flintlock fowling piece and talked grouse shooting to Samuel Robinet, whose name is on the parchment deed signed by Beverley Randolph, Governor of Virginia, I suspect he would have muttered, "Never had the time," much as mountain farmers respond today. A yellowed photograph of a gunner in a bowler standing in the dooryard with a double hammer gun suggests that some of my predecessors at Old Hemlock savored the sporting life, and there must have been game turning golden brown in this fireplace, which would roast a venison whole.

I have kept a gun diary since 1932 and when I'm not doing something with dogs and birds and guns I seem to be talking or writing about them. When Angus Cameron suggested that I do a book on the pleasures of the upland shooting life I was delighted, for it is a book I have always wanted to write. There is camaraderie between the man who writes a book on shooting and the man who reads it. You have been the same places and shared the same adrenalin. You find pleasure in discovering that you agree on certain things, stimulation in disagreement on others. The satisfaction in the experiences of men who shoot is as much in learning as in having learned. I think a book on shooting could be like a conversation between us after a day's gunning, with the dogs sprawled on the hearth. I'd like to hear about that dog you coaxed through gun-shyness; what you did about that gun that didn't fit you. Most of all I'd like to hear about your grouse shooting and where you found them and what they were eating and how they acted; about your days in the woodcock coverts and what you've learned about taking those quick shots in alders; how you handle pheasants; and if you shoot bobwhites, where you go for them. And the men you know who shoot.

There are a given number of days in a lifetime and here at Old Hemlock we try to see that no one of them passes unused. We live a sort of civilized eighteenth-century country life in which there are still values, none of them based on dollars, a life in which the word "spent" means shells. In *Far Away and Long Ago*, W. H. Hudson defined just what, as a young boy in South America, he asked of life: "I want only to keep what I have; to rise each morning and look out on the sky and the grassy dew-wet earth from day to day, from year to year.... to feel the same old sweet surprise and delight...."

Poor Hudson was writing of a life that was fifty years gone. My Far Away and Long Ago is Here and Now.

An Attitude Toward Game

IF I COULD SHOOT A GAME BIRD and still not hurt it, the way I can take a trout on a fly and release it, I doubt if I would kill another one. This is a strange statement coming from a man whose life is dedicated to shooting and gun dogs. For me, there is almost no moment more sublime than when I pull the trigger and see a grouse fall. Yet, as the bird is retrieved I feel a sense of remorse for taking a courageous life. About the time I passed fifty I noticed this conflict becoming more pronounced.

I have considered a miniature camera mounted on my gun in a beavertail fore-end, triggered through the ejector-cocking mechanism to shoot film instead of shells. There would be crosshairs to indicate the center of the pattern and each exposure could determine if the "shot" would have been a hit or miss, with variables to predict my normal swing. I've never got the design on the drawing board but I tell myself I could be content with this substitute for killing.

Kay points out that shooting is a part of me, and that the dogs deserve to have birds shot over them and I know she's right. Giving up shooting would blank out an enormous phase of my existence. Driving through mountains, I evaluate each ridge and every glade as bird cover, and while I admire a woods for its beauty, without considering if it would be a lovely place to shoot, some of the old pleasure would be gone. I could substitute skeet or a clay-target "quail walk" for birds; Kay and I could take the setters out during the hunting season and, without shooting, work them as we do now in out-of-season months—perhaps two times a week. But, when I gun, I'm in the woods every day the weather isn't impossible. We might intend to, but I know we wouldn't seek out those far places to explore the way we do now throughout the shooting seasons. Nor would I push myself to that glorious state of exhaustion, goaded by the need for the emotional climax when a float of feathers settles like the sound of the shot and my dog delivers my bird for me to hold and admire and sniff the dry-feather scent.

How then, can you love a bird and kill it and still feel decent? I think the answer is, to be worthy of your game. Which boils down to a gentleman's agreement between you and the bird, never forgetting that it is the bird that has everything to lose. It consists of things you feel and do, not because someone is looking or because the law says you may or must not, but because you feel that this is the honorable way to do it.

Each man has to decide for himself what his attitude toward game will be. Too frequently this attitude is shaped by environment and conditioning. Of the millions of men who hunt, most of them start with a heritage from ancestors for whom hunting meant meat. Along the line some of these ancestors changed from butchering to sport; some never did. As individuals we progress from a mixed-bag novice to the single-purposed gunner—our first big step toward becoming a sportsman. But, with experience, the specialist in whatever field—upland bird shooting, deer or turkey hunting—tends to become expert, and the expert can be deadly. At a certain level, the measure of a sportsman is the amount of game he can take and stay within the law. The man who ceases to develop beyond this stage is juvenile, no matter what his age.

In states where I shoot I know of no law, and there should be one, that prohibits shooting a game bird that is not flying. With the exception of turkeys, to take a bird in this manner is murder. A child could do it with a rifle. Archers take the position that because they handicap themselves with a bow and arrow they are being sporting to shoot at anything, no matter how easy a mark. A game-management student told me he had shot one grouse with a bow. I was partially prepared for what was coming but I congratulated him, expressing amazement that he could hit a bird flying. "It wasn't flying," he said. "I came to where it had dived into a snowdrift. I held about a foot ahead of the depression and *phttt—*" he made a gesture of releasing the arrow. By this time his story had gone so flat he didn't finish. I'd like to think he wouldn't kill another grouse in its sleep.

If I seem critical of others I am equally critical of myself. I once shot a grouse running on the ground. I was young, hunting with two other fellows in their teens and we were using my father's setter. I

An Attitude Toward Game

heard several grouse flush from a grapevine but the only one I saw was running out the far side for the takeoff and it seemed terribly important for me to shoot it. When I think about it I still feel unclean.

Too often, it appears necessary to kill game to show that you found it and had the skill to shoot it. A hunter in my home town used to walk up and down Main Street with grouse hanging from his belt.

One minus aspect of shooting is that idiot's delight, the Limit Syndrome: "Everyone had his limit except Bill, who had only one bird to go to fill out." This places shooting on the level of a man digging potatoes with a bag of given size, which he feels compelled to fill before he stops. If the law says he may shoot four birds in a day, or five, the potato digger will keep at it as long as birds fly up, with no thought process of his own.

With all my sympathy for and interest in wildlife conservation, I sometimes feel I am floating in an alien medium when I read or listen to discussions on that subject. I have had game biologists tell me that the only problem with game-bird populations is that hunters don't harvest enough. There is something wrong with that statement, chiefly because it asks nothing of anyone, which may be why it is popular. The term "harvest" is unsound until you have learned to grow a crop.

The Indian paid his game the tribute of respect and took care that it was not killed wastefully. After killing a deer or bear he sat down and smoked a pipe beside the dead animal, making a speech of apology and gratitude. Like the Indian who ate the heart of the bear to gain some of its courage, any hunter should absorb a little of the dignity of the hunted. I suppose the Indians had their share of game hogs but they happened to be superstitious. I wish modern game gluttons were naïve enough to fear retribution from forest gods. A member described one Pennsylvania hunting camp in Potter County in the thirties: "We'd shot more grouse than we could eat and we only used the breasts, tearing off the legs with the entrails. Finally we brought in so many we just tossed them in a pile behind the cabin, where they rotted. That was a good year for grouse."

Walking along a dusty road while shooting pheasants on the Amwell Preserve in New Jersey, I looked up a draw and saw my host Dr. Charles Norris, then in his eighties, hunting toward me. It was unmercifully hot and dry—I remember the temperature hit eighty—and Dr. Norris didn't see me. I watched him and his pointer Nellie toddling in front, both of them in what could easily be their last season. It was the sort of day when you can't expect much even from preserve pheasants and a man forty years his junior might have given up or, if he stuck it out, might have sauntered along too indifferent to expect action where it probably wouldn't happen. Not Dr. Norris, and not Nellie. For all his years and the oppressive heat, he moved cautiously, the Purdey held alert for a flush, his gaze never relaxing. Nellie, in spite of age and plumpness, was searching every bit of cover with a narrow but conscientious scrutiny. I watched them as they crossed the opening, still unaware of me—a gallant pair who never had and never would take their game for granted. That, to me, is an admirable attitude toward game.

A part of showing respect for your game is in the way you speak of it. I dislike such phrases as "bust a grouse" and "clobber a pheasant." They suggest hostility between the gunner and his game and, like "knock down a double," should be used for clay targets, not game birds. And there is something lacking in the man who can accept a bird from his dog and stuff it into his game pocket without first smoothing the feathers and admiring it. A reporter once paid me the compliment of asking for my opinions on upland shooting for an article he was writing. When it appeared, it contained the statement that after talking to me about grouse and woodcock he came away with the feeling he had walked into church with his hat on.

If I seem to speak of each grouse and each woodcock and each pheasant as a special thing it is because I feel that way about the birds. If there is one way I could wish to influence the reader by the time he has closed this book it would be to give him a respect for the bird he pursues. The difference between mere killing and a glorious sport is the manner in which you do it—over thrilling dogs, in magnificent country and with a near-reverence for the game. If anyone can dig up something nice to say about me I hope it will be, "He loved bird shooting, but more than that, he loved the bird."

PART TWO

The Coverts

🌸 / THE LORDLY MOUNTAINS SOAR IN SCORN

AS STILL AS DEATH, AS STERN AS FATE.

THE LONELY SUNSETS FLAME AND DIE;

THE GIANT VALLEYS GULP THE NIGHT.

—ROBERT W. SERVICE, *The Land God Forgot*

The Uplands

WHEN I BEGAN BIRD SHOOTING in the 1920's I had the impression that grouse, quail, woodcock and wild turkeys were on the way out, like our native brook trout. Stories of quantities of game in the past convinced me I had been born too late. I realize now that in the twenties when I was doing my original worrying there was, in the upland coverts around me, an abundance of grouse and quail and woodcock if I had known where to go. Since that time, improved roads have opened up even those remote areas and the answer to *where to find them* has, by answering it, once more raised the question.

Knowing where to find birds is important, but there is more to a covert than a place to kill game. October's flaming backdrop for the birds and the dogs makes upland shooting one of the finest things in life. Nonshooters usually consider November a dreary time of year but to the shooting man it is a climax. In the title of his book *There Are No Dull Dark Days*, Percy Blogg, the Baltimore sportsman, said what any man knows who has gunned for grouse or woodcock in a light drizzle or has shot pheasants on a sugaring of snow under lead-colored clouds.

Variety in ranges and in coverts adds to the pleasure of shooting and to experience in handling game, for the same game bird will behave differently in different cover. I've shot in much of West Virginia and Pennsylvania, some in Maryland and Virginia, and have had a sampling of grouse and pheasant shooting in Michigan and preserve shooting in Ohio and New Jersey. I think I know my coverts almost by the square foot, certainly always by name—the Old Sam Place, the Firetower Ridge, Laurel Head, Dark Hollow, Old Farm. Some names, and coverts, are not mine alone: Dolly Sods, Cabin Mountain, The Loop Road. I remember a grouse I missed in Black Moshannon in Pennsylvania—a shot anyone could have made—but that name put its spell on me and gave that bird an extra margin of break. Consider Woodcock Hill in Pennsylvania, Pheasant Mountain in West Virginia and what the shooting must have been when they were christened.

I gun a large number of coverts—from thirty-six to fifty in each of the past six seasons. A covert loses some charm when hunted too often, turning shooting into a process and not a sport. Visiting each only once or twice each season keeps my gun pressure light. When you have owned and lived on game land, you think ahead and your attitude carries over to other coverts you hunt and possess only in your mind. I have "owned" some of my coverts for a generation. Certain ones that I have hunted nearly every season for thirty years hold as many birds now as when I found them, which I like to think reflects my treatment. If I had gunned them closely there might be no birds, as in many heavily shot areas. The gunner has a responsibility to preserve a covert. I prefer to leave too many birds rather than too few. The first is my loss, the second is the birds'—and mine.

Woodcock Coverts

FINDING WOODCOCK, unlike pheasants, grouse and quail, is as much a matter of *when to be there* as *where to find them*. Once you know the right places, woodcock will come to you year after year—in their own good time. This is part of the charm of woodcock shooting.

It will surprise a lot of men who shoot them to learn that woodcock are limited to the area east of a line cutting down through the middle of Minnesota, Iowa, Missouri, and swinging west to include a slice of Oklahoma and Texas. If the northern border of Minnesota were projected in a line east through Lake Superior, southern Ontario and Quebec to take in Maine and New Brunswick, it would fall roughly one hundred miles south of the northern boundary of the woodcock's range, which is about 50° N. latitude.

This northern extreme is breeding range but provides shooting when the birds gather and begin their migration south. Some of them have been reported breeding as far south as Mississippi, but my feeling is that no breeding range south of 40° latitude is significant, except in scattered high Appalachian situations such as the Canaan Valley in West Virginia. And while the northern edge of the wintering range is indicated by a line from southeastern Virginia, sagging under the Appalachians across Dixie and back up to include Arkansas, the real winter concentration of woodcock is in a kidney-shaped area overlapping parts of Louisiana and Mississippi.

The woodcock gunner is concerned not with carrying capacity of fixed range, as with grouse and pheasants, but with coverts that woodcock use during their migratory flight south in the autumn. He has an open season of from fifty to sixty-five consecutive days in each state, with a week or more pre-empted by deer season in some. Any woodcock season after the first five weeks is academic, for by that time the flights have usually gone. But during the flights in a good year the coverts are magically restocked, sometimes overnight.

All alders do not attract woodcock but I have seldom found woodcock in large numbers far from alders. Woodcock have not been as affected as most game birds by changing conditions during the last two centuries. I know alder coverts that haven't changed perceptibly in thirty-five years and unless they are cut and the land drained or flooded, they are not likely to. Agriculture has destroyed some habitat, timbering has enhanced other, but usually the alders remain. When woodcock habitat is changed, the birds cannot adjust and are forced to use other cover.

At the beginning of the season, "locals" or "native" woodcock (if there are any present) have not yet left unless there has been unseasonably cold weather or a severe drought, and the first shooting is usually on native birds. They are less concentrated and not often found in numbers later encountered in the big flights.

All woodcock are natives in their summer breeding range, becoming "flight birds" when they take off for the South. The birds in the northern areas start to move when the first freezes occur about September, seeking local ground still soft enough for probing. Some begin their flight, others linger. I cling to the old idea that the first flights are comprised largely of hens, with the smaller males moving down a couple of weeks later. If this is not the case, I can't explain the preponderance of hens I frequently find early in the season and a balancing majority of males on the last flights. Native birds are often still in their coverts when flight birds come through, as proven by banding records.

Woodcock fly at night and when a "fall of woodcock" drops in, the impression is of an organized flight that started from a certain place and is headed for a given destination, like a body of Canada geese. However, 'cock move as individuals, keeping near water most of the way and stopping to rest and feed in concentrations in limited coverts. They are influenced by the same weather and conditions of drought or moisture, but the birds that dropped in last night may have come from distantly separate sources, and when they leave with the cold snap that will move them out tomorrow or the next day, they may end up in different wintering territory in the South.

On the migratory flight, if it is not alder cover that is used, it will be cover close to water or damp ground. The birds may rest in hawthorns, crab apples, hardwoods and conifers. Soil around such trees doesn't always hold earthworms, so for their nocturnal feeding the birds fly to less acid soil, especially where cattle have used. If the woodcock eats an occasional item other than earthworms, the gunner need not take it into consideration. During the flights, look for a source of earthworms near alders and aspens and you will find that woodcock have left their whitewash calling cards, or are there, or will be there if the season is not too far along.

I have found woodcock in large numbers on a mountain top but, as in the lowland coverts, it was flat land with alders. I discovered one of my best coverts—so far a private one—when exploring for grouse. It proved to hold only a brace of grouse but the second-growth woods with a small run winding through it was stiff with woodcock. I like to blame my poor shooting that day on the surprise of finding 'cock instead of grouse. Toward sunset I came to the reason the 'cock were there—a large stand of alders at the far end.

Although wildlife biologists question the importance of gun pressure on populations of most game birds, for once I find that they agree that the hunting kill is a large factor in woodcock mortality. The woodcock gets hard hammering by guns if he is unfortunate enough to take certain flight routes. It has been suggested that a chain of refuges be established along the migratory lanes where woodcock could drop in and rest, safe from shooting. Some biologists feel these would be unfeasible except at points of concentration such as Cape May, New Jersey, and in the dense wintering range in Louisiana and Mississippi, where the bird should not be harassed. I like the idea of refuges all along the migratory route. If "unfeasible" means too expensive, I fail to see the relation of economy to other appropriations for recreational developments, such as $30,000 to make one mile of hiking trail in Inwood Park in New York, which a dozen hikers could create by walking over it a few times. That sum would buy three thousand acres of woodcock refuges.

Woodcock shooting is a private sort of thing with each man cherishing his own notions and his own coverts. You may find your woodcock in second-growth hardwoods or on hillsides, as I have at times. But for ideal sport give me flat land, aspens and alders, and a good woodcock dog, and enough woodcock to make the day exciting just to see them.

Pheasant Country

THE FIRST PHEASANTS I SAW were a few dozen cocks in my father's pigeon loft, awaiting release by his shooting club. Like almost everyone near the Mason-Dixon Line, I had always thought a "pheasant" was a grouse. An event that occurred two million years ago failed to include my Allegheny mountains in ideal ring-necked pheasant terrain—the birds don't do well much below the glacial belt—and I have to go to the lowlands for my pheasant shooting or rely on preserves.

The introduction and increase of pheasants in America are the best things that have happened to upland shooting, easing gun pressure on our native birds, and in spite of recent declines there is no reason to think the ringneck won't attract many of the growing number of guns. The fantastic pheasant populations of the forties and early sixties may not be seen again, but the bird can be gunned heavily without endangering the species. They can be raised on game farms and, though game biologists do not view stocking as the answer to good pheasant shooting on open range, the bird got its start in every good pheasant state by stocking. South Dakota built to millions of pheasants from an overall release of about 7,500 birds. Given ideal conditions, the pheasant has the capacity to make a comeback.

During the past decade pheasants appear to have been deprived of at least some of those ideal factors, even in what was top pheasant country in the North-Central states. Experts agree that the villain is probably big farming, with its giant machinery making possible huge stretches of cropland without fence rows, "clean" management and wetland drainage, early hay harvests that remove nesting cover before the hatch. Spring weather and severe blizzards haven't changed, but with poor nesting and protective cover and with insufficient year-round food, fewer birds survive. Pesticides are suspected of affecting egg development, reducing broods. Not all modern farming methods are adverse; pheasants do well where there are irrigation ditches. Nor do pheasants find proximity to large population centers incompatible, and they show their recuperative power in the shifts in pheasant populations within states. If they are allowed a place to live, they'll do their part.

Our pheasant is a cross between the Caucasian and the Chinese, two of the original strains introduced into America. The pheasant of the Eastern states more nearly resembles the Caucasian; the bird of the Northwest looks more like the Chinese. The purer Caucasian cocks lack the white neck ring. New York State is experimenting with the Japanese green pheasant and the Korean ringneck, varieties more adaptable to brushland and rolling hills. A cross between the Chinese and the Iranian pheasant has been introduced into Florida. Virginia stocked a similar cross as well as some pure Iranian birds and has had some success with wild reproduction. If these strains thrive in the South, it will suggest that the Iranian blood can take the warm climate. The Caucasian-Chinese pheasant, familiar to millions of gunners in the North, has been a complete failure in the warm and humid land of the bobwhite in Dixie.

I have not shot pheasants in the prime ringneck country in the North-Central states, where the annual kill reached as high as 7.5 million in South Dakota in 1945, and considering what so many birds would do to a well-trained dog I am not likely to. Pheasants are a by-product of wheat and corn farming, particularly in pork-raising country where corn is "hogged-down" in the fields, leaving waste grain. Corn cut for ensilage is of little value because no cover and no grain is left. And, while there is some waste corn when it is harvested mechanically, the stalks are broken down and the remaining ears are covered with snow. Pheasants use wild fruits only as starvation rations.

Pheasants don't do well in dairy-farming country, for grass is of little value to them if it is not near grain. Nebraska is an exception in that pheasants thrive in the sand hills with grassland mixed with thickets and grown-up stream margins, and feed on seeds and wild fruits and greens, but most of the birds are near small cultivated patches.

Even here in our mountains there are isolated pockets where pheasants have reproduced on a small scale, but they are rare. It isn't the cold mountain winters the birds find intolerable—good pheasant country nearly always has bitter winter weather and pheasants can survive −40° temperature. Of millions of pheasants shot every year in America, two-thirds are taken in the northern Great Plains, where mild winters are unheard of. Some preserves near me offer more interesting shooting than farm pheasant coverts, their crab-apple thickets, marshland and greenbrier patches being like grouse cover. Still other preserves I have gunned are in the heart of wild pheasant country and the only difference from the surrounding land is the privacy and the lack of farming.

It is possible for good pheasant country to be outside glaciated land, as I discovered in a highly productive area west of the mountains in southwestern Pennsylvania. Most Pennsylvania pheasants are on unglaciated soil but in outcropping limestone of a type they can utilize. The southwestern Pennsylvania pheasant population is sustained with infusions of released birds, proving that stocking is worthwhile in some situations, for many of these are carryovers with their wild-hatched young. I found no pheasants in similar cover in the same foothills just south in West Virginia, suggesting that the Mason-Dixon Line is the southern boundary of ringneck terrain. This is corroborated in Frank C. Edminster's *American Game Birds* (Charles Scribner's Sons, New York, 1954):

> Why the pheasant should not "take" south of a latitude approximating the Mason-Dixon Line is not understood. . . . some of the best pheasant country in the East is found in Lancaster County, Pennsylvania. Yet just across the border in Maryland the number of pheasants is insignificant. . . . The baffling thing about this condition is that the ranges are practically identical. The same soils prevail, and the same kind of farming. The climate is as nearly similar as would be expected in a 50-mile difference of latitude.
>
> This same clear demarcation of the southern limit of the pheasant's range continues all the way across the humid, low-altitude portion of the country. . . . Continuous exposure of pheasant eggs to temperatures much over 100° F. is lethal. . . . The acceptable range of pheasants on this continent comprises areas with a mean annual temperature of from 40° to 74° F. and altitudes ranging from sea level to 7,000 feet. . . . While the 40th parallel seems to mark the southern limit . . . in the Eastern states, the birds thrive much farther south in the West where the altitude is greater. In southern Arizona

Pheasant Country

and New Mexico pheasants do well on irrigated lands at altitudes of from 5,000 to 7,000 feet. Here the latitude is only 33°.

Kay and I discovered our southwestern Pennsylvania pheasant country in our search for late-summer dog-training grounds in the foothills stretching from Chestnut Ridge to the Monongahela River. The early 1900's coal boom blighted this area with a pall of smoke from coke ovens, the landowners moved "to town" and built gingerbread houses with their coal money, and years later a rugged breed of Central European immigrants bought the old home places and developed the land into farms that look like models of game management, with contour strips of green alfalfa, corn, wheat and grass. Where originally there had been bobwhites, pheasants took over like the alien farmers.

Pheasants require three types of cover: (1) cropland for food (corn, small grains, truck crops, fallow ground); (2) grassland for nesting, roosting and loafing (hay, grazing land, alfalfa); (3) woody or rank vegetation for protective shelter (woodland, conifer plantations, overgrown fence rows, hedges, ditch banks, roadsides, marshland). This prescription describes the cover in the southwestern Pennsylvania counties of Fayette and Westmoreland. During training season we have square miles of this pheasant country to ourselves, where we find nides of young pheasants no larger than quail in the same fields with half-grown birds and adults. With opening day, unless you are a guest on posted land, every field will sprout a group of hunters. A few will be using bird dogs, some will be hunting with beagles, but the greatest number will walk up the birds and a lot of cripples will be lost. After the first day there will be signs of few pheasants where recently we had been moving forty or fifty in two hours of dog training. It isn't that they've all been shot; they're simply half scared to death.

The hordes of pheasant hunters have not endeared themselves to the farmers, but before the season we have always been welcomed to work our dogs—with one curious exception. A cock pheasant flushed across the road, just clearing the hood of our station wagon to glide into a field of new-cut hay. On impulse I turned into the adjacent lane to an old stone house. As I got out, a woman in a smock appeared at the corner of the house, surrounded by at least five white collies. Encouraged by her obvious affection for dogs, I introduced myself and, more as a formality than with any doubt as to her response, asked if we might "run our dogs on pheasants" on her land. It was a poorly chosen phrase, for she neither seemed to grasp the idea nor could she quite let go of it.

"Why," she demanded in a confused tone, "do you want to run the poor pheasants?"

I described the dog work and stressed the fact that pheasants fly on unharmed after the points, but it didn't carry.

"I don't think it's fair," she persisted, unmoved.

In a situation like that there is nothing you can do but bow out. As we drove down the lane we heard her repeat, "I don't think it's fair. Why pick on the poor pheasants?"

She may be right. I think of it every time I miss a big sassy cock.

Grouse Coverts I Have Known

> ❧ / *I dream of upland clearings*
> *Where cones of sumac burn,*
> *And gaunt and gray-mossed boulders*
> *Lie deep in beds of fern . . .*
>
> —Bliss Carman, *The Cry of the Hillborn*

THE RUFFED GROUSE shares my distaste for crowds and my love of mountains and abandoned farms. You may find him in flat country but there will probably be clearings, brush, hardwoods in various stages, and conifers, their attraction for him depending on their size and their relation to each other. Scientists tell us the bird has been in some of its present range for twenty-five thousand years. If man doesn't breed himself and wildlife out of a place to live, the grouse may, if given a sporting break, continue in its coverts for a long time.

If, when you think grouse, you say "partridge" and see Robert Frost country, you probably do your shooting in what the game biologists call the Northeastern Forests. It includes New York's Adirondacks, Vermont, New Hampshire and Maine; Quebec, New Brunswick, Nova Scotia and Labrador to the limits of forest. The grouse of this range is the subspecies *Bonasa umbellus togata*, except in the upper Canadian portion, where it is *B. u. umbelloides*. Other than in the stone-fenced, abandoned apple-tree area of New England's old farms—some of the better coverts—most of it is unbroken forest, government-owned or cut in large blocks by pulpwood companies. Hardwoods are the "northern association"—beech, birch, maple; the conifers are hemlock, white pine, spruce and balsam with tamarack and white cedar in the bogs. The bogs and ponds are the only openings in the northern portion. For brush, the Yankee grouse uses alder runs, aspen groves, whip-size birch and hawthorns ("tho'nplums"). Except in the southern part, regrowth woodland stages are in tracts too large to be ideal. This is all snow country with long winters. The Northeastern Forests rank third among the four large grouse ranges in carrying capacity for grouse, yet, from what gunners tell me, some of the New England terrain offers great shooting.

More grouse are seen, and shot, in the Lake States Forests than in any other range. This includes Michigan, Wisconsin, Minnesota, a piece of North Dakota, and sprawls north into Canada. Like the Northeastern Forests, its grouse are "pats"—the gray-tailed *B. u. togata* and *B. u. umbelloides* (the gray grouse) in the northern parts. Grouse tend to be grayer the further north you go. The land is flat, winters are severe and rainfall is lower than in other grouse ranges. Aspen occurs to some extent in every grouse range but especially in the Lake States Forests, where it takes over after burning. In Wisconsin and Minnesota, grouse eat aspen in some form every month of the year—leaves from May to October, buds from September to May, flowering parts in May. They seem to select the male aspen flower buds, which are rich in protein. The Lake States Forests grouse range, with its swamps and lakes, is Northwoods.

The magnum of all the grouse ranges, the Rocky Mountain–Pacific Coast Forests range, extends from northwestern California

and central Utah to Alaska. Its subspecies of grouse read like a taxonomist's checklist: *castanea* in the southern coastal mountains, *sabini* in the Cascades, *brunnescens* on Vancouver Island and in the Canadian coast mountains, *affinis* and *phaia* in the Rocky Mountains, *umbelloides* and *incana* in the Rocky Mountains and prairie provinces, *yukonensis* in the Yukon and central Alaska. There are varieties of pines, fir, spruce and cedar and there is the ubiquitous aspen. Winters are rugged except for the coastal rain forests. In spite of its size and immense variety of coverts, it is rated below the other grouse ranges.

The Appalachians grouse range is the only one of the four whose largest portion is not in Canada. The name is not exact, for the Appalachian Mountains extend through the Northeastern Forests range to the Gaspé. The Appalachians grouse range as designated includes southern New York, Massachusetts, Connecticut, New Jersey, Pennsylvania, the Virginias, and parts of Maryland, Ohio, Kentucky, Tennessee and North Carolina. Except in the northeast portion, the Appalachians grouse range is what a Virginian would call "full of itself"—the Appalachians. The grouse in the northeastern part is *B. u. umbellus*, the grouse in the mountains is *B. u. monticola*.

I live in the heart of this grouse range, in the westernmost mountains of Appalachia—a beautiful name for a beautiful land, bastardized by the sociologist. In a private collection I recently discovered a map of these mountains published in London in November, 1761, twenty-one years before our house was built, entitled *Two Furthest Settlements, A New Map of Virginia from the best Authorities by T. Kitchin, Geog.* The principal mountains were called "Endless Mts." and my Alleghenies were indicated as "Ouasioto Mounts. a vein of mountains about 30 or 40 Miles right across through which there is not yet any occupied Path in these Parts." By "30 or 40 Miles" the cartographer grossly underestimated, but much of the rest still applies. He spelled Monongahela *Monaungahela* and Youghiogheny *Yo chia Geni*—closer to the sound than most lowlanders ever get.

East of Allegheny Front the mountains are known as the Ridge-and-Valley Province—steep and separated by fertile valleys. West from the crest of the Front they are formally designated Allegheny Plateau all the way to Chestnut Ridge—no more a plateau than areas of the United States are still a sea or a glacier. The Dolly Sods immediately west of Allegheny Front are a big plateau, but if you scramble down Cabin Mountain into Canaan Valley, climb over Canaan Mountain and down into Blackwater Canyon and at last pull yourself up onto Backbone Mountain, you won't have wind or inclination left to say "plateau." And you have only begun. North of this is the Maryland Tableland, and from the Tableland west to and including Chestnut Ridge is the lovely jumble cut deep by isolated valleys—the Intermediate Ridges of my home country.

The Appalachians grouse range usually carries a grouse population exceeded only by the Lake States Forests. Contemplating thousands of square miles of mountains, the prospect of grouse cover appears truly endless but most of it is spotty. I don't find one grouse per fifty acres overall, considered minimum population on occupied range. In good years there is a wealth of grouse in these mountains, but even then you don't simply walk to the nearest ridge and begin moving them.

THE INTERMEDIATE RIDGES

THE INTERMEDIATE RIDGES are about two thousand feet high, with a few reaching above three thousand. Winters are severe enough to keep grouse happy, with temperatures to below zero and snow on the ground from December into March. In the hemlock-rhododendron valleys there are white-water streams, once prime brook trout water—tributaries of the Cheat and the Youghiogheny (pronounced Yocka-gainy, Indian for "water from high ground"). Those not stained with mine acid are still beautiful and wild. Unlike the Ridge-and-Valley and the big mountains of the Blackwater-Canaan further south, you can live almost anywhere in the Intermediate Ridges. Towns in the mountains of West Virginia are too small to matter, a dismay to the economists and a delight to me.

But there is Progress. Coal is called the lifeblood of West Virginia by those who bleed her white on the premise that it is immoral to leave anything underground that can bring a dollar when dug up. I have seen mountainsides I thought no one would set foot on, other than to cut timber or to hunt, ripped open by strip mines and left raw. Since the strip-mine law the fill-backs are planted with grass, pines, locusts and autumn olive.

In spite of my indignation at the ugliness, I can see some benefit to upland shooting from strip mining. The vertical cut forms a thirty-foot "high wall" that extends, unscalable, for the length of the operation. If this occurs near the top it often girdles the mountain, leaving an inaccessible cap. Since most land is timbered just before being stripped for coal, this island forms an excellent game refuge. Grapes, blackberries and greenbriers grow on the brink of the high wall and along the base of the spoil bank, and grouse use these edges. Birds flushed at the bottom usually fly up and over to escape, and a grouse that flushes out over the abyss from the high wall is pretty secure.

Gas and oil pipelines and power lines with their skeletal towers run for hundreds of miles over our mountains. When these rights-of-way are kept cut back, not chemically defoliated, they form good food plots and roosting sites. With managed plantings, these would be enhanced.

I used to resent it but I now recognize timbering as the origin of most prime grouse cover. Lumbering here after World War I was done in small privately owned blocks, creating regrowth in mixed patterns, ideally suited to grouse. Woodland on the slopes of the Intermediate Ridges is laced with miles of log roads converging on clearings where portable sawmills once stood. As grouse cover, this declined in value as it reached pole stage. Pulpwood cutting is beginning to produce these desirable slashed areas once more, as is clearcutting—a controversial issue in national forests.

Small farms lie on tops of ridges with pastures reaching down the sides. Abandoned fields grow to hawthorns and crab apples— thickets for grouse and transient woodcock. Along the streams rhododendron and hemlock are winter protection and year-round escape cover. There was a time when agriculture used more of the land. Photographs around 1900 show many of my coverts in clear pasture, suggesting that perhaps those were not the days of Eden for the grouse hunter. Now, above the hemlock stands, hardwoods offer feeding and nesting cover even in those old pastures. Wild grapes take over after timbering, sometimes smothering entire hillsides. A grouse will hold for the dog in the security of a grapevine tangle, where it knows it has a choice of exits. Greenbrier offers formidable protection for the birds, as any gunner who has tried to force his way through can tell you. Though my flesh heals, my gunstocks bear the scars.

There was a time when the American chestnut provided prime food for grouse as well as turkey, deer, bear and squirrels. I remember seeing entire ridges creamy with fingers of bloom in June. The chestnut was well named *Castanea;* on a windy day after a frost the nuts fell on the leaf-strewn ground with a sound like castanets. The blight finished most of the chestnuts by the middle 1920's and our mountains and our game lost a magnificent tree. Sprouts still grow from old roots, reaching a height of twenty feet and producing burs with withered nuts, but the blight spores are patient and have their way. Nearly every dead chestnut snag has fallen and the last remnant of the big trees, other than sprouts, are the ancient chestnut-rail fences that snake their zigzag lines around old farms.

Some of our valleys are beech coves with trees ranging from whip-size to giants. The stand-by nut food for grouse are acorns from white, red, black, scarlet and chestnut oaks. Summer foods affect grouse cover. "Sarvice" (serviceberry) is typical of early-stage regrowth woods, its lacy white bloom in May like bits of cumulus snagged on bare trees. Grouse use the juicy sarvice berries as well as blackberries and black cherries.

The Intermediate Ridges in West Virginia are like those in southwestern Pennsylvania where I first knew grouse hunting, the streams in West Virginia flowing to the Cheat, those in Pennsylvania to the Youghiogheny. Both areas have high ridges to the west and east; both are primarily wild-grape cover with a variety of foods such as I have found nowhere else.

There was a time when the Intermediate Ridges of Pennsylvania and West Virginia must have held a fabulous number of grouse but those days are gone. It is still good sporting shooting with a change of pace from one type of cover to the next. It is thick, steep and rough, with forest floor formed of rocks, and there are ledges everywhere. Because it is mostly small privately owned tracts, there are NO HUNTING notices on nearly every piece of cover.

I suppose it is because I burned my first powder here that this land of Intermediate Ridges piled up between higher mountains will always look more like grouse country to me than any other. Dragging myself up a long ridge behind a weary setter when my legs and my gun seem heavy, I look out across these mountains to the sunset and know that this is home.

THE TABLELAND

MOST OF MY MARYLAND shooting has been in the Youghiogheny River valley and its tributaries, like the river hills of West Virginia and Pennsylvania, as nearly vertical as anything you can cling to. The Tableland is a different terrain, extending into part of West Virginia to include the Cranesville Swamp and the Snaggy Mountains. The bulk of the Tableland lies in Maryland's Garrett County, beginning north of Deep Creek Lake—once Deep Creek, old Meshach Browning's hunting ground. Below Oakland, Backbone Mountain sidles across the Tableland, and south of that the little streams flow lazily through glades until they pitch into the North Branch of the Potomac and head for the Atlantic instead of the Gulf of Mexico, as do the streams on the north side of Backbone.

This is grouse and woodcock country. Here, grouse go for hawthorns, owing to the comparative scarcity of wild grapes. Sarvice is abundant, in some areas occurring as orchards of round-headed trees. There are greenbrier berries, acorns and blueberries. Winters are bitter, with deep snows, but the grouse of the Alleghenies, like their gray-tailed *togata* cousins of New England and Michigan, do best in cold country.

Glades—shallow basins grown to alders and hawthorn and crabapple thickets bordered by low ridges—occur in both Pennsylvania and West Virginia but especially in western Maryland. Usually grazed by cattle with small runs winding through them, they invite grouse and woodcock. Grouse use them especially in the warm early shooting season but may remain there. In thick thorns and alders they are not easy to hit.

The moment you cross from West Virginia into Maryland you begin to see large white pines, singly and in stands. Where these have seeded, clumps of smaller pines make good winter cover on edges of old fields. The Tableland is not as rough terrain as the Intermediate Ridges nor as thickly covered, and it is not so heavily gunned as it once was.

The B. & O. Railroad was put through Oakland, Maryland, in

1849. In the 1870's the railroad built the Deer Park Hotel, forming a nucleus for a summer colony. This brought an influx of Baltimore and Washington sportsmen who found the fishing and shooting good. During the 1880's one dollar a pound was the going price for brook trout at the Deer Park and other summer hotels and it has been said that this wrote the epitaph for Garrett County streams. Another corrupting effect of contact with the carriage set was the discovery by the natives that there was a market in New York and Baltimore for grouse and woodcock.

To a mountain man who earned $1 for a hard day's labor—$2 for himself and his team—$1 apiece for grouse and $1.50 for a brace of woodcock was too attractive to turn down. He could realize as much from a day's hunt as he could earn working for a week, there was no law against market hunting, and he wasn't the only gunner who thought that loads of "pheasants" and scads of woodcock would always be there, nor the only one who didn't give a damn if they weren't so long as they lasted out his time. Storekeepers' records in Oakland between 1900 and 1910 show shipments of well over a thousand grouse per season. Delmonico's was a regular customer. Considering that woodcock or grouse comprised only the game course of a dinner, it puzzles me that birds could command prices of that sort in the mountains and still provide a profit for the various hands through which they passed. In 1890 grouse brought $1.50 to $2 apiece in New York, with an all-time high of $7 a pair in 1918 in Washington, D.C. It was not uncommon for a market hunter to kill up to fifty grouse in a day.

Laws were passed but it is simpler to pass game laws than to enforce them. Birds changed hands from hunter to storekeeper less openly and the storekeeper continued to ship his barrels of grouse and woodcock, except that now there was a camouflage top layer of Garrett County apples. With strict law enforcement the practice was eventually curtailed, but I suspect the increasing scarcity of game had much to do with it.

I can't share the admiration frequently expressed for the shooting skill of the market hunter. All shots were taken, sitting or flying, and snares were often used. A slaughterhouse lack of sensitivity made him a nerveless automaton; if he became an exceptional shot it was because there was no excitement involved as in sporting shooting.

There is still good shooting in the Tableland. Even had there been no market hunting, grouse might not be there today in such numbers as were there up to the 1920's, but it put a terrific drain on the birds. That grouse survived speaks for the quality of this cover.

MICHIGAN

MANY OF US reach for new coverts when grouse are down, which may account for some of our disappointments far from home. My gun diary opens the 1963 season on an unprophetic note:

"We've had a long dry Indian Summer after probably the most ideal summer weather I can remember. It should have given us a fair grouse brood, which we need after three bad years." I wrote those lines after shooting a grouse on opening day, a heady experience.

At the end of the fourth day our West Virginia season closed because of fire hazard. Less Crowl phoned from Ohio to suggest that we go with him to Michigan, and Kay, Shadows, Dixie and I drove out on November 1. When we reached the white-birch belt south of Grayling we entered large flat expanses of pines with light snow, adding to the feel of North Country. Our cabin was on the famous Au Sable River at the edge of Grayling. After a hasty unloading, Less and I tried a short hunt in the late afternoon but found no birds.

Next day we drove to the Deward area. It was swamp cover, much like our Blackwater spruce bogs but with tamarack, cedar, jack pine, white pine and a similar tree they call Norway pine, but no rhododendron. There are open areas with maple scrub and aspen almost as white as the birch. The land is mostly flat and I have never seen so much pine woods. But the grouse were almost nonexistent.

I learned a lesson about swamp hunting. Covering the edge of a bog with Dixie and Shadows, I heard Less whistle and hurried toward him, thinking he must have got into birds. A narrow neck of swamp separated us but a fallen log beyond a shallow pool offered a way across. I took one step into six inches of water and sank into silt to my waist and kept going deeper. There are things you're supposed to do in this situation, such as throw your gun away and fall flat on your back. Instead, I held my gun high with one hand, my other arm going full-length into the ice-cold muck, floundered to the log and crawled up on it like a slimy sea serpent. I'm accustomed to sphagnum bogs but they rarely suck you in. I carry a change of clothes in a period-piece leather suitcase in the station wagon and I was soon back in action.

Next day we obtained a guide. We had the dogs and we knew what to look for, but this Michigan Northwoods is too big and too unbroken; grouse were in pockets and the pockets are as difficult to locate as the birds.

Our guide was an unsavory little weasel who got under my skin by announcing that he had shot sixteen grouse in one day earlier in the week. There was implication that all sixteen were available if we cared to buy them. The guiding, at twenty dollars per day, consisted principally of riding in the rear seat of the station wagon and directing us along miles of back roads where I guessed that this individual made a practice of ground-shooting birds beside the road. Road hunting accounts for half the grouse shot in this part of Michigan. The birds encourage this by using the roads for want of other breaks in the forest.

When the guide got it clear that we wanted to hunt grouse with our dogs, he took us to three coverts. The first two were empty but in the third I saw Dixie hit a point. Before I could reach her a grouse flushed wild well ahead of her. The guide began counting—flushing a new bird with each exclamation until four or five had gone out, which he said were seven or eight. I'm convinced his experience was limited to hunting from a car, for he talked incessantly and loud. Altogether we moved five grouse during the day and I didn't fire a shell—not even at the guide.

The following day we tried another guide with the unbelievable name of Egbert Bugsby, as refreshing as the first one was not. We picked him up at a house with a front yard fenced by palings made of discarded canoe paddles. "Eggy," who is no longer living, came out—a little fellow about seventy years old—and greeted Less, whom he had guided on trout float-trips on the Au Sable.

Guides feel their first responsibility is to jack up your hopes, so you hear of the birds that have been shot during the early part of the season, which to me seems mathematically negative. After moving two birds in the first covert, Eggy took us to an area west of the Manistee River, miles away. The fatigue in this kind of hunting comes from riding, not from walking. Eggy too had a sharp eye for a "pat" along the roadside and he brought us up short with a "Whoa! There's one." I'm certain he thought Less and I were crazy for passing it up and wanting to hunt the woods with dogs, and perhaps he was right for we made several circles with no results.

About sunset he took us to a basin covered with low brush that I think was gray dogwood. Almost immediately we moved a group of five. As we followed, trying to relocate them in the failing light, I was startled by a form rising from the ground in front of me—a bow hunter in camouflage who warned me not to walk into a blind where his friends were dug in, waiting for a chance at a deer. I could never decide whether his concern was for my safety in the uncertain light or that I might spook a deer and spoil their shot. These risks are one of my objections to concurrent deer-grouse seasons.

Though the Michigan trip was disappointing in that birds were scarce, the grouse country around the Au Sable and the Manistee is impressive. But from what I saw of the coverts you would almost have to know the birds personally to find them. The grouse are the gray-tailed *togata*, which they call "pats," a term that crops up wherever the *togata* occurs. A Northwoods hazard we didn't encounter is the porcupine, which can make life miserable for your dog.

As in any pine woods, there seemed little for those grouse to feed on. They eat blueberries, of course, and greens, and aspen and other buds, and there were some acorns. The biologist, Bill Goudy, tells me they use gray dogwood and poison-ivy berries. I saw none of the wealth of food I find in the East. But it is a mistake, when hunting in a strange land, to look only for the kind of food you know birds use in your home coverts.

The day we left, we met George Griffith of Trout Unlimited. He has gunned a lot in that area and was having no trouble finding birds, proving that it is important to know your country.

WATOGA

GROUSE FLUCTUATIONS ARE almost never the same over all parts of the country. Southwestern Pennsylvania had plenty of grouse in '63 and again in '64, when we were tramping half a day to move two or three birds just across the Mason-Dixon Line in West Virginia. Reports from West Virginia's Pocahontas County led me to try there. On Sunday, November 22, with top maps and a cabin reservation, we drove to Watoga State Park about 150 miles south of Old Hemlock.

Our cabin was at the foot of a steep ridge near a small trout stream running through rhododendron. Except for the park superintendent's family and a lone game biologist we didn't see, Kay and I were the only people staying in the 10,052-acre park. There is excitement about moving into terrain you've never gunned that even the setters sense.

Most of that area east of the Greenbrier River is white-pine country. By 1875 some of the pure stands were being cut, yielding up to forty thousand feet per acre, and the logs floated down the Greenbrier to the big mill at Ronceverte (French for greenbrier). Like all West Virginia state parks, Watoga is closed to hunting, but it lies next to the Cal Price State Forest, which is open to shooting and holds grouse in its dense second-growth pine and hemlock cover.

Small valleys and streams squirm in all directions. The dominant mountains on the east are Brushy and Beaver Lick with contour lines so deeply convoluted they look on the top map like suture interlocking on a deer skull. East of this lie the two forks of Anthony Creek and then Allegheny Mountain, whose crest forms the state line between Pocahontas and Greenbrier counties of West Virginia and Bath County, Virginia. This is the border between the Monongahela and the George Washington national forests, both open to public hunting. Approaching the top of Allegheny Mountain from the west, it seems no mountain at all until you start the long descent into Virginia, when you realize that you have been in very high country. On top maps showing wooded land in green there are few breaks in this section; what clearings are indicated are in the valleys—unlike our Intermediate Ridges.

Shooting in thick white pine and rhododendron is sporting, with odds stacked for the grouse. They are too inclined to flush out of trees only to land in others, giving the dogs no chance to work them. The road along Cochran and Anthony creeks reminded me of cover around Grayling, Michigan, with a few pines on low-ridge scrubby oak cover, much cut-over and with many brush piles. There were acorns and teaberry everywhere and a few hawthorns. One grouse I shot there was crammed with haws, seeds and leaves. There were a few grapevines and a bird I shot the next day several ridges away was full of withered grapes.

West of the Greenbrier River but within easy reach of Watoga lies an entirely different terrain. The mountains are higher by a thousand feet and the forest is hardwood with spruce topping the highest crests. To reach this we left the Greenbrier Valley at Mill Point with its old water-wheel mill and drove up Cranberry Mountain.

Hunting to the 4,215 foot peak of Cranberry, we looked down on Cranberry Glades, nestled between Kennison, Black and Cranberry mountains. This northern-muskeg-type bog is famous for plants and animals that occur here at their most southern stations. I didn't hunt the actual bog—a large, wild area—but the cranberries should attract grouse. There are many alder stands but I wouldn't expect woodcock because of the acid soil. The margins of the Glades are good grouse cover, ten miles around, and I don't suggest any short cut across.

We chose to hunt the top of the mountain among dotted thorn full of red and yellow haws. Birds were scarce there and south of Kennison Mountain along Hills Creek so we drove on over Point Mountain and hunted some of the tributaries of the North Fork of Cherry River. The cover is mixed evergreen–northern hardwood and lies in small ravines. There, young Bliss made the day memorable by making her first productive point on grouse.

On that trip we didn't get into the nearly inaccessible area between the North and South forks of Cherry River but just looking at it on the top map gives me the itch to go there. This is primitive country; panther tracks were seen on Kennison Mountain in June, 1936, by two members of the Smithsonian. Watoga Park is within easy reach of almost unlimited grouse terrain—country that in good years could be excellent.

THE BLACKWATER-CANAAN

FROM THE CREST OF Canaan Mountain east of Davis, West Virginia, you look down the far side into a thirty-two-square-mile basin rimmed by spruce-and-rock-topped mountains. This is Canaan (rhymes with *might rain*) Valley, a frost pocket with a floor altitude of 3,200 feet—the headwaters of the Blackwater River. Like most streams in this high region, its clear water is the color of strong tea, from tannin compounds derived from the hemlock and spruce through which it flows, combined with iron oxide. In this water, submerged rocks appear golden but are bone-white when exposed, and trout take on gorgeous color.

A few grazing farms break the big alder flats and the spruce-hemlock swamps in the southern end of the Canaan Valley, but the northern two-thirds is almost entirely tundra and bog, dotted with golden aspen clumps and laced by the Blackwater and its tributaries, which can be traced by beaver ponds and stands of spruce. There is only one place where the water will flow out—at the gap between Brown and Canaan mountains in the northwest corner.

Parts of Canaan Valley and the 4,000-foot plateaus to the east are misplaced Canadian wilderness—a relict flora following the Ice Age. Up to 1890 one of the world's finest climax red spruce forests grew on these mountains and in the Valley. Today, in what look like dry river beds, roots of skeleton tree stumps clutch rocks yards above ground level. These once were giant spruce and hemlocks rooted in moist sphagnum moss up to two feet thick beneath an understory of ten-foot rhododendron so dense a man had to cut his way through. The lumbermen's multimillion-dollar rape from 1890 into the 1920's opened this to sun and wind and when the fires that followed their operations swept over it, the dried humus burned off like peat. But Nature produced a regrowth cover that for forty years offered exceptional shooting for turkey, bear, deer, grouse, and woodcock. Most men hunt this terrain without realizing it was not always like this.

The southern end of the Valley is being converted into Canaan Valley State Park, with a lodge designed by Walter Gropius Associates, cabins, a ski lodge, and a golf course on lands where I've shot grouse and woodcock. The Allegheny Power System plans a pumped-storage power plant by 1977, to include a dam on the Blackwater at the northwest gap to form a 7,200-acre lake that would cover most of the unspoiled northern portion of the Valley. To sugar-coat the pill, Allegheny Power proposes extensive vacation and recreation complexes on the shores of a lake that will form acres of mud flats with each recycling process pumping to a storage reservoir on Cabin Mountain above. Canaan Valley has been manhandled before but, unlike former situations when natural regrowth took over to form game cover, unless conservationists can prevent it, this lake and recreation development with boating and hundreds of cabins will destroy a rare wild area.

When we say Blackwater-Canaan, those of us who gun it include all of the terrain from Allegheny Front west to Backbone Mountain, most of it within the Monongahela National Forest. Although there are some privately owned tracts within the forest, you could hunt for years and never be on posted land. Beyond this sense of freedom to hunt where you please, there is the feel of wilderness. The country has been, and is, heavily gunned. Yet it is so big it is rare to see other grouse hunters except during the first week or two of the season in certain well-known sections.

One of the most popular is the Dolly Sods—Dolly (Dahle) a family name, Sods to denote the moorlike character of some of it. Accurately, Dolly Sods is a specific area but the name is commonly applied to the entire top of Allegheny Front, from the unpaved Laneville-Petersburg road north to Bear Rocks. The more applicable name for this region is Huckleberry Plains. It is in this high country that the connotation Allegheny Plateau really fits. From Allegheny Front, almost sheer on the east, the land rolls west in highland moors to the peaks of Cabin Mountain, where patches of spruce show like cloud shadows among the pattern of autumn color. This is grouse country but you must jeep or walk long distances to get into it. The overall effect is bigness—big sky, big distances, big mountains showing beyond the edges of the plateau.

Hundreds of acres of blueberry bushes turn crimson in the fall, carrying dried blueberries that attract grouse. Much of the year Blackwater-Canaan grouse make do with greens, but I suspect it is the wealth of summer foods like blueberries and sarvice berries that bring on broods. There is scrub thicket of red maple and yellow birch. Some hunters feel that grouse feed on the red mountain holly and mountain ash berries but I have rarely found holly and never ash berries in birds I have shot. Mountain ash with its yellow foliage against a pewter autumn sky grows with fire cherry and mountain laurel on some of the rockier terrain. The rhododendron on rocks is impenetrable but is good for edge hunting; spruce grows in thick stands around the bogs. Over everything is the silence.

A Forest Service road runs north for eight miles like a white chalk line to Bear Rocks before pitching down the steep mountainside on the east. Hunters spot-hunt along this road, which passes through isolated clumps of red spruce distorted by the winds into one-sided signposts pointing east. Occasional grouse move out from these.

The most challenging coverts are in the swamps. Pushing to the inside you come to typical Canadian muskeg with expanses of sphagnum and hair-cap moss, and beaver ponds that give the illusion of being at eye level. There are small red globes of cranberries in the green sphagnum, which holds ice-cold water. This is good cover in mid-November after the birds are bunched. One of my memories is of Ruff on point in one of these cranberry bogs with a brace of grouse pinned—both birds flying low and straight for an arm of spruce cover. Next to a grape-fed grouse I rate a November bird that has fed on cranberries until its flesh has acquired the cranberry tang.

I saw my first snowshoe hare up here, its large slate-blue ears alert, the dark eyes regarding me. It moved slowly at first, showing its white belly under the brindle saddle, then was off with big hocks flashing.

Never hunt this country without a compass. The east-pointing spruce give you bearings or you can use your watch and the sun—until the fog moves in. One sunny October afternoon we saw a wall of white vapor on the east, writhing up a hundred feet above the brink of Allegheny Front. We were eager to hunt and followed the dogs into the scrub growth to the west. Twenty minutes later the sun was blotted out and the thicket grew indistinct. In a cold fog we groped our way back until we felt the Forest Service road under our boots. It's not nice up there in fog without a compass. These sudden fogs are characteristic of this high country and sometimes hover for days. I have enjoyed sunny shooting in the Canaan Valley with the tops of the surrounding mountains obscured by clouds rolling like a white sea.

Unlike the mountains that were timbered, no one is certain what the original cover was like on the Huckleberry Plains. One opinion is that it was similar to the present low growth, stunted by almost constant winds. There are no large stumps to suggest big timber. Another opinion is that fires started in 1863 by Confederate campfires on the plains burned off the original growth; certainly there were many fires. The results are much the same as in the timbered and burned areas except for lack of old lumber railroad grades. South of this the roadless Red Creek, Flatrock and Roaring Plains stretch miles of black-dark spruce against the sky to Mt. Porte Crayon a little higher than the rest.

In the Canaan Valley, pioneer man seemed determined to prove himself unworthy. The virgin spruce forest was not only cut but some of it deliberately burned to clear it for bluegrass, which followed the fires in some sections. The slopes of the surrounding mountains are now largely forested in northern hardwoods—beech, birch, maple—and offspring of the original spruce grow along the Blackwater branches and in bogs. Alders and aspen-dotted tundra stretch for miles. No woodcock gunner needs to be told what this means. Grouse also use the alder thickets and the lower ridges. When hunting in this country, you dress for sudden rains and soaking fogs. Canaan Valley is notorious for snow—166 inches fell during the winter of '69–'70. If there is any doubt in your mind about its wildness, try hunting the head of the Blackwater.

In November, '65, after a blizzard the previous day, I started with two companions for the upper basin of the Blackwater. We had to leave the Land-Rover at a stream and proceed on foot. The Blackwater in its upper reaches flows through spruce bog. One of our trio thought he knew the area well enough to get across and hunt up the far side to the head of the swamp, where Less and I, who had never hunted in here, would meet him.

After Ed left us we worked up the north margin to what appeared to be the upper end, where Less and I sat down to wait for our friend. Nothing had been said as to what to do if we didn't get together. It was nearly four o'clock when I suggested that I hunt around the upper neck of the swamp to meet Ed and that Less should start back the way we had come and wait for us at the lower end.

The "upper neck" turned out to be a small peninsula of swamp and I found myself going farther and farther. Bliss was working nicely and I kept going, enjoying the sense of exploring an area as untamed as it must have been a century ago. Huge deer tracks emerged from a tunnel-like opening in the dark spruce and I started in, knowing Bliss and I could get through anything a deer as large as that could penetrate. When I came to the main branch of the Blackwater, a mere trout brook here, the path ended but I saw breaks in the thicket on the far side and crossed over. I hadn't gone far before I was in a rhododendron hell over my head. Rather than take the long backtrack, I pushed on, feeling a responsibility not to leave Ed up there. If you look carefully you can usually find a place to crawl through the thickest rhododendron, although it isn't comfortable in deep snow.

Fighting my way over a shoulder, I got out of the main spruce stand and started along what looked like the far side. I had been blowing my dog whistle and calling and I knew by now that I was alone. The thing to do was to hunt down, recross the swamp and join Less and Ed, who were probably waiting for me.

I tried several openings but they led to dead ends or beaver ponds. All the while Bliss was hunting as if we had the day before us, though the sun was down behind Canaan Mountain at my back. The main muskeg along the Blackwater stretched wider the farther downstream I went. I knew I had to either cross here or tramp all the way to the highway in the Canaan Valley. Feeling a little drastic, I started into the frozen swamp. The ice was too thin to hold me but I leaped from one to another of the tussocks of swamp grass and hair-cap moss until I came to the main current, where an accommodating beaver dam gave Bliss and me footing across.

On the far side I came to Ed's tracks, where early in the afternoon he had turned back and had taken an old road out. With Ed off my mind I set out to find Less, whom I pictured sitting on a log smoking and waiting for me in the dusk. Bisecting his probable line of march I came to large bearlike tracks that turned out to be Less's number 14's leading to the log with the ample imprint and his cigarette stubs where he had waited; but he had given me up and moved on. When I overtook him he still had not seen Ed, whom we found back at the Land-Rover.

As grouse hunts go, the day had been less than memorable. But I felt that I had, for a while, been in tune with Robert W. Service and his big country. I had somehow strung my soul to silence, I had heard the challenge, and I had, by God, got back.

Another celebrated grouse country of the Blackwater-Canaan is the Loop Road or Twenty-two Mile Grade. This was once a standard-gauge lumber railroad that followed the crest of Canaan Mountain to its southern end, looping back along the brink of Blackwater Canyon to the big sawmills at Davis. Sparks from the Shay locomotives caused recurrent fires in the tinder-dry spruce slashings and left Canaan Mountain barren. The term is not overstatement. When the U.S. Forest Service began reforestation there in 1925, some places did not have enough remaining humus to plant a seedling tree. Soil from the Canaan Valley was hauled to the mountain, where a bushel or more often had to be used for each spruce seedling. From 1925 to 1933, twenty-five hundred acres were planted to red spruce. This is now splendid forest along the top and western slopes of Canaan Mountain, too dense to penetrate except on the network of trails and "fire lines" connecting the upper and lower arms of the Loop Road. Unfortunately, the Loop Road in its relation to the cover lends itself to the unsporting practice of road hunting.

In the mid-1800's the entire Blackwater-Canaan was uninhabited. Philip Pendleton Kennedy in *The Blackwater Chronicle* described one of the first sporting trips into the region when he and some companions reached the North Fork of the Blackwater in 1851. The following year they returned and his cousin, David Hunter Strother (Porte Crayon), wrote of it in *The Virginian Canaan*. Their headquarters was Tower's Mountain House, eighty-seven miles west of Winchester, Virginia, on the North Branch of the Potomac near the present town of Gormania. Tower's was described as a place where sportsmen "resorted to fish for trout, hunt the deer, shoot pheasants [ruffed grouse], wild turkeys, woodcock in their season."

The Kennedy and Strother group trekked into the wilderness by horse and in the final stages on foot. They described "fallen hemlocks six feet high as they lay 150 feet along the ground, coated with moss half a foot thick with thickets of their own kind growing out of them. Laurel brakes [rhododendron] extend for many miles, waving up and down as far as the eye can reach like a green lake, either shore walled by the massive forest. The Blackwater, the same color as streams and lakes of Nova Scotia, had never had a line thrown into it before. . . . Below the second falls we caught some fifty more trout on gullets cut from other trout, or the red fins used as flies." These were, of course, native brook trout. They wrote of bears, wolves, panthers and badgers. "The rattlesnakes were not to be feared because the temperature was too cool."

On their second trip, these fishermen and hunters got as far as the confluence of the North Fork and the main Blackwater in a canyon that is still almost as impressive as when they saw it, except for second-growth instead of virgin forest. They worked up the Blackwater to Pendleton Run. Each time I see Pendleton Falls I see again the Porte Crayon sketch with big spruce trunks fallen crisscross between the narrow walls, and I almost think I see tiny figures of his friends as he drew them crawling over the boulders.

In 1858 George and William Dobbin of Baltimore built a twelve-room log hunting lodge on the high peninsula of land between the North Fork of the Blackwater and Pendleton Run. They owned twenty-six thousand acres from Canaan Mountain on the east to the crest of Backbone Mountain on the west and entertained a cosmopolitan group of hunting and fishing guests—actors, artists, writers, sportsmen, politicians. Names of two of these—*Catherine and Isabella Scott of London, July 10, 1859*—can still be seen inscribed on a boulder in the Blackwater above the big falls.

In *By-Paths in the Mountains*, Rebecca Harding Davis wrote of a trip into this country in 1879, describing the climax spruce forest as "a nightmare of trees stretching from horizon to horizon. When you have gazed on through them past the first sky-line, new horizons open of interminable hills shouldering hills, lifting to the sky the same monotonous growth." Not long after Mrs. Davis's trip the lumbermen took care of all that.

In spite of this destruction or perhaps because of it, certain species of game are more plentiful in the Blackwater-Canaan today. Certainly there will never be brook trout like that again, but there are many more deer. Turkey and bear are less plentiful but in good years there have been far more grouse than in the virgin forest. Blackwater grouse populations have dropped steadily since '61. Studies in Wisconsin and Minnesota indicate that grouse do well following forest fires, and in Pennsylvania the game biologist Ward Sharp recommends controlled burning for cover management. Perhaps too many years have elapsed since the big fires in the Blackwater-Canaan.

Upland gunners are the first to arrive in October. Kay and I take one of the Blackwater Falls State Park cabins, but if you don't insist upon your own log fire and a hearth knee-deep in setters, you should sample the old-fashioned Worden's Hotel in Davis. With its brood of four-wheel-drives and station wagons, it is the true headquarters of the hunters. At the Worden's they treat you as if they really cared. They have prepared not only grouse, woodcock, and wild turkey for their clients, but turtle eggs and rattlesnake. The lunch counter in the restaurant is a massive carved wooden bar from one of the saloons built when Davis was a roaring lumber town. During opening week the Worden's is filled to its third floor with bird hunters, and a few diehards maintain quarters throughout the season.

There are many other grouse coverts in the Blackwater-Canaan —the Beaver Creek drainage, Backbone Mountain, the Bayard country. But as Riley Worden would invariably tell you, "If grouse are any place you'll find them up on Stony River."

From the Canaan Valley side, Stony River is a jeep-type safari. Lurching across a plank bridge over Sand Run in a Land-Rover, my host jerked his head downstream. "One day in the thirties, four of us shot seventy-six shells in here and didn't kill a grouse." The road ended at a lonely sheep shed and the Land-Rover nosed down a rocky gully that shook growls from the setters and pointer in the rear. At such times you know you sit on two bones. Bumping over ties of the old Babcock lumber railroad grade, we began climbing Cabin Mountain. We followed the grade over the crest and parked by a rusty fragment of a Shay locomotive near a patch of Scotch heather and crossleaf heath, natives of Europe whose presence here is unexplained. One theory is that a lumberjack, receiving sprigs in a letter from the old country, set them out. Scottish red grouse cannot exist without Scotch heather (*Calluna vulgaris*) and presence of this species here suggests a soil favorable to grouse.

Stony River country is fire-succession growth with enough coverts to last a month of shooting. Grouse are usually grouped here, offering fast low-flying shots in the clearings. As in many Blackwater coverts, Stony River grouse can be difficult to locate because the country is so big and wild—in 1950 a deer hunter shot a coyote up here.

Back at the Land-Rover at sundown, we sat half-frozen in falling temperature and drank coffee while a raven uttered its curdling sound above us. On our way over the brink of Cabin Mountain we paused to look down on the northern end of Canaan Valley with its tortuous rivers and beaver ponds like fragments of green sky. *I am the land that listens, I am the land that broods.* Robert Service couldn't have described it better if he had seen it.

PART THREE

The Birds

❦ / THIS WILD THING I SEEK IS THE LIVE THING

SOMEWHERE AHEAD—

THE QUARRY CEASES TO BE QUARRY

WHEN THE QUARRY'S DEAD.

Woodcock Shooting

> ❦ / *A fall of woodcock, like aspen leaves under the October moon—*

THE WOODCOCK MOON

IF ANYTHING SETS my gypsy blood astir it is the combination of flaming October leaves and woodcock. The birds themselves are like gypsies on the move ahead of fall storms, eventual destination South but unable to resist prolonged bivouacs along the way.

Foliage is still dense when our grouse and woodcock seasons open in mid-October, and going into our home coverts with a gun and dog is nearly hopeless. Kay and I solve the problem by taking a state-park cabin in the high mountains where the leaves have fallen, and spend the first week shooting woodcock.

I particularly remember one of those trips. We were going up Backbone Mountain with a full load of setters and gear and halfway up we came to a sugaring of snow on the screaming color. As if especially for us, there was a caravan of gypsies stopped along the road, their scarves and vivid skirts and blouses looking like the leaves around us. They were in vintage cars but I kept expecting hooded wagons and guitars, and we waved as we passed. From the light in their dark eyes I think we shared a quickening pulse from the time of year. Or maybe, seeing our loaded station wagon, they thought we were gypsies, too.

To me, the woodcock has a special quality, with its enormous eyes, its harmony of browns and black and dusty-orange breast with

The Birds

black underdown. Its name has an enchantment as mysterious as its ways. The old English form, *wude-coco*, evokes images of sportsmen in tall hats shooting flintlocks over spaniels. I don't know who thought up such an asinine name as *timberdoodle* for so lovely a game bird but I suspect it wasn't a shooting man.

Few nonshooters know a woodcock as anything but a plate in a book. For those who shoot the bird, the words "a fall of woodcock" hold magic. One afternoon there is an empty covert of thinning aspens and alders. During the night a flight, or fall, of woodcock drops in silently and the covert is alive again. Woodcock and salmon share an unpredictability in making their appearance. You know *where* to expect them and almost *when*, but when they show up is something else. You can expect woodcock when Canada geese come over. Or when robins begin to bunch up. Or when you see juncos down from the North. I shoot through at least four Hunter's Moons, but to me the first one is the Woodcock Moon and it is auspicious when it is full about October 25, when the big flights should begin.

When woodcock are coming over in their main flights they appear to be almost everywhere until you try to locate them, when you find they can be choosy. We made a long trip to an extensive alder and hawthorn covert to shoot woodcock. Bliss made the first point, a hot one, in high alders. I walked in to take the shot while Kay got ready with her movie camera but instead of a 'cock, a grouse zoomed out, dodging the bases of the alder clumps until it was forty yards away, then topped out and sailed off. We found five single grouse in that "woodcock" covert but not one woodcock. In 1967, the following year, it was full of them.

The season of '65 was a dry one after a summer of severe drought and we never did get normal flights. Passing up my best coverts, the woodcock used high country where fogs provided moisture the lowlands lacked.

Of my shooting friends, the most experienced woodcock gunner was Dr. Charles Norris. His woodcock shooting in Pennsylvania, New Jersey, Maine and New York was minor compared with the shooting he did in New Brunswick and Nova Scotia. He used to say that when the flight is late the birds seem to sense they are overdue and stay only a short time; also that late flights and those resulting from rough weather often arrive in a body rather than in small groups or singly. Dr. Norris blamed heavy winds for making wood-

Woodcock Shooting

cock wild. He hadn't encountered the group of five guns I tried to dodge, together with their pellets, one afternoon. I don't think they got many birds but each flush triggered from two to six shots. When they got through, the woodcock were frantic, though not a breeze was moving.

A good woodcock covert, like a good grouse covert, should be a well-guarded secret and I see no reason to hedge about it. Few woodcock coverts are large enough to hold comfortably more than a pair of gunners at a time. Two or three parties shooting the same area are dangerous. Knowing that subsequent flights will put in new birds within a few days doesn't reduce the annoyance of trying to keep out of the way of other gunners or of having them working ahead of you.

It's not so awkward if you select different times of day, for woodcock move about. But woodcock hunters who know their sport are apt to be on hand just when you are. I realize that I am no welcome sight to another gunner who arrives to find me assembling my double, ready to start out with my brace of setters. At such times, or when you meet someone while shooting, it is well to ask the other fellow where he plans to hunt, giving him his choice so you can keep out of each other's way. Aside from winning his gratitude, I have discovered that the other man's choice is usually not in the direction I planned to hunt. Few things appear more ungracious than someone hurriedly parking ahead of you and slinking off into a covert without exchanging a greeting. If you discover that hunters are shooting a covert too frequently—and a lot of them do—it is best to abandon it and look for other places, for it isn't pleasant to take part in pounding birds—even woodcock passing through.

Going into strange woodcock terrain "cold" can be disappointing. Two coverts may look alike, yet only one may attract 'cock. Whitewash is the best clue, next to seeing actual birds. The white splashings disintegrate rapidly and when you see them you can almost count on woodcock being nearby. Resting sites may show some whitewash but not the boring holes. I came across whitewash splashings in an old lane while grouse hunting. It was on a stony hill and a woodcock would have needed a diamond drill to bore into that ground. This was where the birds rested. The feeding covert was an alder swamp in the bottom. Sometimes feeding and resting sites are combined.

The Birds

Moss indicates acid soil, unfavorable for worms. Some grass is good but too much complicates boring. Cattle enhance woodcock cover by keeping grass eaten and tramped down, and their droppings attract earthworms. Hillside spring seeps are good isolated spots to expect woodcock. Just as they can't bore through baked earth, woodcock can't probe through frozen ground. Earthworms don't remain near the surface at much below 35°, and though I have found woodcock late in November, most of them have moved on by that time. Gunners in England and Ireland believe European woodcock lie better after a clear moonlit night. Our woodcock, *Philohela minor*, frequently do this, probably because the long feeding period of the previous night leaves them heavily fed and less active.

Woodcock are neither the hardest nor the easiest bird to shoot. I think if your shooting average on 'cock is one bird for two shells fired you are doing well. Your gun must fit so well that you aren't conscious of it. Both barrels should be open—50 percent right and 60 percent left is nice. I'm not enthusiastic about anything as small as a .410, in spite of the notion that lighter gauges are more sporting. Though most woodcock drop if a single pellet finds its mark, it isn't sporting to spread a pattern thin.

I was surprised when a friend who shoots a lighter gauge said, "I wouldn't have expected you to use that twelve-gauge on woodcock." From his tone I might have been beating a dog. The gun was my nice old Fox and to me the only thing incongruous about it was its 28-inch barrels and 7¾ pounds, which I thought in that cover gave the woodcock the edge. When I began shooting the little 6-pound 7-ounce Purdey 12-gauge (26-inch barrels) I was more comfortable, but I shot about as well with the Fox as with the lighter Purdey because both guns fit me, using a 3 dram 1 ounce No. 8 load in both.

Inaccurate gun mounting accounts for a lot of woodcock misses in thick alders or thorns, and the close flushes don't help. While an ounce of shot can demolish a woodcock up close, you don't wait the bird out if you are going to make the shot. I've never used No. 9's, as many woodcock gunners do; in the kind of close, fast woodcock shooting I do, even No. 8's often put more pellets into the bird than I would wish.

I remember only two woodcock flying on after being hit. One of them Shadows found—one of his last birds. The other bird seemed to go on forever with a leg dangling. We searched hard but didn't find it, the only woodcock my dogs have lost.

In October of '65 in a thick woodcock covert I caught my foot on a queer arrangement of chicken wire. It was a barrier about twelve inches high with enclosures at both ends—one of a dozen in the area. I found no woodcock in the traps, but from my experience with quail I could predict injury to a bird if it struggled to escape. I later talked to the biologist in charge and was told the traps were visited at least once a day. In addition, he erected nylon mist nets in open areas when he was in attendance. He trapped and banded about a hundred woodcock that year, most of them in nets. The ground traps were left in place until mid-November and, whether or not owing to this disturbance, the birds seemed less inclined to lie for a point. There were placards WOODCOCK HUNTERS! GIVE US ONE WING FROM EACH WOODCOCK YOU SHOOT, there was a mailbox on a post to receive the wings, and wing envelopes and a map of the area were tucked under your windshield wiper to be marked where each bird had been shot. The following year, signs WOODCOCK HUNTERS, REPORT KILL HERE were placed along the highway and a

THE BIRDS

game technician at the roadside recorded your kill. Banding studies provide valuable information, but this activity in the coverts during the season takes something away from the pleasure of gunning.

I am interested in the wing-study program and for years have sent a wing from each woodcock I have shot to the Migratory Bird Populations Station, Laurel, Maryland, in envelopes provided. From twelve to sixteen thousand wings are sent in annually. In the 1967–68 season, the U.S. kill was estimated at over one million.

If you shoot a banded woodcock and mail in the band you will receive a card with the band number, age and sex of bird, banding agency, location and date of banding, and location and date of recovery. All of the banded birds I have shot had been banded nearby, less than a month earlier.

About the time Rachel Carson's *Silent Spring* was published, there was concern regarding the exposure of woodcock to DDT used against the spruce budworm in the nesting areas in the North, and to heptachlor used against the fire ant in the woodcock's wintering grounds in the Gulf states. At Patuxent Wildlife Research Center at Laurel, Maryland, traces of heptachlor had been found in the tissues of woodcock in increasing amounts up to 1961. Since accumulations of pesticide remain in the organism that consumes it, it takes little imagination to see effects from a cycle beginning with earthworms that become capsules loaded with heptachlor, consumed as the chief diet of woodcock that in turn may be eaten in quantities over the years by woodcock hunters. Since heptachlor is considered a potential carcinogen, the Food and Drug Administration has set a human tolerance level of zero for heptachlor.

There appear to have been no marked effects on the bird and its ability to reproduce after exposure to heptachlor and/or DDT. On the brighter side, these pesticides are stored in the organs and fatty tissue. If care is taken to remove the skin and fat as well as to refrain from eating the liver or heart it would seem that a moderate number of woodcock could be eaten without ill effects. This restriction would not allow for serving 'cock in the old manner, with head and entrails.

In the autumn of 1970 the woodcock season was closed in New Brunswick as a result of tests on woodcock indicating excessively high levels of DDT (reports quoted levels up to 200 parts per million). Concern led to contemplating closing U.S. woodcock seasons but further tests here were reassuring. New York State found a mean level of 'cock tested there to be .27 ppm. Replying to my inquiry, Calvin M. Menzie, Chief Toxicologist, Division of Pesticide Registration, U.S. Fish and Wildlife Service, wrote on October 13, 1970:

"The newspaper stories are incomplete and the latest word is that the woodcock season in Maine will not be closed. Analyses of woodcock collected in Maine for the Bureau of Sport Fisheries and Wildlife showed a mean level below the 7 ppm level at which the Food and Drug Administration prohibits sale of beef. Those woodcock upon which the Canadian government based its action were collected in an area that had been treated annually with DDT from about 1954 through 1968. Other woodcock collected in New Brunswick, in an area not treated with DDT, exhibited a mean DDT level of 6 ppm."

U.S. woodcock seasons were open in 1970 but uneasiness about rising levels of pesticides in woodcock is felt by more than shooting men. To shoot a woodcock over a dog is one thing. To poison it—and ourselves—with pesticides is another. It shouldn't happen to a bird.

ONE OUNCE NO. 8

ONE DAY WHEN DIXIE was very young, she pointed along the base of a mountain in alder cover. I walked up a woodcock, which I shot. Dixie held steady and I marked the fall in a clearing and sent her to retrieve, pushing my way after her. It hadn't been a long shot and I expected to see her coming back with the woodcock, but she was quartering the clearing empty-mouthed.

When a bird falls dead it is not only air-washed from the fall but is more difficult for a dog to locate than a wounded bird that flutters and gives off scent. I repeated my command to fetch and Dixie combed the area with no results. Even if my bird had not been killed outright, a wing-tipped woodcock falls and stays there, unlike a grouse or pheasant.

I called Dixie to me and we started over, circling the clearing in a widening radius. Suddenly she paused and I saw my woodcock lying dead, breast up, in a spot where it could not have fallen. I think Dixie had gone directly to the bird, picked it up and brought

The Birds

it part way toward me, then laid the unsavory thing down and moved on.

Like many dogs who love to retrieve grouse or pheasants, Dixie does not enjoy picking up woodcock. She will do it if she thinks I don't know where the 'cock has fallen, but if she feels I have seen the bird go down, she may go to it, nose it and walk away. I know better than to try to force her; Dixie is the kind that could be turned against retrieving by harsh methods. If she's the only dog I am using I now make a practice of kneeling down to peer through the cover, watching her as she locates a fallen woodcock. On grouse or pheasants I have no need to worry—Dixie brings them on the double.

The length of a woodcock's flight is influenced by the height of its flush. Woodcock usually "go for the light," and having cleared the thicket through a hole at the top, level off. Birds flushed in tall alders are likely to fly longer and therefore farther than birds going out of lower cover. I remember one 'cock I flushed from a point of Ruff's in an aspen grove. It looked as if it were climbing one of the tall trees until it topped out and I don't think it ever stopped. When

Woodcock Shooting

the trees are wide-spaced, woodcock usually dart low and dodge around the trunks, earning their reputation—a doubtful one—for zigzag flight. The zigzag illusion is also created by a low straightaway flush when the gunner sees the woodcock's characteristic roll from left to right, but the line of flight remains relatively straight.

Flushed from bare ground or low cover, they don't waste time rising but get under way fast. One day Dixie pointed, stretched out in her intense manner reaching for body scent. A 'cock flushed as I moved up and I tried to pull the trigger with the safety on—a right-quartering flush that looked so easy as the bird seemed to float away like a toy balloon. I followed around a neck of alders where the woodcock had disappeared but failed to locate it. Coming back from a wide cast in knee-high tundra I unexpectedly walked onto the bird. It flushed at my feet, low and straightaway. I snapped twice at its flashing underparts and it went on, the tweet-tweet of its wings mocking my shots. A quarter of a mile away at the car, Kay heard my *"damn!"*

What did I learn? That a low bird can't fly directly away in your line of vision (and line of gun pointing) without flying into the ground, unless it is flying down a slope. If it is below your eye level it has to be, relatively, coming up and you must hold a bit above it.

I don't always miss, but perhaps I need a talisman. On our way to Blackwater, driving up through Roaring Gap we saw small forms huddled in the road ahead of us. Kay and I sometimes get involved with puppies or kittens some sweet-scented character has abandoned on the road. We can't leave them to starve or get run over but we have spent weeks finding homes for some of them. When you are in a station wagon loaded with setters and headed for a shooting trip, you don't welcome complications of that sort.

As we drove closer we saw that these were three baby raccoons, about the most appealing little things in the wild. Kay began taking movies of them as they scampered to the side of the road and climbed a few feet up two maple trees—two up one, the third up another—and peered around the trunks at us. There is an urge to do something about young wildlife, apparently helpless, but usually the mother is nearby and we decided it was best to leave them.

Down in the big mountains we got hunting by mid-afternoon. We were after grouse but it was a poor year and birds were scarce. At last I saw Shadows on point on the brink of a ledge of rocks above me. I tried to get to him, but before I could make it, a woodcock flushed out over the cliff and folded at my shot. Shadows plunged down into a thicket, emerging in a moment with my bird.

Further down the mountain Dixie began unraveling scent, head up and into the wind. I felt it was a grouse moving in front of her or one she was winding from far away. As I stepped into a small draw, remembering a group of seven that had flushed there three years before, a grouse exploded below me and tumbled when I shot. Dixie found it where it fluttered along the ground and retrieved it.

Later, beyond a large patch of greenbrier, I came to Shadows and Dixie pointing shoulder to shoulder like an Osthaus painting. Walking up, I was surprised to flush another woodcock, which went out low and left-crossing, falling at the shot.

I was using my second pair of barrels on the Purdey for the first time since having the choke changed to 50 percent and 60 percent for woodcock. I was also using a 3 dram 1 ounce No. 8 load my shell dealer assured me was inadequate for a 12-gauge. "A women's and children's load," he had called it.

With our grouse and brace of woodcock, Kay and I walked toward the car and on the way I almost stepped on a buck. There is a scent I find in damp fall woods that appeals to me, not because of fragrance, for it is almost offensively pungent, but because it means autumn. It resembles the redolence of a long-used dog collar, or ripe blueberries; it has been suggested that it is from some of the viburnums—arrowwood or wild raisin (*V. cassinoides*); and a mountain friend identified it as raccoon. I caught this same scent seconds after the buck sprang.

We reached the station wagon and drove to one of my woodcock coverts for the late-afternoon shooting. There, Dixie made a couple of points I was unable to act upon until one 'cock flushed away-left and I saw it drop as I shot. Shadows got there first and retrieved. Toward sunset a rising flush gave me my last shot and woodcock for the day.

A string of five hits is not something for me, or my dogs, to forget. I don't know what the magic was—perhaps because it was the first of November, or maybe it was the reworked Purdey barrels, or the "women's and children's" shells, or seeing the little raccoons. Or maybe there had to be a combination.

One evening after sunset Kay and I were sitting in the station

Woodcock Shooting

wagon eating a sandwich while our dogs licked themselves dry. There were three woodcock on the seat beside us and we were watching the dusking flight. The light was dim, but from where we sat we could see something move at the edge of the old road twenty-five yards ahead. It was a woodcock and it ran in short spurts, as fast as a bobwhite quail. I had pictured woodcock waddling awkwardly, not moving far in their search for worms. Seeing this one, I understand why a dog may find a maze of scent, especially in late afternoon if the birds are feeding. I turned my lights on and the woodcock walked to the far side of the road and tested it for worms, unperturbed by the lights until I drove close, when it flushed. Moving on, we flushed more along the road. The ditches were soggy and they were searching in the black muck for worms. Once they have begun to feed, woodcock eat voraciously, letting little disturb them.

I have had good woodcock shooting in drizzle with clouds blocking out the mountaintops around me. Light rain, unless it makes pushing through cover uncomfortable, enhances any kind of upland shooting. The dogs handle scent well and birds seem indifferent to the weather.

Woodcock gunning is exciting because you never know what's going to happen. When a 'cock comes up, nearly fanning your face, there is little you can do but obey reflexes and take the shot the best way you can. However, when your dog is pointing, you have some choice, for a woodcock is obliging about lying tight. It does little good to plunge into thick alders and fight branches with your free arm and shins unless there is no other way to handle the situation. If possible, I like my dog to range the alders while I walk outside. If the point is just inside cover, rather than go in to flush in thicket where I can't shoot, I try using my voice. If the voice won't put it up, sometimes moving back and approaching once more will flush the bird if you stop abruptly. They are not as jumpy as grouse, but like grouse, a sudden stop can trigger woodcock into action.

A woodcock flushed from a double point by Bliss and Dixie on my right, crossing an opening in front. I fired and saw the bird go down in an arc into hawthorns. Both dogs marked the fall but after a minute of searching neither of them made the find. I was never more certain of a bird, but when I joined the dogs the leaf-plastered area under the thorns was empty. As if to reassure me, I could see a feather still floating past my shoulder—then another, and another. I looked up and saw my woodcock, hanging in the spiked branches. I dislodged it with my gun barrels and it fell in front of Bliss, the most surprised setter that ever picked up a bird.

Regardless of whether flight birds may refill the coverts, woodcock should not be shot without restraint just because they are there. With a legal quota of four or five a day and no season limit, it can become a game of collecting. The first or second 'cock—each a particular experience because of the point, or the shot, or the setting—loses its identity and becomes merely another bird in a long string. The woodcock deserves better.

The 'cock's fastidious choice of coverts, its good holding to a dog, the speed and irregularities of its whistling flight, the delightful weather during the shooting season, the way the birds appear and just as suddenly are gone, the beauty of the bird, its excellence on the table, all combine to make woodcock shooting one of the best sports enjoyed by the upland gun.

WOODCOCK REVISITED

IT'S HARD FOR ME to realize I haven't been shooting woodcock every autumn of my life, but for years a woodcock was a bird I flushed in grouse coverts—two or three stragglers each season that wandered off the flyways into our area. Shooting woodcock in that manner wasn't too exciting, and unless a bird was in front of a point I lowered my gun, wished it *bon voyage* and got on with the serious business of grouse shooting. I had occasionally run onto a concentration of perhaps four, which constituted my idea of a flight. So I don't think I'll ever forget the 22nd of October, 1958, not only as a date in Dixie's first season but for the meaning the 22nd holds for me when October comes around.

The day began partly sunny with increasing masses of clouds as we topped the Brieries and hit pockets of fog. By the time we met Walt Lesser with Dixie's brother Jeb in front of the old Worden's Hotel in Davis, it was pretty certain we'd be hunting in drizzle.

As a wildlife biologist, Walt had discovered some coverts that promised woodcock in numbers if we could hit the flight. He had given Jeb intensive pre-season training, and Kay and I had just returned from the Amwell Preserve in New Jersey, where Dixie had been introduced to the gun on pheasants. But nothing, I think, equals work on woodcock for a youngster and this seemed exactly the thing for two nine-month-old grouse dog puppies with a lot to learn.

We drove into the Canaan Valley and took an old road into immense alder flats. A watery half light shut out nearly everything except the foreground but I sensed big mountains as a backdrop. We parked Shadows in the station wagon and took Ruff to set an example for his offspring, Dixie and Jeb.

The valley floor is flat and the extent of alders difficult to grasp until you've tried to cover even a small portion of them. A few cows grudgingly made way as we started out and we saw where they had been using over most of the area. Kay walked behind us with her movie camera and Walt and I kept well apart with the three dogs quartering in front. Ruff at eleven and a half held to a comfortable woodcock range and the pups were not yet at that stage when they wanted to take the world to pieces.

We made a sweep to the Blackwater River and circled back. The cover looked perfect—alders, grass, black mud trampled by cattle, but no whitewash and no birds. Standing on the road we contemplated the cover on the other side—identical with what we'd just hunted except for clumps of aspen beginning to show through the mist like scattered pines in southern quail-country savannah. I suggested that we try a couple of aspen clumps before we moved to another place Walt had in mind.

In the second stand of aspen Ruff pointed. A woodcock flushed and as we watched it go, two more went out to the left. Ruff soon made a second point that produced a fast bird I missed. I lost sight of Walt after we entered some alders, then heard a shot. From then on, action remained at a high with one or the other exclaiming, "There goes one!" and "Another one!" but with no shots.

I realized that, for the first time, I was into a flight. Whitewash was everywhere, even on cow pads, with probing holes through the cow dung to the earth beneath. Without warning, a large hen rocketed up from my boots with that weightless quality woodcock have and I got off both barrels before a rational man would have mounted his gun. Following two birds, we doubled back to the area of Ruff's first point and moved two more, all within a few hundred yards of

[59

what had proved barren cover across the road. So far, the young dogs had made no contact with game other than to bump birds we saw going out wild.

We pushed deeper into the alders and came to stands of a shoulder-high woody shrub called "hardhack"—a spirea so dense I suspect you could walk on it if you could climb on top. The thing to do is detour unless you find a cattle path to crawl through. Walt dropped the first bird of the day in the middle of this stuff.

Further on, Ruff pointed at the margin of some aspens and Dixie got a noseful. The 'cock rose in a right-quartering flush, dropping at my shot. It seems so easy when you hit. The next flush was a double going Walt's direction, one of which he dropped. At the crack of his gun, a third bird flushed and it fell within yards of the first. Circling with Dixie, I saw her swing on point. She changed position and pointed again a few feet from Walt's woodcock, lying breast up. Pointing dead birds is excellent training for a young dog, and while Dixie pointed, I handled her.

By the time we reached the car at four o'clock I had shot another bird. Kay stayed with Ruff while Walt and I took Shadows with the two youngsters to another part of the covert and immediately began moving birds. One flushed from in front of Shadows and came at me, weaving to miss my head where I stood in hawthorns. I let it pass and caught it in a low right-quartering clean hit. I had grasped a basic fact about woodcock shooting—take the shot quickly or not at all but, as with grouse, wait for a sharp focus on the bird, then mount and overtake it. I doubt if the entire sequence takes two seconds. Shadows came barreling in, hit the thread of scent to the bird, snapped it up and delivered in style. Some dogs may be squeamish about woodcock but Shadows would retrieve anything that fell.

I fought my way to the old road and waited for Walt to emerge. My abrupt stop flushed a woodcock from the far side—a straight-away I should have dropped but didn't, consoling myself that my pattern might have holes large enough to slip over the two-and-a-half-inch circle of a tail-on woodcock with only edges for wings.

We had done a lot of shooting over two such young dogs and Walt decided to leave Jeb in the station wagon with Kay and Ruff while we went on with Shadows and Dixie. After her baptism of fire on preserve pheasants, Dixie was eating this up. We soon found

Woodcock Shooting

two woodcock. Walt shot one, his fourth, which Shadows retrieved to me.

The low clouds were still with us and there was intermittent mist but we pushed ahead, Walt no longer shooting, hoping for another chance for me. I soon had it, a rising shot I missed. Fifty yards farther along, a 'cock showed against the sky and folded at my shot. For a while it seemed that, even with Shadows, the bird would be lost in the wet tangle of weeds. Then Dixie found it, dead.

As we walked back toward the station wagon with a gratifying plumpness in our game pockets, several birds went over us in the drizzle. It is difficult to estimate separate woodcock but we had moved at least thirty for forty flushes. It had been a revelation of what 'cock shooting could be. Compared with grouse, woodcock on this level offer more action for both the gun and the dog, and closer-lying birds for young dogs.

The Birds

THE FLIGHT IS IN!

Oct. 23-'62

Mr. George Evans
Dear sir—

If you want two hunt woodcock you had better come up this week they are on the move.

Yours Respt.
Melvin Heath
Davis, West Va.

In woodcock shooting, along with a close, reliable dog and a perfectly fitting open gun, a friend on location to notify you of the flight is something to value. Four hours after receiving Mel's note, Kay and I were in the Canaan flats with their miles of hoary alders, shoulder-high spirea, and aspens.

With the flight in, almost every clump of golden aspen held one, two or three woodcock. When we reached open tundra we simply turned back and worked more alders and aspen. Dixie was giving us thrilling points but I was hitting more aspen bark than feathers.

My first open shot came after Dixie's bell went silent in almost impenetrable alders. I was unaware the 'cock was in the air until Kay called and dropped (a well-broken wife) and the bird seemed to come out of my cap and dart over her. As it climbed I had a safe shot, which I fluffed, but the left barrel caught it well out. In spite of her cramped position Kay got her movie of the falling bird, a yearling hen.

It is possible to identify a male or female woodcock in flight silhouetted against sky. The hen is conspicuously larger. I think it is her bulk of body that shows up, although her bill is about one-fourth inch longer than the male's and her wingspread is greater. When examined, the outer three flight feathers—the ones that make that wonderful whistling sound in flushing—are not only longer but wider than the male's, with a more distinct concave curve on the trailing edge.

For years woodcock specialists used these outer flight feathers for sex and age determination in their wing studies. Size determined sex; age was determined by the amount of wear on these feather tips. Yearling 'cock grow these feathers when they develop full plumage in early or midsummer; adults replace theirs in their late-summer or early-fall moult. By the shooting season these outer three flight feathers on young birds are more worn than those on adults, showing under a microscope as notched around the tip. This method loses accuracy in the late season when adult feathers also show wear.

At Patuxent Wildlife Research Center at Laurel, Maryland, I was shown a newer aging method that remains accurate through the season. First, spread the wing and examine the secondary feathers on the *underside*. Begin at the "wrist" bend of the wing and count inward—the first five feathers being the most typical. Examine the marking at the tip on the underside. On young birds the narrow buff-colored band at the tip will show a well-defined contrast with the darker portion next to it. On adults this buff tip is merged into a smoky border with the dark portion, or the dark subterminal band may be missing. Sharp contrast indicates a young woodcock; smoky or less distinct, an adult.

Whether the woodcock you shoot is a male or female, young or adult, may presage your chances for good shooting. Woodcock gunners have long believed that the earlier flights are predominantly females. If I'm still flushing mostly females in early November, I remain alert for the males to come down later than usual. Conversely, if I find mostly males during late October I feel I may have missed the first flights. William Goudy, the research biologist, tells me that immatures migrate earlier than adults. An early mixture of adults and immatures of both sexes usually indicates a concentration of locals with no bearing on the main flights.

A high autumn ratio of young to adults is good news. If wing studies are accurate, the autumn ratio of juveniles to adult females was between 1.8/1 and 1.9/1 from '59 through '62. In '67, a year of splendid shooting, it was 1.95/1.

Grouse have made it clear that they are the most difficult bird for me to shoot, but woodcock have done more to improve my shooting than anything I have tried. They offer varying flushes and a lot of action. Some seem to float while others get out like rockets. In alders you are usually too close to take the bird rising, it is out of sight a moment after it levels, so you must shoot when it tops the cover. The varied speed in different situations makes it necessary to forget preconceived notions of how to lead certain angles. If you pause to think, you'll have nothing but the memory of whistling wings and the report of your gun. Take each shot when and as it comes, focus on the bird and mount and shoot instinctively; then decide afterward how you hit it. Which isn't a bad rule for any wing shooting.

The sun was almost touching Canaan Mountain, black against a green-gold sky, but true sunset was twenty minutes away. This is the hour, with cold creeping in as time runs out, when woodcock seem to take form out of the ground and you can almost smell them and your dog moves in a trance, scanning the terrain for the richest of the scent. Under these conditions, a good woodcock dog works with its head down, not actually ground trailing but working scent like ground fog on a damp evening.

With Dixie in her top form, something good seemed to happen between the little Purdey and me. 'Cock tend to fly faster toward evening; some men think it is because, being nocturnal, the woodcock sees better in dimmer light. I may be like the woodcock, for I brought off shots I never seem to manage on grouse—perhaps the difference between the gentle tinkle of a woodcock rise and the nerve-shattering burst of a flushing grouse. In a crab thicket ahead, Dixie was solid in a stand-up point unusually high for 'cock. Anticipating a grouse, I hurried up, feeling myself tighten. When I reached her, a woodcock bounced up twenty yards to her right. I thought I'd missed, then saw it settle at the edge of the thicket, and there were feathers floating toward me. Dixie was gone and back in seconds—a white ghost with the dead 'cock in her soft mouth.

The dusking flight began after we reached the station wagon and Kay and I sat and drank coffee as we watched. We had lost count of separate woodcock we had moved during the afternoon's shooting. Now we counted new birds flying in for the night's feeding. In spite of biologists' estimate that a large portion of the woodcock in the Canaan Valley are local birds, the big flights provide the outstanding shooting. One fall we had no discernible flights and the difference in sport was amazing. Flight birds or locals, there are no grander birds for sustained action. This was only a tiny fraction of the Valley and it was a safe guess that there were a thousand woodcock tonight in the alder flats of the Canaan. As I fell asleep back at our Blackwater Falls cabin, the vision was spinning in my brain.

Woodcock Shooting

A NOVICE AND A VETERAN

ONE OF MY MOST GRATIFYING SHOTS on woodcock was in October of 1964. Bliss, double granddaughter of my old Ruff, had been given pre-season training on local woodcock and now we were going to play for keeps. On our way into the coverts we met two pairs of gunners coming out. They reported poor shooting, which sounded as though local birds had moved south and the flights had not begun. Or that they had been trying too early in the day.

I gave Shadows a half hour's turn in deference to his eleven years and got a point with no shot. At four o'clock I brought him back and Kay and I put down Bliss and her mother Dixie, our brace of matched "snow beltons." I used a sleigh bell on Bliss, Dixie wore a small brass bell that was a legacy from an old Pennsylvania grouse dog, and the bells and their movements were pure harmony.

Within minutes Dixie made one of her stretched-out points at the edge of a clearing but Bliss came in too fast to stop. The woodcock bored directly at me and I turned, brimming with confidence, and missed both barrels. But the setters shuttled through the alders like lightly ticked gyrfalcons, it was our first day on woodcock, and life was good. Then in a dense expanse of cover Bliss's bell went silent. I had her located but it was two minutes before I could push my way to where I found her solid, looking like a dream.

Knowing a kill was impossible in that thicket, I wedged in beside her to honor her point by at least flushing her bird. The 'cock went arcing through the tops of the alders and I tried for it anyway, shooting through branches. By a glorious chance it folded. Bliss ran to the site of the fall, mouthing the bird in a bewildered, gentle manner. A kill over a puppy's perfect point at not yet ten months of age is, perhaps, routine to an outsider. But that bird enhanced the entire trip for me in the way one small thing can become something splendid for a dog and a man.

On another point by Dixie, Bliss swung toward her and, at my hand signal, backed. This is the time, knowing you've got a good one, that being so fortunate goes to your head. The 'cock gave me an easy shot but it took two shells to drop it. Dixie retrieved.

To emphasize the need for caution, I was passing up shots at birds young Bliss might have bumped. When the sun was dropping toward the ridge, one came over my left shoulder far from where either dog could be and I tried for it and saw it go down far out in the sea of alders. I plunged in with Dixie and Bliss but couldn't get them on the scent, though Kay joined in and all of us searched until dusk. At last we were forced to give up and we drove to our cabin with the fine day tarnished.

Next morning after breakfast at the cabin I hid one of the previous day's woodcock that had been in the refrigerator overnight, then sent Shadows into a rhododendron thicket to fetch. He made four prompt finds and retrieves, regarding it as kid stuff. With the idea of a cold bird fixed in his mind, we drove back to the scene of the previous evening's search.

Locating my empty shell, I re-established the direction and distance of the fall and Kay and I took Shadows in alone. Within minutes I saw him turn, put his head down and pick up the woodcock, which he retrieved and sat proudly to deliver—a nice hen.

A bird shot and lost seems tragic, while a bird shot and found— but just as dead— is a matter for rejoicing. Like so much about gunning, it appears illogical, but that's the way it is.

Woodcock Shooting

ONE MAN'S FOLLY

AT OUR COUNTY SEAT a stranger stopped by our parked station wagon to admire the setters. "If I had the time—" he reached through the window and rubbed Dixie and Bliss about the ears—"these would be my folly."

A special "folly" of mine, and I like the word, was shooting over Dixie and Bliss as a brace. Locating a pointing dog in dense woodcock cover with the bell silent isn't always easy. With a brace of light beltons you usually see the backing dog first—which is the purpose of the backpoint. Two reliable woodcock dogs working in coordination offer additional ground coverage and extra assurance of recovering fallen birds. But I may as well stop pretending it was for efficiency. I did it for the exquisite pleasure of seeing a well-trained brace work 'cock.

Although it was a mid-November day we couldn't help trying one of our better woodcock coverts one more time. We started at the same hour, we covered the same alders and aspens where we had been finding birds, but something was different. Now the pasted-down aspen leaves were tobacco-brown instead of golden, and there were no white splashings. Finally we moved one woodcock over a point by Bliss.

Next day we hunted grouse on the high plateau. In the last hour of daylight we stopped, with not much hope for success, at a covert where I had shot several 'cock earlier in the season. It had been a good woodcock year, Bliss in her third season and Dixie in her ninth had given me lovely work—so lovely I had been shooting only over points, woodcock shooting at its best.

This afternoon Bliss was overeager from too few contacts with birds and was into the woods ahead of us. It was not classic alder-aspen cover, but hawthorns in second-growth woodland with a few alders on the edges. By the time Kay and I reached the woods both dogs' bells were no longer tinkling. In spite of their light color I could see neither and repeated blasts on the whistle got no results.

With time slipping, I hurried into the thicket. Far ahead, I saw Bliss doubled on herself in an intense point and, to one side, Dixie backing loyally. Both had held like angels while I had whistled and

The Birds

called. Oddly, when I walked in there was no bird. I have had this happen when I've been long in getting to a point. There is no doubt they'd had a bird but I suspect a long wait occasionally inspires the 'cock to slip out on a silent "floating" rise. Which poses the question: do woodcock produce their wing twitter only in alarm when walked up, but go up silently when not frightened?

Bliss, now frantic, dashed on fifty yards and froze again. This time there was a bird—probably the same one, for those quiet ones usually make short flights—but it flushed without giving me a chance. As I swung the dogs ahead, we found whitewash on leaf-covered rocks over a large area as if a fall of woodcock had dropped in. Just then Bliss hit another point. This time there were three 'cock and again I didn't get a shot. After the next two flushed without offering me a shot I was as jumpy as the birds.

When shooting only over points the gunner puts himself at a disadvantage, for in thick cover the shot is close. Walking in on a tightly lying woodcock is like pulling a piano string to the breaking; when it comes, the twitter-up can destroy me. I could stand back and let Kay walk it up but I feel that wouldn't do honor to the bird. I am never certain which is the best way to approach a point on woodcock. If, as on grouse, you come in from the side or from the front, the woodcock lies so tightly it comes up between your feet—unnerving, and when hit it is usually demolished. Walking in from behind the dog most often produces a going-away flush. If the cover is open enough, this may be low and can be a good shot; if thick, look for the bird to fly toward an opening overhead, when again you get only a short view but at better range than birds that come up inches in front of your face.

In the shadow beyond the far edge of the covert a sudden flutter from a hawthorn spun me around as a grouse started up. My nerves were in no condition to deal with an unexpected grouse, and I missed and missed again. At the second report a woodcock bounced up a few yards beyond the grouse's hawthorn and settled in the opening beyond.

Both dogs moved in and went on point. I walked it up and the 'cock fell in a low going-away shot and Dixie retrieved what would seem to be my final woodcock of the year.

We turned back and picked our way through uncertain footing over a forest floor that was mostly rocks. I was thinking what a miracle a sinking red sun can be with tree branches etched against it when I saw a white specter far in front with the straight-out tail that is Dixie's stance on woodcock. I hurried up and heard the whistling flush somewhere ahead and to the left, got a short look at the 'cock high against a piece of red sky that, even then, said *hen*, fired and to my surprise saw the bird fold. Dixie was nearly under it and made the retrieve.

There is no predicting woodcock, from the time you expect the first flights until they go. Yesterday we had said our *adieux* to what appeared to be the last 'cock of the season. Today we had moved eight in slightly over half an hour. These birds, if I'm not presuming too much omniscience, would be gone, if not this night, then surely by another night or so. And after that these coverts would take on an almost desolate emptiness. The Woodcock Moon was past.

SONG AT TWILIGHT

WITHIN THE LAST FEW YEARS, my affair with woodcock has expanded beyond Indian-summer days. I have discovered the pleasure of dog training on woodcock in September and again in March when the birds come back north. You have the 'cock, the dogs and the coverts—everything but the shooting. In spring there is, in addition, the courtship sky dance of the males. At such times I prefer to forget there is anything like a gun and simply look and listen.

On the second day of April, 1965, I flushed a woodcock in our lane. It disappeared in a plantation of young pines north of our house. After sunset when I stepped onto the north porch I heard a tentative *beezp* at the edge of the pines. Gradually the sounds became more frequent until seven, when the bird made its first flight. While he was in the air we heard a second male in the pines. As we moved closer we flushed a third woodcock, the lady being courted, identified by her size. The first male gave up and moved away, but the second one made repeated flights. He landed so near where we were hiding we could hear a curious *took-koo* sound before each *beezp*, like the cooing note of a pigeon. Once we saw him on the ground. He didn't strut but at each *beezp* his body and small tail jerked from the force of his delivery.

The Birds

Most biologists call the buzzing a *peent* but the woodcock's pronunciation is a nasal buzz, like a cicada on a summer afternoon, lasting about a second. I would guess he makes the *beezp* by vibrating his long tongue between his mandibles like a reed instrument. He did it six times at three-second intervals, then there was the twitter-up of wings and he flushed horizontally into a spiral with a diameter of 150 yards. We watched as he came around, higher on each loop, until he climbed nearly out of sight. Vertical distance is misleading but we estimated that he went up two hundred feet or more. He seemed suspended there, then started down so abruptly that we lost him, but we began to hear his wonderful liquid song in irregular bursts of four rapid notes. As the music grew louder we saw him in a zigzag dive, there was the wing twitter again and he put on the brakes and sideslipped into the pines almost at the site of his takeoff. The weather was cool with thin overcast, there was a new moon in the west and we had a good performance until we came into the house at seven-thirty.

The woodcock starts his act when the light diminishes to a definite level after sunset, or increases to this intensity after dawn. On a clear evening this occurs about twenty minutes after sunset. Rain, snow or fog discourages the show.

On the second evening the buzzing began at six-fifty, within a minute of the time it started the previous evening. After a five-minute warm-up he made nine flights in nineteen minutes. Once he skimmed in so close he nearly touched our heads where we crouched in the dusk among the short pines.

Singing woodcock behave within a general pattern. One bird may sound the *beezp* in groups ranging from as few as three to as many as fifty, and we heard one series of sixty-five. The warm-up often continues for five or ten minutes; the *beezp* seems always to last about one second, but may be spaced three to five seconds apart. If you knew what the woodcock had in mind you could count down with him to zero and be prepared for his launching; instead, you wait for the twittering takeoff whistle of his wings.

The male doesn't always ascend in a spiral. One woodcock zoomed off like a rocket fired at a low angle, turned back and came almost directly over us but climbing. He made two or three forward and back ascents until he reached what a falconer would call his "point of pride," where he flickered, a mere speck in incredibly high and joyous flight. The descent is like the falcon's stoop, except that it zigzags, and the accompanying clusters of *chirp-chirp-chirp-chirp* rising vocal notes have a ventriloquistic character—one moment seeming directly overhead, then behind, followed by a split second of silence before the bird splashes down from a completely unexpected direction. If you are at your car you can lie back on the hood and keep the woodcock in view throughout his climb and dive. The sky dance may go on for a half hour or longer. No two birds perform exactly alike and even individuals vary from night to night. On bright moonlit nights they have been known to continue all night.

In '65, our woodcock sky-danced here from the 2nd to the 6th of April. The next evening the weather was warm, cloudy and breezy and two males buzzed near our house for ten minutes but there was no flight. The following evening, April 8, there was not even that haunting sound. The woodcock had moved on. A display for only a few evenings indicates passage woodcock. In breeding areas the sky dance may continue into early June.

I'm not likely to witness it but the woodcock does his sky dance at dawn as well as at twilight. Most books state that the courtship display begins when woodcock return to their breeding grounds, that mating takes place on the singing ground and that the female nests nearby. This is true in places where woodcock breed and summer, but where we live near the Mason-Dixon Line any woodcock that raise young here keep their existence a secret. On April 8th, 1971, Kay found a woodcock egg on the edge of a farm road within inches of tractor tire marks in the clay. Almost as large as a grouse egg, it was gray with brown splotches and was pointed at one end. It seems incredible that so small a bird can lay an egg that large. We moved a woodcock in the area but I have no doubt this was an odd egg dropped, as quail and pheasant eggs frequently are, more on impulse than with intent to nest. I have never seen a woodcock with young in this area during the thirty-one years we've lived here, but we do see the sky dance.

After the abnormally large flights in October and November of '67, an unusual number of woodcock dropped into our coverts on their way north in March and April of '68. Spring "singing counts" are made to estimate woodcock population. In our local coverts these counts record mostly transient males on their way to breeding grounds further north, not birds that will produce young here. I

THE BIRDS

have visited coverts in early October where numerous males had been counted in the spring and, with a pair of good woodcock dogs, have failed to turn up a bird. Singing counts to determine resident birds should be made after the migration is over. I suspect that singing males in our area either play to an empty house or, if matings result, that the hens continue north to lay their eggs. According to William G. Sheldon in *The Book of the American Woodcock* (University of Massachusetts Press, 1967) most of the males fly north first, singing on the way; the females arrive later and mating takes place.

Banding records show that woodcock, after their first winter migration, return to breed in the same area where they were hatched, returning each spring for as long as they live. An early shooting season before migration begins exposes them and their progeny to "captive" pressure and may decimate native breeding stock. Woodcock raise only one brood each year and normally lay four eggs. Populations would be endangered if a large number of hens did not live to lay a second year.

I'm sure passage woodcock have been sky-dancing in favorable spots in our terrain, even on our own land, every spring we have lived here. An open field near swampy land or alders is a likely place. Flat areas with scattered hawthorns or plantations of young pines appeal to woodcock. Listen for the *beezp* soon after sunset. Face west and keep the lighter part of the sky behind the woodcock when he takes off. As you watch that fluttering form, listen with your mouth open and your hands cupped behind your ears and you will hear one of the loveliest sounds on earth or above it. The woodcock was probably making his astounding flight more than a million years ago and, if treated half decently, he may be doing it at twilight on spring evenings a thousand years from now.

Grouse Shooting

🌺 / *Her bell goes silent and I find her,*
  Eyes glazed, a blue belton sculpture
With choke-bore nostrils endlessly reaching.
At my step, a flare of fan,
  A black-barred flash of breast climbing,
As much sound as motion.
The gun becomes my eyes and recoil jabs my cheek
  But only yellow leaves spin down—
Empty echo to the shot.

WHY?

WHEN I THINK OF shooting, which is often, I think of grouse. For if woodcock shooting is one of my delights and pheasant shooting a dalliance, grouse shooting is my addiction.

The novice has his concept of grouse shooting: you have a bird dog, you have a gun, you have grouse spread through the woods in groups; your dog quarters in figure eights and points with one forepaw raised at contact with each grouse, you walk up to him with a repeater shotgun (the more shots, the better your chances) and if the flush is a straightaway the grouse will fall, for a straightaway is the easiest shot. It may take him years to learn how rarely it happens this way.

There is nothing sensible about grouse hunting and a man can't be entirely sane who will put himself through what he calls the pleasures of the sport. In most gunning—quail, dove, woodcock, waterfowl, pheasant—there is frequent shooting. With the exception of dove shooting, I know of no bird shooting that offers so few hits for shells fired and, other than turkey hunting, so few chances to shoot as does grouse shooting, unless you indulge in idiot shots. One season I hunted grouse in deep snow for twenty-eight days and fired exactly three shells. Only the dedicated are grouse hunters.

Psychiatrists speak of "incompleted action" and resultant ten-

sions. When grouse hunting you push hard, alert, with eyes straining at each grapevine or thorn thicket, your muscles and nerves unconsciously set for action. The build-up reaches exquisite proportions when your dog checks, then points. You hurry to him, your nerves tightening further, but the dog reconsiders and moves on. As you proceed, your pulse returns to normal but you haven't unwound. At the end of the long day you get a productive point. It is now nearly dusk and your eyes bulge in an effort to see the bird as it goes out. The roar of the flush pours an additional jigger of adrenalin into your bloodstream, and you start the swing just as the hurtling form disappears behind a tree. You lower the gun, undischarged like all the high-octane stuff boiling through your system. An incompleted action.

After a week or more of this I have asked myself why I go on hunting grouse, especially in a bad year. But I know. I am certain the moment will arrive, if not today, tomorrow. It may not be an easy shot but I'll make it, probably without knowing how I do it— the swing, the report I rarely hear, the grouse immobilized and falling out of a circle of feathers that looks like the pattern of the load. As I accept the soft, warm form from a gentle mouth, my interbrain sends messages of good will to my glands and my juices flow in a way that produces euphoria. The grouse is the loser here, I can't forget that, but with a clean hit I don't believe it knows what happens. This is the moment when the gunner, the dog, the grouse become an entity. It passes almost with the echo of the shot, but it lives in your brain for years. At this level, grouse hunting achieves the intensity of a passion. If it doesn't, you're not a grouse hunter; you're just a shooter who goes out occasionally for grouse.

The appeal of grouse shooting is the appeal of the bird itself. Not the dead bird you bring home, but your experience with it. It is not just because they are so difficult to hit, or so delicious, or so hard to locate, so brave, so beautiful, so clever. Even nonshooters sense the grandness of the bird, its disdain and refusal to come to terms, its explosive wildness. It is not only what the grouse demands of the gunner in endurance and patience and reflexes, and even more of the dog in inbred bird sense and brilliance. It is all of these in combination, and where it happens, and the unpredictability of how. And, perversely, it seems to be the failures as much as the successes that keep you coming back.

Someone gave names like "titmouse" and "dickcissel" to perfectly good birds. Others have felt moved to call a woodcock a "timberdoodle," a pheasant a "Chinaman." To them, wild things are "critters" or "varmints." To my mind, giving the ruffed grouse a nickname is like calling a gentleman a "gent."

I don't consider "partridge" or "pheasant" nicknames, nor do I consider them below the dignity of the grouse. I was reared hearing my grouse of the Alleghenies called "pheasants," or "mountain pheasants" further south. When I hear them spoken of that way I know I am in back country. There is a similar quality about "partridges" or "pats." But for years now I have preferred to call a grouse a grouse.

When grouse hunters—serious ones—discuss their bird, it is from a variety of angles, its food preferences, the kinds of coverts, the way the grouse behaves, effects of weather, its predators, diseases, population cycles, conservation measures, and, most personal of all, their experiences with grouse and grouse dogs and shooting.

The scientific approach has been covered by competent men, though there are exceptions that contradict the books. There is also the how-to angle, which need not be a collection of tricks to hoodwink the grouse. Learning how to locate birds, how to handle your dog, your gun and yourself more efficiently are refinements of the sport.

I doubt if there's a man who shoots grouse who doesn't indulge in considerable self-questioning following each day's gunning. No matter what the gratification of a grouse bagged, of dog work stylishly performed, there remain unsolved problems about bird behavior, what weather had to do with it, the seemingly impossible way to walk in on a certain point. Worse yet, the agonizing doubts that keep nagging after a day of fluffed shots or lack of understanding between man and dog. Or sometimes it is just the simple poser: why weren't the grouse there in perfect cover and abundant food?

One overcast day in November when Bliss was not quite three, Kay and I were using her solo. We had moved two grouse wild during the first hour and, after a long period with no action, Bliss suddenly hit scent. Winding with her head up, she took several cautious steps and froze. I circled to one side but the grouse went out behind greenbrier vines. We watched it fly through a neck of cover, then emerge and, sailing low, cross an open pasture to second-growth woods more than a hundred yards beyond. I like to follow a grouse promptly, for I get tighter-lying birds when I keep my dog moving right after them. Furthermore, Bliss had an eye for a grouse flight and genius for going to a marked bird. But all we found was a tangle loaded with grapes, though Bliss covered it thoroughly. I don't think the bird ran out, for she would have hit the scent. Some grouse flare after entering cover and fly on.

We climbed through grapevines and rocks and tried the ridge in the opposite direction. Bliss began reaching for birds, moving too far out and away from me, rather than across in front. Line-bred to Ruff, I had planned her like a blueprint, but you don't build grouse dogs, you polish them, like gems. When they disappoint you, it hurts and it's easy to become irritated. She came in at my whistle, cringed to my overloud scolding and then moved straight out as before. I knew what I wanted her to do and I thought she should have known, but obviously she did not, or thought she had a better idea. During one of these clashes of intent, she bumped a grouse. Hacking at a dog impairs its concentration on finding birds. I should have called her in and, instead of negatively scolding, I should have encouraged her to work closely, imparting a sense of excitement and expectancy.

A grouse chose this moment to flush from some boulders Bliss had missed in her forward casts. It came over me from the rear and I watched a good overhead-away shot go untried because I was complaining to Kay about Bliss and not alert for shooting. Reaching a bench of the ridge, we stopped to relax before turning back, probably the most sensible thing I had done.

On the return swing I found Bliss on point near the edge of a field. It was open woods, and before I could get close the grouse

Grouse Shooting

flushed low across the field as the earlier one had done, disappearing into cover. We followed, and half a grouse flight inside, Bliss wheeled and went solid, her nostrils distending. As I hurried to her a grouse flushed, giving me a right-quartering shot, which I missed.

Bliss made four more productives—five points in fifteen minutes. I can't remember having had three identical right-quartering shots in one day, but it happened here, and the last bird folded. It was as far out as the others, as short a view through the same thick cover, but I felt myself mounting and overtaking with a faster, smoother motion and there, for me, is the difference between a hit and a miss. Within seconds Bliss was delivering a lovely black-ruffed cock. I found the day suddenly perfect, and Bliss the most brilliant of setters. We had moved ten grouse for fifteen flushes in four hours; Bliss had made ten productives and a retrieve. The bird, a yearling, had, in spite of all the grapes and greenbrier berries within an easy flight, been eating only cinquefoil and greenbrier leaves.

But, viewing it critically, I had performed raggedly on two shots and had passed up another; I had handled Bliss poorly and for a while she had done less than ideal work; all of the grouse had been in typical grouse terrain but not over three had been in what could be called food cover. With a grouse in my game pocket it seems like arguing with success to ask why. Yet these are the thoughts that mill around in my brain when I am back home before the fire. They in no way detract from the glow of a day in grouse coverts but, instead, add something, for I think somewhere there must be answers.

WHAT A GROUSE EATS

IF AN AREA CONTAINS woodcock, pheasants or bobwhites they are usually not far from the foods they depend upon. Unlike these birds, a grouse has such a wide choice of food he can find some almost anywhere. The adage "grouse are where the food is" persists, but locating food is not, in itself, the magic many hunters think. If you doubt this, tramp through grouse food areas and see how many of them contain birds.

In my gun diary I have kept a record of the crop contents of each grouse I have shot for the past eighteen years. Year-round food records tell why grouse are in certain areas, but a shooting man is most interested in what a grouse eats during the shooting season. I have selected the ten seasons 1957 through 1966 as typical, with the crop contents of 178 grouse, listing the number of crops in which the five major foods of Allegheny grouse appeared, and the number that were empty. Some crops contained more than one variety, which affects the totals.

Grouse Shooting

	GRAPES	GREENBRIER BERRIES	GREENS	HAWS	ACORNS	EMPTY
'66	4	8	15	1	0	1
'65	3	6	17	2	0	1
'64	11	0	10	1	4	4
'63	1	0	2	0	0	1
'62	3	0	4	1	0	3
'61	3	4	12	2	0	0
'60	3	0	8	0	0	6
'59	10	3	12	2	3	2
'58	16	0	8	0	0	4
'57	9	0	11	0	2	6

178 crops: 63(35%) 21(12%) 99(56%) 9(5%) 9(5%) 28(16%)

WILD GRAPES. A grape-fed grouse is the most delectable game bird of them all, and the wild grape is the favorite of Allegheny grouse. Grapes don't, in themselves, assure a high grouse population. Nineteen sixty-four was a poor grouse year in the coverts I gunned, yet it was nearly impossible to walk without stepping on fallen grapes. Only three of the sixty-three crops containing grapes were from birds shot in October. The others were shot from November to January. During thaws grouse use fallen grapes that have been protected from freezing by the snow. It is easier to locate grouse when the grape yield is limited, for the birds concentrate on the few fruiting vines. Late spring frosts restrict grapes to protected hillsides and, when severe, destroy the yield entirely. Even then, grouse use the grapevines for cover.

GREENBRIER BERRIES. The bluish-black berries of the greenbrier (*Smilax*) are the number-two grouse food in my coverts, if you discount greens. In '61, '65 and '66, limited grape years, I found them in more grouse crops than grapes. Six species of *Smilax* tangle the coverts I hunt. Some vine into trees, others form impenetrable snarls, and the smaller wiry "rip-shin" cover old fields. Some of the high vines retain their leaves, appearing like foliage on the trees they cling to. In good years fence rows are blue with the berries, and it is rare that greenbriers fail entirely. Being persistent on the vine, greenbrier berries are reliable grouse food during heavy snow. They remain firm and plump within easy reach when the few grapes that haven't fallen are mere raisins. I more often find greenbrier berries in late-season crops, as though grouse providently waited to eat them when they would be most needed.

If grouse can be found where any specific food grows, it is near grapes or greenbriers. During heavy snow, grouse remain under the tangled vines for a day or more. But, like grapes, neither abundance nor lack of greenbrier berries has a relation to fluctuations in population.

GREENS. I find greens of some form in more grouse crops than any other kind of food. The most common are: ferns, cinquefoil, rubus, teaberry and greenbrier leaves. I also find sheep sorrel, mountain laurel and leaves I have not identified. One November morning we watched a cock grouse eating grass in the clearing of our Blackwater cabin. Each time he cropped a blade and swallowed it, his tongue flashed pinkish-tan. As long as we stayed indoors the bird fed calmly, but the moment I slid the door ajar for a closer look, the head went up, the crest rose, and the grouse ran into the rhododendron.

Being evergreen, the marginal shield fern and intermediate spinulose shield fern are good winter food, the latter growing almost everywhere grouse are found. I have shot only one grouse that had eaten Christmas fern. Cinquefoil, called "sink field" by an old-time grouse hunter I knew, is a small five-leafed plant found in acid-soil clearings and log roads and resembles a wild strawberry plant until you remember that strawberry plants are three-leafed. You see it, still green, through the winter; in summer it is conspicuous with its little yellow blossoms. Teaberry leaves ("wintergreen" or "mountain tea"), eaten most often in late season, were in a high proportion of the 178 crops. There were a few of the red teaberries in one crop in '57, one in '60 and one in '65. In '68 I shot a grouse with its crop stuffed with teaberries, acorns and buckberries.

There have been stories of poisoning from eating grouse that had fed on mountain laurel leaves. In *The Ruffed Grouse*, Bump, Darrow, Edminster, Crissey (New York State Conservation Department, 1947), Gardiner Bump reported eating two laurel-fed grouse with no ill effects, "though the taste of the flesh was distinctive." Kay and I ate a grouse that had some laurel leaves in its crop and felt fine. Mountain laurel is poisonous to some livestock, and grouse fed laurel leaves exclusively have died, but from malnutrition, not poisoning.

It has been suggested that when you shoot a grouse you should determine what it has been eating, then proceed to such food to locate other grouse. I shot a grouse in late morning in the Blackwater-Canaan and through the skin and feathers I could feel the crop jammed with bulky material. When I opened the crop a double handful of rubus leaves spilled out, nothing else. There are eighty species of rubus in West Virginia, mostly blackberries and dewberries. These leaves were from a low variety that turns maroon in the fall. It covered the ground where I stood and I knew it grew in nearly every clearing within a hundred square miles. Locating a grouse by looking for rubus leaves is like locating a steer in Texas by looking for grass.

HAWS. Haws ("thorn apples" or "thorn plums") are generally considered a favorite grouse food. More than eleven hundred varieties of hawthorn (*Crataegus*) have been described in North America, most of them in the East. There are at least thirty-seven species in West Virginia, from a little over a yard in height to the big dotted thorn growing to forty feet, with fruits from reds and orange to yellow and yellow-greens, from almost pea-size to the size of wild plums. Until a hard freeze, fallen haws remain in good condition on the ground. Of the 178 crops, only 9 contained haws, yet I was shooting grouse in hawthorns. Were they there for food or for protective cover?

ACORNS. I have found large acorns in grouse crops, swallowed whole with the shell on, but usually they are broken into peanut-size chunks. Acorn-fed grouse accumulate fat deposits, which help the bird winter well. Good acorn mast is irregular but some biologists think it is often followed by a successful breeding season. I found acorns in crops in '57, '59 and '64; good grouse years followed '57 and '64.

BEECHNUTS. I have shot grouse with crops filled to bursting with beechnuts—birds that made delicious eating—but there is beechnut mast about one year in five. I found beechnuts in 4 of the 178 crops. Some years beech trees develop burs, only to yield "blasted" shriveled nuts.

DOGWOOD BERRIES. Five of the 178 crops contained the red capsule-shaped berries of the flowering dogwood. In all but one, they were in combination with grapes. Two of the crops contained a single berry. I remember only one season, 1955, when grouse were using dogwood berries to any extent; 6 of 27 crops contained them.

CRANBERRIES. You have to gun the sphagnum bogs of the high country to find grouse using cranberries. I have memories of days when I had only to work my dogs further along the spruce edges to locate one more grouse feeding in the sphagnum flats where the cranberries grow. Cranberries impart a pink tinge as well as a delightful tang to the grouse when served.

OTHER RED BERRIES. Because grouse use some red berries it might seem that they eat all brilliantly colored fruits. Only one crop of the 178 contained berries of the hardy mountain holly (winterberry), two contained berries of the more common *Ilex montana*. I have never found mountain-ash berries in a crop.

One October day Kay and I were hunting along Yellow Creek above Davis surrounded by flaming mountain-ash berries, haws, and mountain holly with berries not yet frozen and translucent. Everything was red blended with gold, even the matched brace of orange beltons quartering in front, and Kay was preserving it on movie film. Pushing our way through waist-high golden bracken we flushed three grouse near the stream, the last bird giving me a long left-crossing shot through trees. It folded at the crack of the gun, cartwheeling the way wing-broken birds go down. Within seconds Feathers located it in the water, missing his first pass as he plunged in. One more lunge and he had the grouse, carrying it up the middle of the stream. He paused and shook, water and feathers flying, then sedately climbed out, dripping a trail over the rocks, and delivered the bird to hand. Its crop contained leaves and birch buds, but not a single red berry from the thousands around us.

We hunted to the Blackwater and drove up to Number 70. The lumber camps now live only as numbers spoken by hunters. There, we walked an old lumber railroad grade into the upper flats of Canaan Valley, silent and enormous. We had changed to our blue beltons, Shadows and Dixie, who became suddenly busier in a stand of alders to my left. It was a woodcock and I missed it as it topped out.

We were a long walk from the station wagon but I kept working further along the flat in the shadow of Canaan Mountain. Seventy yards out in a low growth of blueberry loaded with berries still unfrozen, the dogs found a grouse, which flushed straightaway and low. I waited that important pause, fired, saw it drop and heard a second flush behind me. Dixie delivered my bird, a young hen. The crop contained blueberries, wild raisins and a grasshopper, but none of the red holly, mountain ash or haws that were all about.

BLUEBERRIES. Blueberries and huckleberries grow by the square mile in the Blackwater-Canaan, are important summer food and hold enough berries into late fall to feed hundreds of grouse. The Huckleberry Plains on Allegheny Mountain are famous, yet the presence of blueberries does not assure grouse—there are too many to concentrate the birds. The only crop among my 178 that contained blueberries was the bird I shot in the shadow of Canaan Mountain.

WILD RAISINS (*Viburnum cassinoides*). These grow all over the Blackwater country and grouse use them casually. I found them in two crops in '60.

SUMAC. In some grouse coverts sumac ranks high as food but not in mine. Among the 178, one crop contained a few sumac seeds, though sumac grows almost everywhere I hunt. Yet, one day in the Blackwater country Kay saw a grouse land in a sumac, walk to a terminal head and devour the entire cluster, seed by seed. It took about fifteen minutes.

BLACK CHERRIES. In the Intermediate Ridges, wild black cherries are a prolific late-summer food and available well into the season. But, while 1966 had an enormous black cherry yield, I shot only one grouse that had been feeding on them.

MAPLE SEEDS. Four of my 178 crops contained winged maple seeds —two packed full, suggesting a craving for bulk. Two of the grouse were shot in early season, a third on the 17th of November, the fourth on the last day of December. Three were Blackwater birds, which rely on almost any edible material in autumn as opposed to a wide selection in summer.

BUDS, CATKINS, SEEDS. Grouse eat leaf buds of many varieties, from trees to shrubs as small as blueberry, often with short lengths of twig. In 1960, two of my Blackwater grouse had eaten rhododendron buds. When a grouse has been budding on black birch, common in the Alleghenies, the flesh takes on an aromatic flavor that detracts from its normal deliciousness.

I find catkins in a number of crops, mostly alder and yellow birch. A few crops have been jammed with nothing but buds and twigs, but most buds and catkins are eaten with greens. Seeds often accompany this mix. Buds, catkins, twigs or seeds were in 36 of the 178 crops. There was no relation to early or late season or to kinds of weather but most buds were eaten in poor grape years.

APPLES. The statement of mine that raises most eyebrows is that, with one exception, I have never shot a grouse that had been feeding on apples. On November 12, 1965, I shot one whose crop contained apple flesh and seeds, together with a variety of greens. Stories of New England grouse and apple trees are so persuasive I can't approach an abandoned farm without checking its orchard. Once, I shot a grouse that flushed from a woodland clearing that had several apple trees and a huge hydrangea to say this had been somebody's home. The grouse may have been considering the apples but what it had in its crop were wild grapes. It may take a Yankee *togata* to prefer apples.

Like most New Englanders, Dan Holland found this surprising: "It was quite a revelation to read your findings in regard to apples. I was sure grouse would take advantage of them where possible. Like you, I have been a crop watcher from the beginning. Throughout the Northeast they eat the fruit and occasionally the seeds from a decayed one in autumn and are particularly fond of the leaves. The latter becomes important from a hunting standpoint late in the season since some of these hardy old apple trees remain green after other green foods have been frosted. So I am much the wiser for your letter."

Grouse Shooting

Wild crab apples lie rotting in most grouse coverts in the Intermediate Ridges. A crab thicket is a wonderful place to find a grouse on a sunny fall afternoon, but the hard green little crab apples seem to have an attraction only for rabbits and deer. The gun-barrel-blue spiked branches are more formidable than hawthorns and your dog may come on point among them, but from my experience the grouse is there for protection, not food.

WATER AND SOIL. Studies suggest that grouse, like bobwhites, obtain adequate moisture from succulent foods and from dew without drinking from streams or ponds. In thousands of observations in New York by the Ruffed Grouse Investigation (*The Ruffed Grouse*, Bump *et al.*) no wild adult grouse was seen drinking from open water. They did not suggest that grouse never do but that food and cover exert a greater influence upon grouse distribution than does water. I find grouse along small alder runs and streams and on the edge of swamps, especially during dry hot weather. At the other end of the thermometer when there is snow on the ground or when the ground is frozen, the open flow of small spring runs and seeps seems to attract grouse. I have not seen grouse drinking—they are alerted by the dog pointing them or flush at our approach—but I have found grouse at the edge of open pools with no cover of a type to attract them.

The kind of trout stream that flows over a white sand or quartzy bottom is likely to have grouse nearby. The factor here is not the water but the gravel. Up on big Allegheny Mountain there is a formation geologists call Pottsville conglomerate, a typical outcrop on the higher Allegheny peaks locally called "bean stone." The small white quartzy pebbles that form the "gravel" in this concrete separate as the conglomerate disintegrates. I find these small white pebbles in many grouse gizzards. The authors of *The Ruffed Grouse* note that "White quartzy pebbles seem to be picked up more often than would be accounted for by random taking." Certain soil types appeal to some species of game birds—pheasants do best in glaciated terrain, the red grouse of Scotland is found only on soil that will grow heather. While ruffed grouse are not limited to soil with Pottsville conglomerate, it seems to me they find it exceptionally desirable. Whether because of grit material or because such soils grow the heaths—rhododendron, mountain laurel, huckleberries, teaberry

—as well as hemlock and spruce, I find grouse where I find this formation.

I have, in a container before me on the table, the dried contents of the crop of a grouse I shot on a fair January day at 35° with no snow on the ground. In late afternoon Bliss pointed in the middle of a power-line right-of-way. Three grouse went out before I could reach her, two flushing straight out the ridge. I followed and got a shot at one when it flushed from some slashings—an adult hen.

The bird must have been feeding in the low plants on the right-of-way, although I suspect the three had settled for the night. There are countless tiny seeds from some kind of dried flower head with several of the heads intact, each on a portion of stem. There are some long purple leaves I don't recognize but have seen growing, and there is an entire cinquefoil. This grouse had also been feeding either within the second-growth woods or on the edge, for there is a single dogwood bud for the next year's blossom. There are the tip of a spinulose shield fern and portions of catkin that might be black or yellow birch or alder. There are several half-inch twigs with buds too small for tree buds, and an inch length of bulky twig with no buds. And, most interesting to me, a number of small yellow button-shaped blossom forms that I didn't recognize until I saw them on witch-hazel shrubs—blossoms after the orange-fragrant fringes had fallen or frozen off.

This one heterogeneous meal shows how unrestricted a grouse is in obtaining all it wants to eat. Grapes and greenbrier berries may be favorite foods but, with the enormous supply of greens and rough food, there would appear to be times when it isn't worth the effort to the grouse to go where these special items grow. And in years of poor yields, the stand-by foods permit grouse to do well enough without fruits.

The longer I hunt grouse, the more I see the importance of cover in relation to food—cover in combination with food, and cover in proximity to food. I have found grouse habitually using small food coverts surrounded by open fields, protected by a clear view that would reveal approaching man and dog. Cover without food can attract grouse when flushed. We all have seen grouse escape to cover, such as rhododendron, too dense for a man to penetrate. The

Grouse Shooting

fact that it was near may be the reason the grapevines where we found the birds proved productive when another tangle of grapevines just as full of fruit held none.

Even with food and cover in ideal relation, I have hunted all day and moved only one or two grouse or none. There is some feeling that grouse feed rapidly and for only a short period, so it isn't surprising that they are not always in food coverts any time you choose to look there. Nor does a grouse spend the remainder of its time when it isn't feeding, in the spot where it spent the night. I used to be naïve enough to think, when I couldn't find grouse where I had recently moved them, that some other gunner had been there and cleaned them out. This is almost never the case. There is a factor, actually a combination of conditions, that I consider as critical as the presence of food and cover—weather.

WEATHER

Two kinds of weather affect grouse hunting: weather that happens, and weather that does not. Here in the Alleghenies it usually hasn't rained for weeks before the opening of the season and the woods are so dry they would explode if touched off.

After a dry spring and summer in 1966, on October 15 the temperature rose to nearly 80°. We hunted anyway. There was glorious autumn color, the tea smell of drying leaves, the familiar feel of fingers curled around fine-checkered walnut, and the setters and Kay and I in tune with life, but going into the woods was like sticking our heads into a salad bowl. What leaves were down sounded like cornflakes underfoot. As if to tell us their troubles, the dogs came in at every pause and threw themselves down, gasping with foam-flecked tongues a foot long.

We hunted a covert with brushy areas where late the previous season we had found a nice lot of grouse. There were greenbrier berries but today the slashings and thickets held no birds. Passing through a neck of tall woods, we moved one grouse. The bird wasn't in typical cover but I would guess it had been loafing in the shade. In late afternoon, Bliss pointed on a wooded hillside just inside the upper margin. There were four grouse but I could only sense their flush through the mass of leaves. Brushy cover attracts grouse later when the leaves are down, offering protection in the denseness of bare twigs. But in hot weather with foliage still on, the birds pass up brush for the cool, tall woods.

No matter how hard a bird dog tries, in hot weather he can pass within yards of a grouse and miss it. The high rate of evaporation dries his nasal passages, reducing his scenting ability, what scent exists is quickly carried off in the dry air and, baffled by this combination, he becomes discouraged. He covers his terrain less efficiently, and if you hack at him with directions, he does not respond. I have shot grouse under these conditions but I realize as I do that it is more than I could reasonably expect. At such times, fine old grouse dogs refuse to retrieve—it isn't pleasant for a dog to carry a mouthful of loose feathers that choke him at each breath—and it's wise not to insist upon delivery.

The other kind of weather is the sort that happens, and nothing can happen to you more personally. When my shooting was limited to escaping from New York for two weeks in the southwestern Pennsylvania mountains, I took pride in hunting in all kinds of weather. Nothing short of a blizzard or dense fog could keep me in, and I recall hunting in a few of those. When we moved to West Virginia I arranged my life around shooting. With long seasons, I became choosy and while I often gunned six days a week when the weather was nice, I found it not unpleasant to stay indoors when it rained.

And so I lost sight of the advantages and pleasures of gunning on a wet day. I don't have in mind icy rain running down your gun barrels and saturating your gloves, each drop drilling in where the last one left off, but rather a drizzle that seems to hang, barely precipitating, when leaves are spongy underfoot and even a light shooting coat will turn the moisture. In a pounding rain, grouse are covered up under old logs or in grapevine tangles or huddled in hemlocks close against the trunk. But on misty days when a slight fog veils the other side of the valley, grouse move about as if they loved it and a dog can handle them like a dream.

There is another kind of wet shooting that weaned me from my dry-hunting notions. It was November of '64 and Kay and I were hunting from a cabin in West Virginia's Pocahontas County. A gentle sprinkle had begun in the night, increasing to a driving rain

Grouse Shooting

that continued past noon. If I had been at home I would have given up, but rather than waste the day I phoned Wayne Bailey, the wildlife biologist, and arranged to meet him in Huntersville at three. The rain had stopped but mists persisted in the coves of the mountain as we drove north.

We parked at a watershed and hunted up the headwaters of a small stream. It was at flood stage and the mountain laurel and rhododendron were still dripping. As we climbed the mountain, white pine gave way to hardwoods with laurel still dense along the path. I walked into the first grouse under a hawthorn in a clearing. The path crossed the stream repeatedly as we worked higher, and because the woods were too wet to penetrate without getting soaked, we had to walk single file. There weren't many grouse anywhere in West Virginia that year, but after the rain what few were in this covert seemed to have come down along the path. We each shot a grouse and with Dixie and Bliss working nicely as a brace I discovered once more that near-perfect conditions exist either immediately after a rain or during light sprinkles. It is possible to move silently through wet woods, and though you can't walk up on a grouse without its being aware of you, it is likely to lie better to the dog. Scent on a cool wet day, like the steam off the dogs' coats, seems to hover about the grouse, held there by damp air.

I have found, when training a puppy, that a grouse wing dipped in water gives off more scent than a dry one. Wet feathers on a grouse seem to produce a similar effect. Even heavy rain doesn't appear to wash scent out of the air and I have seen productive points on days when it was pouring rain.

It was such a day in December of '65 in an isolated valley where I was sure of grouse. The drizzle set in soon after Kay and I started hunting and increased until it became steady. Young Bliss made the first point standing on a log road, pointing down the steep slope, but the grouse gave me no shot. We tried an old field where we usually move birds but they seemed to be covered up.

We were halfway back the ridge on a lower path when I saw Bliss hit scent on the slope above me. Quartering furiously, she began working scent as if it were a layer of vapor just above the ground. Her head well up, she crossed the path and froze twenty yards below, pointing into a tangle of grapevines. I was certain the grouse would go out through a hole in the cover over Bliss or flush

THE BIRDS

up across the path. Instead, it flushed below her, giving me a short right-crossing shot headed for dense branches. I knew as I fired that I didn't have time to swing through and saw the pattern splash a perfect circle in the wet twigs in line with but just behind the grouse.

We continued along the path, trying for a second chance. It came 250 yards further on when Bliss swung left and pointed toward a large rhododendron. To get a better shot, I moved several feet beyond where I stood. As I did, I heard the flutter and the grouse rose in a curving flight that would have given me a good shot if I had stayed where I was.

A grouse that has shown preference for rhododendron will often do so again, so we worked the cover along the stream. I was about to say to Kay that my bird must have crossed when I saw Bliss on point again, turned toward a small clump of rhododendron, and I could tell by her glassy stare that the bird was close. I stepped in front of Bliss with no reaction until I kicked a branch, when like a charge of explosive the grouse came out inches from my boot and dodged around a sapling. If it had climbed and leveled I might have made the shot but I had to take it four yards away. It was the last look I had at that bird. Possibly because of the heavy rain, we found fewer grouse than usual but the rain gave us almost perfect dog work and my two misses were not because the gun was wet.

Grouse hunting can't be reduced to equations and not all drooly weather makes good shooting, especially the period before a rain. This is usually accompanied by a falling barometer, which seems to have an adverse effect. Although it has been suggested that reduced atmospheric pressure makes better scenting by releasing odors normally held down by higher pressure, some of the poorest days I have experienced have been at these times. I not only feel that scenting is poor when a storm is impending, but at such times I find fewer grouse for the dogs to scent. If the birds sense the approach of bad weather, they might logically be feeding to last out the storm, but if they do, I haven't observed it as a pattern.

On a warm and almost cloudless October day with a slight breeze, I discovered a remote glade of hawthorns lying under the wooded slopes and fields of an abandoned farm. On our first visit we moved thirteen grouse for eighteen flushes, had some nice work from Bliss and shot one grouse and moved woodcock.

Grouse Shooting

Nine days later we returned. The day was dry and warm but there were clouds of a storm system moving in. We parked the station wagon above the blind old house sleeping away the autumn afternoon. Today the covert looked even better, with hillsides thinning and thickets red with haws. Bliss worked just as diligently, but where I had left twelve grouse, today we moved four. The lay of the land is such that grouse are nearly contained and there were no signs of other gunners having been there. I blame it on the changing weather, which turned rainy and foggy the following day.

On the 5th of November I visited one of my favorite coverts. The overall grape yield was spotty but this knob was a mass of grapevines blue with fruit, and there were greenbriers heavy with berries. The previous season I had found a good number of grouse here and had shot only two, so I had reason to expect shooting. But the day was cloudy, with falling barometer and a forecast of rain or snow. I was lucky enough to shoot a grouse but we moved no more. That evening the rain set in. Later in the season I took a turn in this covert just to satisfy my mind and moved eight. It is this effect of weather that can give an inaccurate impression of a covert if it is visited only once.

Some gunners say they find grouse feeding actively before a snowstorm. Songbirds will feed excitedly for a short period at the beginning of a snow, especially if it is changing from rain, but with one exception my experience has been that grouse do not. On that day I hurried out in the face of a forecast calling for a severe snowstorm. The barometer was falling and clouds hung like gray smoke. I moved six birds and shot two in a little over an hour. It began raining while I was out and by the time I reached my station wagon it had changed to sleet. We were snowed in for two days. This is the only good shooting I can remember preceding a storm of any kind.

Wind often accompanies pre-storm periods and, of all conditions affecting shooting and dog work, wind is the most adverse. A moderate breeze can stir bird scent to a dog's advantage, but when wind is high it whips the scent off the birds and a dog may quarter his ground perfectly and still miss them, especially when the wind is gusty and changing directions from moment to moment. Wind stirring dry leaves from the ground makes grouse nervous and they flush ahead of dogs. On such days they take off almost silently and what sound they make is masked by the wind. When it is windy I look for grouse in valleys and protected coves, not on ridge tops or exposed slopes, but grouse do not always avoid windy situations.

On the premise that grouse prefer to bask in the sun rather than stay on the shady side of a valley on a chilly day, many grouse shooters hunt the sunny slopes. I find dust baths on sunny hillsides and I find grouse on the sunny side if grapes or other cover make it attractive. But if I must choose grapevines on the shady side or barren cover like scrub oak and mountain laurel on the sunny side, I'll take my chances on finding grouse in the shade, even on days with snow on the ground. I have never found that grouse prefer a sunny exposure for the sole reason that it is sunny.

Sunny, cool days can offer magnificent shooting, especially if the day has been preceded by rain, leaving the ground pack of leaves still damp. Walking is quiet and scenting conditions seem ideal if it is not too cold.

There was a time when I thought optimum scenting conditions occurred below freezing, when the differential between body temperature of the grouse and air temperature was extreme. But I have learned that temperatures between 35° and 45° produce the best scenting for dog work, particularly if the ground is damp. There have been days when I've had nice points in the sixties but they are exceptions; what moisture may be on the ground evaporates rapidly on a warm day and by noon the fallen leaves are dry. If the thermometer drops below freezing, the ground pack becomes crisp, creating as much noise as dry leaves. If you will notice on those days when your dog seems to do it all perfectly, the temperature is most often in the 35° to 45° range.

A sunny day has disadvantages in late afternoon. The obvious one is the unpleasantness of hunting into a low sun. I remember grouse that flushed into the sun, leaving green spots on my retina. I became aware of another condition during the past season that may have been the cause of wild flushes that have puzzled me for years. On this day grouse seemed inexplicably jumpy. Footing was quiet but in late afternoon birds kept going up as if released like clay targets too far out. We had been hunting with the sun at our backs and when I stopped to wait for Kay, who was above me and to the rear, I saw something moving through the woods thirty-five yards ahead of her, darting from tree trunk to trunk and across rocks and uneven ground. It was her shadow, elongated by the lowering sun, and I realized that our shadows or the shadow of the dog had been spooking the grouse.

Falling snow, if it is thick, wipes out hunting the way it obliterates a view, but snow, after it has fallen, offers advantages along with limitations. Some men say grouse hunting isn't worth the effort until there is snow on the ground. These are usually the trackers who don't use dogs. Tracking may appear to be taking advantage of the grouse, but most often it is inefficient. Going along with head down, unwinding a maze of tracks that frequently bring him back to where he started, if he succeeds in following the tracks to a grouse the hunter may road into it like a ground-trailing dog and flush the bird without a shot. Most grouse tracks end in a pair of curved wing marks in the snow and all that waddling around and the flush may have taken place hours before the hunter entered the woods.

Observing tracks is a way to determine if there are grouse in a covert, though immediately after a snow it is possible to walk through excellent grouse cover and see neither birds nor tracks. There may be no tracks for two or three days if the weather stays cold and the snow remains powdery, except where a bird has waded up to its hocks from its hiding place, gone a short distance and flushed. In deep snow it is difficult to determine which direction the grouse was walking. According to a grouse, the time to walk about is when rising temperature has softened snow enough to leave clean, sharp tracks that almost show his fingerprints. This is a chance to take a census of a covert. A single grouse can leave an impressive number of tracks when it is in a mood to stroll, but you can tell when there have been two or more birds; the lines of tracks may not be parallel but they follow a general direction. Tracking snow will give you a concept of how thoroughly a good grouse dog covers his terrain.

It is possible to move noiselessly over snow-covered rocks and logs and they are no hazard provided you are alert for crevices between rocks. When there is what I call a cotton snow clinging to every twig and clump of vine, any grouse that isn't literally covered up will be in a tree and will tree-hop when flushed, offering no chance for dog work. I have given up trying to hunt in cotton snow, for it seems nearly impossible to locate grouse. There was a memorable exception.

The Birds

In November of 1954, Less Crowl came for his first shooting visit with us and I was anxious to show him birds. With six inches already on the ground the night he arrived, the weatherman's "intermittent snow" kept coming down like a bleeding Christmas card and by morning the woods were full. In spite of the snow, I drove to one of my better ridge coverts, where I put Less on a tramroad and I bucked the thicket. We were using Ruff and Feathers and Less's dog Shell, Ruff's son. Although dog work appeared hopeless, we soon moved two single grouse.

Snow clung like white foliage and shooting seemed improbable, but we had gone only a short distance when I heard the report of Less's double, muffled by the snow, and he called that the bird had gone back down the run. Less knows what he's doing when he swings on a bird and when he misses he only grunts. We began to hear grouse going out but could merely mark the flushes by sound. As we followed up the mountain I heard one go up and from its piping knew it had treed. In a moment it reflushed, crossing to the right, and folded at my shot. Ruff retrieved it—an adult cock.

We continued to move birds so closely bunched they had to be new. One went Less's way and I called, "Mark!," heard the shot and Less's "Go fetch."

Topping a ledge of rocks, we hunted into a shallow crater. There, in deep snow, Less got his number 14 boot wedged between a root and a rock and we had a struggle getting him disengaged. After our efforts we paused to eat lunch and then hunted to the shoulder beyond. The cover was pole-size sassafras, and suddenly we were into more grouse—six of them going out one at a time but again mostly sound. We each missed some less than probable chances but it was so exciting we lost sense of time. Clouds were pressing lower when we started back down the mountain. It was nearly dark with dull red on the horizon when we dragged ourselves into the station wagon and collapsed over hot coffee. Less was delighted with his first taste of Allegheny grouse shooting but he had no concept of how unusual it had been. In the worst kind of cotton snow, we had moved twenty-two grouse for thirty-four flushes—my only experience of the sort. That we had had shooting at all was luck, that we each shot a grouse was that extra measure of good fortune that makes grouse hunters go out in adverse weather against better judgment.

Grouse Shooting

When hunting in snow, expect more than one grouse to flush. It is common to find a brace—frequently adult birds. We hear of broods breaking up by mid-November but in the Alleghenies I move what appear to be unseparated broods in January and February. In snowy weather, these groups cover up in greenbrier or grapevine tangles or perch in evergreens. I have seen only a few snow burrows and these were empty. Unlike the *togata* further north, our Appalachian grouse prefer snow-covered brush piles and rhododendron to snow burrows.

When you are moving through snowy woods, it's wise to remove the shells and look through your gun barrels frequently; a barrel choked with snow can be disastrous. I carry a heavy cord with a brass weight on one end and a chenille gun cleaner on the other. When I find snow in my barrels I wrap a Kleenex around the chenille and draw it through, or you can swab the barrels with tissue on a whip-size sapling. I also carry Kleenex to wipe snow off the exterior of the barrels and rib.

The pleasure of grouse shooting in snow is directly in proportion to your ability to keep warm. I have never found a satisfactory way to keep my trigger finger warm in bitter weather. Deerskin gloves with wool liners do well to about 25°; below that, any glove warm enough seems too bulky for shooting. Wool wristlets keep snow off your wrists and a knitted turtleneck dickey will do for your neck. A small whisk broom to brush off kicked-up snow will keep pants from getting soaked. With insulated rubber boots, warm, dry feet are no problem.

Winter weather follows a pattern: a snowstorm moves in, the next day clouds break and the sun comes out but the snow is still too deep and powdery for good hunting. On the third or fourth day, just when the snow has begun to soften, another storm moves in and delivers a new load. You find yourself sitting out one weather cycle after another, waiting for favorable conditions underfoot to coincide with a moderately decent situation overhead.

Snow makes it difficult for a dog to handle grouse, not only because it affects scent but also because the maze of grouse tracks confuses him. He identifies them by sight and will often waste time following day-old tracks when he should be quartering for scent. In snowy cover, a heavily marked dog blends against patches of dark brush, while a light dog seems to dissolve on snow. Unless it is solid plastic, most orange collars soon lose their color. Streamers of "shocking pink" or "flame orange" plastic ribbon of the type surveyors use as markers, if tied to each side of the collar, will make a dog—whether quartering or on point—stand out on the darkest snowy day. In spite of limitations, some of my most vivid memories are of hunts on, and in, snow.

It was Dixie's first season on grouse and I was using her with Shadows. I had shot a grouse within the first half hour and, not wishing to shoot another in the same area, moved to the far side of a low ridge, where I came to tracks lacing the hillside, singly and in pairs, but no birds. On the principle that if the grouse weren't up high they might be lower, I headed for a ravine. There, from a fallen oak across a little run, six grouse flushed wild. I took a long and foolish try for the last bird and missed. Swinging the dogs, I followed a neck of woods. Reaching an open field I heard a flush and a grouse bored out in a low right-quartering flight. I swung through and fired and the bird dropped on the open snow, where it lay with wings spread, fluttering to stillness. Shadows came in and I watched him quarter excitedly for scent and observed how little a dog uses its eyes. There was a stiff wind and though he circled the bird, head down, he failed to find it. Young Dixie arrived and I let her work it out, circling as Shadows was doing. But instead of going to the ground she kept her head up and, once downwind, wheeled and followed the stream of scent directly to the grouse, which by this time was limp, its head falling back over its shoulder from the force of the wind. There is nothing more sadly beautiful than a fallen grouse on snow—rich browns and tans of outspread wings and tail, iridescent ruffs, the red stain on white, the closed eyes, and like a stir of life already gone, the small motion of feathers drifting across the snow. Dixie picked up the grouse and brought me out of my thoughts, delivering it in a nice retrieve.

A Christmas grouse—and any bird shot during Christmas week counts—is about as nice as you can shoot, if one grouse can be more thrilling than another. You should have deep snow under pewter skies, or a sugaring on crisp-frozen leaves, or there can be brilliant sunshine on snow so soft it will take a grouse track clearly enough to read his lifeline.

I remember one bitter cold Christmas Eve hunt when only a half-pint thermos of hot tomato bisque and the right clothes enabled

Grouse Shooting

me to stay out. Grouse exploded from snowy hemlocks like puffs of white smoke or were mere sound, followed by a segment of snow falling from a branch. The birds were here but my dogs couldn't handle them in trees. I found myself in failing light, high on the mountain, miles from my station wagon. Before starting back, I ate my last half sandwich leaning against a tree while Ruff and Wilda gnawed ice balls off their feet and flanks. This was the day I learned never to carry a banana in subfreezing temperatures unless you have a taste for brown banana mush. As I half-walked, half-skied down the mountain, I could feel the temperature drop with the hidden sun and my fingers go stiffer. Then minutes through a woods that would have been nearly dark if it had not been for the strange snow light, I came to Wilda on a point so hot she seemed to steam, the bloody tip of her ramrod tail fluorescently visible in the dusk. I knew my brace well enough to expect this to be a backpoint. Probing with eyes sluggish from the cold, I could make out Ruff on a glorious point beside a mass of greenbrier. I sensed Wilda's step forward as the grouse flushed and glimpsed the dark form as it leveled, my numb finger searching for the trigger. The echo of my muffled shot was motion, not sound, as the grouse tumbled. Ruff came out of the dimness, sitting in deep snow to deliver the bird, a large cock shot over a double point—a precious gift at any season.

And so weather, whatever it is doing—coming down on you or refusing to—affects grouse shooting more than food or even cover. It affects your ability to shoot; it affects the location of the grouse, their behavior and your chance of finding them; it affects scent, the most critical factor of dog work. It takes a courageous man to go grouse hunting in some of the weather we have in our Allegheny Mountains, sometimes a stupid man. It takes a wise man to know enough to stay at home—and miss the fun.

GROUSE FLIGHT AND BEHAVIOR

MUCH OF WHAT a ruffed grouse does under stress is instinct but a lot of it must be something else. Some young grouse will flush into a tree and perch there with raised crest, piping as they would in the presence of a fox; others that have never seen a pointing dog or heard the sing of pellets will behave as adult grouse do, whether or not you fire a shot. How do they know to go up with a roar of wings, to take the far side out, to travel a long distance and to pitch into thick cover instead of landing in an open clearing?

You may say it is instinct to get far away from any animal—dog or man—once it is obvious that hiding is useless. But why doesn't the yearling that perches in a tree feel that fear? (Pen-reared grouse return to the "fool hen" state of innocence in one generation.) Why doesn't man on horseback or in a car appear threatening? A grouse will stand in the middle of a road to be murdered by a man in a car.

It is easier to understand responses acquired from experience. Methods of escape that have worked are used again—and again, if they are good enough. But what about that yearling that couldn't have seen a gun and yet flushed on opening day like a veteran? I suspect that some of this is a sort of "inherited experience" from ancestors who survived because they learned to do it that way and lived to pass it on. For there must be instincts that have evolved since the prototype. Canadian grouse, which have not been gunned as much as the more sophisticated grouse in the eastern United States, behave differently before a dog. If their responses were entirely basic instinct this would not be so. Grouse in hunted areas have become increasingly wary. Not every generation was bred from parents that escaped shot—and this may explain those young birds that act less wisely—but enough experience has been infused to put its mark on the blood.

Grouse Shooting

Traces of old tramroads lace the mountains in Pennsylvania, Maryland and West Virginia, following the contours of the ridges. From the 1890's through the 1920's these lumber railroads hauled logs to sawmills that operated throughout the Alleghenies. After they were abandoned and the rails removed, weeds grew up in the roadbeds, then blackberries and finally trees. Most are so obliterated that only close examination reveals old crossties rotting in the forest floor. For forty years I have known these tramroads to be good places to find grouse. Being on contour, they make easy walking and once were open paths from which to shoot. More than that, grouse stayed near them because they found grapes and berries along the roadbed and because grouse like an escape up and out of cover. When flushed, if the birds didn't top out they often crossed or even flew along the tramroad corridor.

As the woods reclaimed the tramroads, grouse have continued to use them. They can no longer find them attractive as openings, for overhead cover has closed in and few food plants remain. I suspect that today's grouse use the ghost tramroads because, having been raised along them, each succeeding generation has seen its parents and other grouse use them, though recent generations have derived little benefit. Some tramroad grades were later utilized as log roads, keeping them open and extending their usefulness to grouse and the hunter. If you haven't gunned for grouse along a tramroad winding through autumn woods you have missed a memorable experience. With a conscientious dog quartering left and right across the grade, it is a productive and delightful way to shoot.

One of the fascinations of grouse shooting is that, no matter how long a man pursues it, he seems to encounter something new. On a cold sunny day in November of 1957, Kay and I were exploring a tributary of Stony River up on Allegheny Mountain in West Virginia. This high terrain seemed too open but it was as near to being wilderness as anything in the East and that was excitement enough. We were using our father-and-son brace of Ruff and Shadows. At a little run bordered with rhododendron, hemlock and spruce a grouse flushed ahead of Shadows, and he went on point. Two more flushed without shots and we followed them to dense spruce farther up the stream, where, obeying my impulse to hunt the woods, we spent the afternoon attempting to ferret birds out of nearly impenetrable spruce. We would find Ruff on point and be treated to only the sound of grouse going out with no chance to shoot. When the sun reached the treetops we started back.

Rather than return by the long way we had come, I headed for a knob I judged to be in line with our station wagon. This led us across a big flat grown to waist-high blackberry canes. Both dogs were working it nicely when I saw a grouse flush to the right of Shadows. Finding grouse in the open two hundred yards from woods was new to me and equally surprising to young Shadows, who took one look at the bird heading for a beech woods and started after it. As he broke, two more grouse left the same spot, then a fourth. The air seemed full of birds, all out of gun range, with Shadows leaping at them as if he'd never heard of stopping at flush. As number six took off I swung through and missed with my left barrel, only to see number seven flush even farther out. It was too far for the right barrel but I was frantic. I might as well have saved the shell. Number eight took off, with me a shaking wreck holding an empty gun.

We reflushed a few of them in the dry, noisy beech woods—wild flushes too far ahead to shoot. With cold and darkness overtaking us we pushed for the knob. On the way we saw grouse roosts in open grass. We had moved twenty-two grouse and the only thing I managed to do right was to get us out of that wilderness before pitch-dark. I had not known that grouse will roost in an open area on a cold night, though I later read that flat lands seem to be most attractive to grouse when weather is colder than normal. In that high country, every night is cold.

My next experience with grouse in the open—again in cold weather at the end of day—was in 1959 in the Blackwater-Canaan. It is difficult for a grouse shooter accustomed to grapevine ridges and hawthorn bottoms to immediately appreciate this strange terrain. One day a shooting friend stopped at Old Hemlock with a glowing account of a trip to the Blackwater country. "Forget the way we hunt grouse up here," he advised. "The birds aren't in the woods down there. They're lying out in the open."

He was right. Grouse went for thick cover when flushed but we found them in the open, not only during the day but settled in to roost for the night. One evening at sunset I walked into a brace of grouse in frozen grass when it was so cold I could scarcely focus

Grouse Shooting

my eyes on them. If you haven't tried them, don't underestimate the difficulty of low, open shots.

Grouse don't suffer from cold as long as they are in good condition. One December day in western Maryland I shot a large cock grouse, one of a group of five that were on the shady side of a valley in preference to the sunny slope. The grouse had frost on one of its tail feathers—not loose frost from contact with the frozen ground but frost frozen hard on the feather. Feathers may not transmit sensation but a bird that can't stand cold doesn't get frost on its bottom.

Grouse often roost in the open right-of-way of high-tension power lines that cut across our mountains. Sometimes two or three roost together in the low cut-back growth. If there are blackberry canes, there are often yearlings together as a brood and I find them in such places as late as February. The last day of the '66–'67 season ended for us on such a right-of-way. It was February-cold, with deep snow on the ground, and Kay and I found ourselves in an unproductive covert. Rather than end in a negative mood we returned to the station wagon and drove to another valley for the last half hour of daylight and, as a final splurge, used all three setters. We came to grouse tracks almost immediately, but though we hunted until nearly dusk we had no contact with birds.

Turning back, we followed a log road that held to the side of the ridge through slashings. As we approached a power line with big cables sagging from one side of the valley to the other I saw Bliss stiffen in the path, a brisk wind hitting her in the face. Step at a time she moved, reaching, until she was pointing at the edge of the right-of-way, her head high with both ears swept back by the wind. This would seem to locate the grouse either in the open swath or in dense cover on the far edge. Dixie joined Shadows, who, almost blind with age, stayed in front of me, nearly tripping me as I advanced into the right-of-way. In the half light neither dog had seen Bliss pointing. There is some feeling that grouse flush into the wind if they have a choice, which would still give me a shot if the bird lay in the open. Instead, the grouse went out above and behind me, the wind carrying the sound away with the bird, and I turned to see it sail back over Bliss. Seconds later, another grouse took off from the same spot, following the first but to one side of Bliss, and I in my eagerness fired the right barrel knowing as I pulled that the bird was too far off. It was stupid shooting, but it had been a fine piece of dog work, from the first hint of scent in the wind to the established point.

As for the grouse, they had behaved about as should be expected —unpredictably. They had selected that open situation on a bitter night in preference to brush piles all around them or to heavy rhododendron in the valley; they had held tight, not unusual at such an hour but exceptional in a high wind; they had flushed back over the pointing dog, and true to form, they had disconcerted me.

I try not to look for the bird on the ground in front of my dogs' points, for to stare at the sitting bird will slow your focus at the flush. Much better, keep your gaze at "universal" in front and above the dog, where sudden motion will draw your eyes to the flushing bird. In spite of intention I occasionally see a woodcock or grouse under a point. The woodcock is almost always flattened with head drawn back into the body, and from that position it jump-flushes nearly straight up with legs like springs. Some grouse stand erect before a point, neck elongated and crest raised, but many lie flattened like woodcock, a bright eye following your every move. A grouse held this position on a drumming log and let me pass within six yards without flushing.

Driving along an old mountain road I saw a grouse standing in the middle about seventy yards ahead. Interested only in a point if possible, I reached back and carefully opened the rear door of the station wagon and let Bliss slip out. She knew what to expect but not where, and when she cast in front, the grouse saw her and instead of flushing squatted like a brooding hen. Trying to put a dog on sighted birds is rarely successful. As Bliss swung into the side cover a second grouse flushed from the bank above the first bird, which also took off. It was a fair picture of what grouse sometimes do as dogs approach, long before it is possible for the dogs to scent them.

Except in obvious situations the grouse's takeoff is unpredictable and may be anything from nearly vertical to a low skimming flight. The classic evasive tactic is the flush that dodges behind a tree trunk. Many grouse hunters believe the bird intentionally keeps the tree between itself and the gun until it is beyond range for a

Grouse Shooting

shot. I can't go along with this notion. Darting behind the nearest obstacle is understandable, but anyone who has tried walking a line from a given spot without looking back or taking sightings will realize it is chance when a bird continues in line behind the tree instead of showing itself.

Some grouse take the wide-open way out; others crash through twigs and leafy branches. I tell myself to shoot as though the trees weren't there and I sometimes drop grouse in early season by completing my swing and firing after the bird has disappeared into dense foliage. While some grouse come straight at your head, I don't believe they do so knowing it will unnerve the gunner, though God knows it does.

The closer I am to the flush, the more devastating the effect on my nerves. Late on a cold February day I came to Bliss pointing into a grapevine tangle with Dixie backing. I waded in behind Bliss in deep snow, each step letting me down into concealed brush and vines. At such times passages from books on shooting flash through my brain—*toes of the boots should be about nine inches apart, heels about three . . . balance and poise of the body must be even.* In the terrain I gun I'm lucky if I'm on either foot when I shoot. There was no flush but Bliss held while I backed out and circled to the opposite side. I got to within eight feet of her and kicked the grapevine but still nothing happened. Looking as if she couldn't believe it, Bliss

moved three steps closer and froze again. Suddenly, what I thought was a rabbit bored out of the snowy tangle at my feet, spread its wings like a fast-motion movie of a flower blooming, climbed vertically and topped a pair of saplings that jutted from the mass of grapevine. I waited until the grouse reappeared before I shot as it leveled. I missed, but it took talent to do it.

Each grouse flush is influenced by the character of the cover. I have hunted coverts that seemed stiff with grouse and have yet to shoot a bird in some of them. In other coverts with few grouse, I have had good shooting. I love to hunt where there are plenty of grouse, if only for the excitement of dog work and hearing the birds go out. Heavy rhododendron-hemlock is this type, as is dense spruce; tall beech woods never produce good shooting for me; whip-size regrowth choked with blackberry canes offers no footing; climbing a rock ledge is no way to get a shot. Yet there are often grouse in such places and when they flush it is in a manner distinct to each type of cover, and it is hard to resist hunting there. "Probable" shots as compared with "possibles" can make a lot of difference. Much of it is luck and the way the birds are coming up on any particular day, but some coverts with few grouse offer better breaks by the nature of the place. Being aware of these subtle differences in grouse country can contribute that extra bit that makes Lady Luck smile, and sometimes grin most pleasantly.

One of the "rules" is that grouse will be on top of a mountain in certain kinds of weather, or on the slopes or in the valley under different conditions. Grouse often use upper levels of a low ridge during the day, then drop to the valley a hundred feet below to spend the night, or for protection from wind, or during low temperatures, or for cover in rhododendron in heavy snow. But I am not persuaded that grouse that live on high plateaus around four thousand feet, such as the top of Allegheny Front or Cabin Mountain, ever get to the valleys miles away. In the big mountains when grouse are found on the lower slopes or in large valleys, they are there because they spend their lives there, not because they have temporarily dropped down to escape fog or wind.

Another rule some gunners cling to is that the best times for grouse shooting are early morning and late afternoon. I think it was Samuel Johnson who said, "It is but lost labour that ye haste to rise up early," and for my part, that goes for grouse hunting. I love to hunt grouse in the late hours of the day. If weather has been warm and dry, scent becomes more perceptible during the temperature drop of the last hour before sunset, a tired dog and a tired man gather strength and grouse seem to lie best, possibly because having settled for the night they hope to be passed by. You may not shoot at your top form during this late hour, especially if you haven't had a shot all day, but if you make a hit, there are few times when it means so much.

However, I shoot as many grouse between noon and three o'clock as at any time of day. The authors of *The Ruffed Grouse* list the hours in which more than eighteen hundred grouse flushes occurred during the autumns of 1930 through 1936. Far more grouse were flushed in each of the midday periods than in early morning or late afternoon. Early afternoon, considered by many grouse hunters to be the poorest time of day, produced four and a half times as many flushes as the highly touted early morning. Even my favorite late afternoon produced fewer birds than any of the middle-of-the-day periods.

No experienced gunner will question that grouse fly faster at certain times, and there are times when they take off silently instead of with a roar, affected by weather and especially wind. The wind behind or against the bird, the character of the cover and accessibility of escape all have bearing on the speed of grouse flight.

It is nearly impossible to measure accurately a game bird's flight speed. The New York Conservation Department carefully clocked a grouse at 47.2 mph, which included takeoff time and a flight of 251 feet slightly downhill to a definite spot where the bird entered a woods. Using the easy approximation of 1½ times mph equals feet per second, this is about 70 feet per second. Most estimates are not this accurate, and a bird shot at and hit by a fast swing appears to be flying slower than that same bird if snapped at and missed.

I have seen tables of flight speeds indicating that a pheasant flies half again faster than a grouse. But *which* pheasant and *which* grouse and *when*? I've shot pheasants barreling downhill that required as fast a swing as a grouse, and I've shot pheasants after they had leveled that were so slow it was difficult to swing slowly enough. To tell me that, in general, pheasants fly faster than grouse doesn't reach me. I've shot, and missed, both woodcock and bobwhites that moved like bullets, and I've shot, and shot at, a lot of grouse. One thing remains clear—nothing is, for me, quite so hard to hit as a grouse. Some of it is psychological (I almost said, psychotic). It is also because a grouse is fast.

The grouse flight that most concerns the gunner is the flight before the gun. I have often wished I could have been at the far end of a flight to see what the grouse did. Not to ferret it out when it had sportingly evaded me, but because much of the time I am so damned bewildered as to where it went. Sometimes tracks in snow will give the answer; at others, your dog will give you circumstantial evidence and your imagination fills in the blanks. But many grouse disappear in contradiction to logic.

A large number of initial flushes is often luck, but a high number of reflushes is a sign of good dog work aided by careful marking. I've become fairly adept at marking grouse flights in relation to a distant snag or conspicuous contour. This is elementary but I have known men who simply couldn't mark a grouse. If a bird topped out over the trees they were certain it had left the country; if it took off low they were sure it had gone only a short distance; and I've seen some of them follow "a straight flight" in a beautiful curve. With grouse that flush unseen in front of a point it is sometimes possible to estimate direction by sound, or by the attitude of the dog—a quick turn of the dog's head or a short break-at-flush, preferably only a few steps.

A grouse that climbs, then levels over high timber does not always go the great distance it may appear to. Conversely, starting with a low takeoff a bird may zoom up after it is out of sight and travel far. Few flights can be observed to their completion. It is important to watch the bird as long as you can see it—a slight change in direction in a grouse flight is magnified at the far end.

If I have marked the flight by a tree I walk to that tree and, before passing it, line up another tree or object ahead. Two or three alignments usually take me close to the area where the bird landed but you still can't be certain what the bird has done. Many of them bank before landing. Considering the cover and topography I try to visualize what I would have done if I had been the grouse.

In flat lands grouse may flush any direction. When you are gunning steep hillsides you will notice a general pattern, with birds remaining pretty much on contour except those flushed near the top, which often fly over the crest, and those flushed low on the ridge, which sometimes pitch for the bottom. The downhill flight is the one that seems to go on and on. Last season I flushed a grouse from a small patch of woods high on a mountainside. The bird came out a few feet above the ground, skimmed down a steep pasture and, setting its wings, glided almost between the legs of some grazing cattle and with no more than an occasional twitch of wings bored all the way to a woods a quarter of a mile below, still going. I've heard hunters tell of grouse that sailed from one side of a valley to the other, implying an air line across. I have never seen a grouse fly across a valley at higher than a normal grouse flight above ground; they always dip to the bottom.

In cover, I find that most grouse fly at least 200 to 250 yards. I recently flushed a brace on an edge of woods bordering a paved road. Both birds took the middle of the road down a straight stretch and banked into the woods, where I marked and reflushed them. I checked the distance on my car odometer as .25 of a mile—440 yards—and yet it didn't appear an excessively long grouse flight. Flight length varies with birds and cover—young grouse occasionally landing sooner than adults, with thick cover encouraging shorter flights. Unless it is a very young bird, I find it rare for a grouse to land within 150 yards of where it was flushed. If it does, expect a wounded bird.

There have been a few times when I've been privileged to see what occurred at the far end. Shooting with a friend in spruce cover along a sphagnum bog, I heard "Mark!" and looked up to see a grouse pitch and land on the floor of the spruce forest forty yards from me. The bird righted itself, stood a moment and then reflushed at an angle to its original line of flight. The sound of the reflush couldn't reach my friend, who had no way to know that the bird was not somewhere ahead in the direction of the first takeoff. I'm certain this is what has taken place when your dog makes a stanch but empty point somewhere along the line of flight when you are following a grouse. You may call it ground scent but it is actually lingering hot body scent.

I hear that grouse are learning to run out on a dog's point, like pheasants. I suspect most of the running takes place before the dog points (those that move out from under a point most frequently flush). When a dog makes an unproductive point, then follows scent to finally pin a grouse, he has usually struck hot ground scent laid down before he arrived. In a year of low grouse population birds seem wilder, suggesting a heightened instinct for survival, or it may be that the wildest individuals have survived.

Another opportunity to observe a flight from the far end occurred in the Blackwater-Canaan, shooting over Dixie. She had cast toward me and a grouse flushed wild. For a moment I thought it was going away low, then saw that it was boring straight at me. Before it could have seen me it made a 60° turn, climbed and was topping the trees when I caught it with a long right-barrel shot. Seen from the site of the flush, the flight could have been misjudged as a straightaway—many birds that appear to fly straight ahead aren't there when you and your dog arrive because they never went there. Direction of flight is more critical than distance in relocating grouse.

An old hunter where I grew up always followed the first grouse he flushed because it would "take you to another grouse." There is some wisdom in this. By following, there is at least one bird ahead, and it may be one of a scattered brood flushing back to the group. Probably the best reason is that a grouse will usually lie tighter for a dog on subsequent finds, especially if it has been shot at—unlike woodcock, which are inclined to be more jumpy after a shot.

Again unlike woodcock, grouse don't plop down at the end of a flight and just sit. They may not run far but tracks in snow reveal that they go at least to the nearest hiding place. Underestimating the length of grouse flights can give an inaccurate impression that the bird has run a long way after landing. I have watched a grouse fly through a stand of good cover and cross a field rather than settle too soon.

Grouse frequently flush to the same type of cover they were flushed from. A grouse flushed from a tree will often land in another tree after flying a normal distance, especially on a wet or snowy day. Many grouse flushing from rhododendron land in rhododendron at the end of the flight; the same thing often happens in grapevines. But, when a grouse is flushed in a clearing, you can bet on its heading for protective cover.

Next in fame to the grouse that keeps a tree between itself and the gunner is the grouse that lets the gunner walk past and then flushes behind him. The man who finds grouse doing this is probably barreling through the woods as if he were in a hurry to get it over with. I like to keep a steady, moderate pace that does not tire—one my dog can depend upon and adjust to. Tearing through cover at high speed is not conducive to pleasure, and arriving at a point blowing like a spent horse is no way to make an effective shot. The other extreme is the man who pokes along, pausing every few minutes to wait for a flush. Sudden stops sometimes flush grouse, but where? The bird you flush may go out ahead where you would have been if you had continued walking. If a grouse lets you pass, it will probably go out within seconds, whether you stop or not. I don't suggest never stopping, but the walk-and-pause method is for the man who hunts without a dog.

The way you move through grouse cover affects your chances for a shot. Taking paths or log roads is part of hunting efficiently, not laziness. This not only offers better footing from which to shoot but usually greater probability of moving grouse. There have been times when I've stepped off a path to look over a piece of cover, only to have a grouse flush further along the path, where I would have had a good shot. It's best to let the dog do the bird-dogging.

I first read of the mad moon when I received Ernest Thompson Seton's *Wild Animals I Have Known* on my tenth birthday. I had not begun to shoot and I found his story of Redruff very moving. He placed the mad moon as November and described the unpredictable flights of grouse at night, with daylight finding them in odd places far from their normal habitat, calling it a trait of young birds exhibited during the first and sometimes the second season, never afterward.

Some authorities consider infestations of stomach worms responsible for the unusual behavior; others suggest it as Nature's way of dispersing surplus young in a sort of shuffle into other coverts. Falling leaves have been considered cause for abnormal nervousness, but Seton's November mad moon occurred after the leaves were down, especially in Ontario, where he described it. Some suggest that it is a residual migratory instinct.

I believe, like songbird collisions against windows and screens, that "crazy flight" accidents are just that. I have lived for thirty-one years at Old Hemlock in typical grouse terrain and have only once seen anything that could even loosely be credited to a "crazy flight." In mid-October a cock grouse flew into one of our screened porches, boring through the copper screening and tearing it in its efforts to escape. The grouse, too large to be a bird of the year, was unhurt and made a beautiful flight to the nearest woods when I held the screen door open. There was a heavy acorn mast that year and I suspect the bird was coming in to feed at the springhouse white oak and simply cut his corner too acutely.

Perhaps freak flights with grouse flying into wires and windows are seen mostly in congested areas, where, please God, I'll never be again. Woodcock have a high mortality from collision with wires during migration. As for a crazy flight as Nature's way of breaking up grouse broods in September and October, I don't think it occurs among our grouse, for I find groups of first-year grouse together throughout the shooting season into late February. In the Alleghenies, dispersal takes place in March and April in the mating season. The extreme forms of the mad-moon phenomenon seem to be reported in the northerly grouse ranges and I wonder if, like more clearly defined grouse population cycles, it may be more characteristic of the *togata* subspecies.

Grouse Shooting

AFTER THE SHOT

THE GROUSE YOU CENTER and kill cleanly and the grouse you miss cleanly are both exciting parts of a wonderful sport. In the first, you have won more than the beautiful thing in your hands. In the second, the grouse has won an immeasurably higher stake, and if you're honest, you're glad the bird made it, even while you bemoan your shooting or heap blame upon your poor dog. You know it's part of the sport and you move on, determined to do better on the next one.

The situation isn't so pretty when the birds are hit but brought in with their heads up. My setters are gentle-mouthed retrievers, partly by nature and partly as a product of training, and my birds are delivered to me unruffled except for occasional lost tail feathers, but still alive when only crippled. This calls for dispatching the bird immediately.

I saw a television program about grouse shooting. One gunner was a celebrated woodcock and grouse hunter, whose dogs were used, the other a sports columnist. A grouse was dropped and the latter broke shot and beat the dogs to the retrieve, carrying the struggling bird to the camera. He worked the shattered wing back and forth, showing where it had been hit, then spread the tail fan and demonstrated at length that the bird was a hen. Actually, it was a cock. What annoyed me was his callous attitude toward the wounded bird. After the monologue, he stuffed the grouse, still fluttering, into his game pocket as he walked away.

Shadows, bless him, was the most effective retriever I've had. Although gentle-mouthed, he developed a technique of dispatching birds with one firm clamp over the back before delivering them. Wringing a bird's neck is an efficient *coup de grâce*. Another way is to grasp the bird firmly with wings held against the body and strike the head sharply against a tree trunk or boulder. None of this is pleasant, but unfortunately no one can make clean kills consistently. Do it quickly and get it over. The alternative is to give up shooting.

To suggest that a wounded bird feels nothing is rationalizing. A game bird is in many ways a highly developed organism, but a wounded bird could not act as most of them do if it felt extreme pain. I haven't been on the receiving end of a blow for many years, but I recall that the sensation is one of numbness with some delay before pain sets in. Men have described gunshot wounds as at first feeling numb or like a stinging blow from a lath. And, while wild things show fear, I don't think they anticipate death. In the wounded bird, shock and fear of being overtaken may obliterate pain for a short time at least. A bird that is dispatched promptly before the initial shock passes may suffer no more actual pain than the bird killed outright—or so I hope. If remorse as to wounded birds tarnishes the pleasure of shooting—and for me there are times when it does— remember the joy of your dog in his share of the moment and treasure it as a thing between the two of you. You and he have all too short a time together.

Lost cripples comprise a regrettable aspect of shooting and no effort should be spared to find them. Years ago I was shooting over Blue—our first Old Hemlock setter—along a mountain stream at flood stage when a grouse flushed and quartered toward the cover along the bank. The bird was hit solidly, but momentum took it out over the water, where it was carried downstream. Fortunately Blue didn't see the fall, for a dog would have had small chance in that flood. Hoping the bird would be washed into a backwater, I ran along a deer path until I came to a bridge where I thought I might reach it with a pole, but it had been swept past by the time I arrived wheezing with my lungs full of foam. I don't think I would try such a chase again.

Beyond the excitement of dog work and the greater number of birds found, no man should gun for grouse unless he uses a dog that retrieves. Retrieving as a ritual is beautiful: the find, the carry and the delivery to hand bringing a gunner and his dog about as close as they can be, equaled only by the shot over a point. From the standpoint of conservation, retrieving is more important than pointing, and I am surprised that any gunner is satisfied to do without that aspect of dog work.

From 1939 through 1948 I lost only two grouse over Blue—one was the bird carried down the stream. During his last two seasons, hunting almost blind, he made some impressive retrieves. I shot a grouse that cartwheeled down—I hadn't learned the significance of that kind of fall—and I hurried to help him locate the bird. The

Early symptoms. The author with his first setter.

(Above) *Orange, blue, orange, blue—perfect beltons. Shadows and Feathers, from different litters, flanked by their parents Ruff and Wilda.*

(Opposite) *Old Hemlock Blue on his thirteenth birthday with his son Ruff.*

(Below) *A full hearth that has seen Christmases since 1782.*

(Above) Dixie, second from right, and her seven brothers when life was very new. Belton puppies are born snow-white.

(Left) *Postprandial.* Dixie cleans the kettle.

(Below) *The same litter, all blues, at nine weeks.*

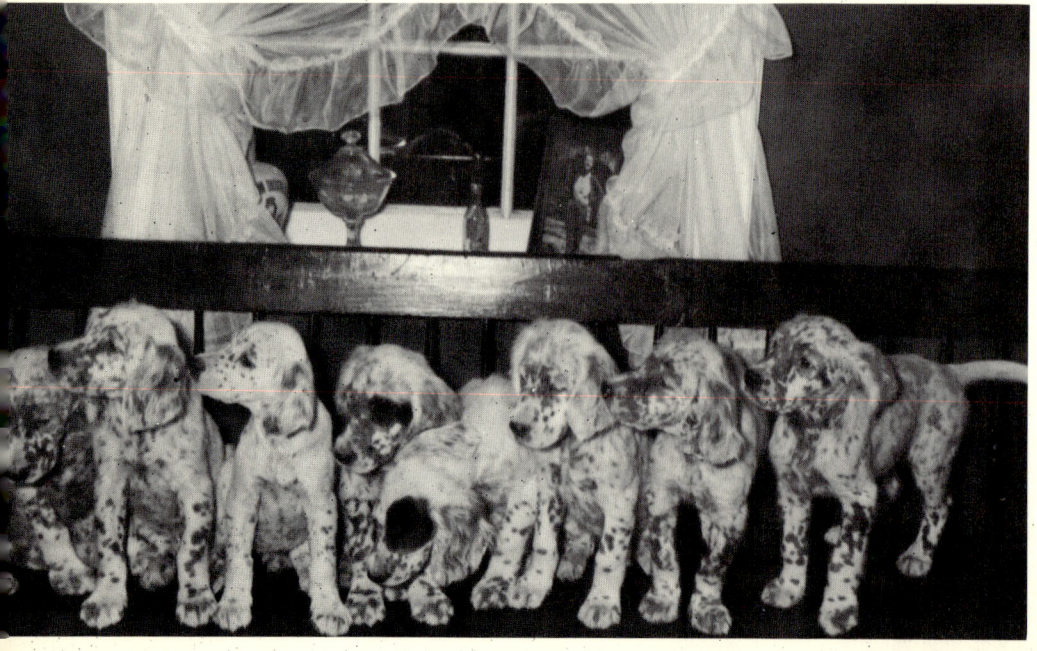

Graduated to the next step, Bliss scent-points the wing hidden in typical cover situations.

Dixie holding steady as bobwhite hen runs out from point.

Dixie pointing training quail at Old Hemlock.

A triple point on pheasants, with young Shadows being taught to back-point.

Bliss playing the indoors retrieving game, the dummy hidden and the dog sent to search with the command dead bird, go fetch.

A mock-up grouse with wings and tail fan and wrapped with heavy wire to discourage chewing. Retrieving a feathered dummy should wait until after *the young dog is stanchly holding his points.*

(Above) *Dr. Charles C. Norris in 1930, with Lad and Sadie, and Dr. Norris at eighty, with Nellie and Charm at Fairhill.*

(Opposite) *A good overhead chance in an old clearing.*

(Below) *An old-time Pennsylvania grouse hunter, Cliff Springer, at nearly ninety-three with his Parker.*

Shadows's points were always a production.

Group portrait of some of my shooting friends' alter egos: 20 ga. Remington pump gun, 16 ga. Fox double, 28 ga. Parker double, 20 ga. Winchester Model 21 double, 12 ga. Ithaca double, 12 ga. Ithaca pump gun, 12 ga. Breda over-and-under, 12 ga. Browning automatic, 20 ga. L. C. Smith double, 20 ga. Browning over-and-under, 16 ga. Francotte double, my 12 ga. Purdey double.

Preserve shooting appeals because the gunner is almost certain to get action, or he at least knows the birds are there. With his own dog he can make it about as sporting as he cares to.

Bliss loved the Purdey...

...for as long as she lived

Double granddaughter of Old Hemlock Ruff, Bliss proved what can be achieved by line breeding.

Mother and daughter, two snow beltons like lightly ticked gyrfalcons.

A finished retriever delivers the bird from a sitting position.

Difference in marking on grouse breast and throat as sex determination: hen left, male right.

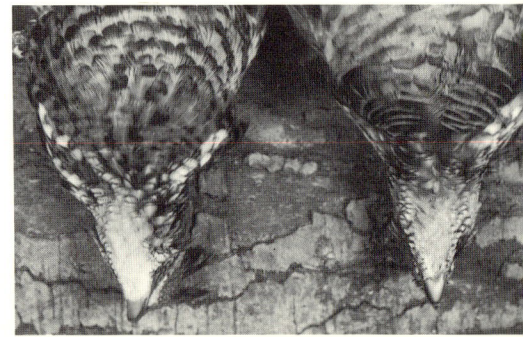

A stylish point on 'cock. Briar, at less than two years, shows the results of selective breeding and of careful handling to preserve natural intensity on birds. The gun is in position for a straightaway bird, fore-end raised to cover the bird with the left hand before bringing the stock to the shoulder for a fast shot.

Grouse and woodcock provide the loveliest mixed shooting and dog work.

A gun diary makes those precious moments last.

Upland shooting is at its highest level when the bird-dog-gun triad is balanced by a gun and a dog worthy of the bird.

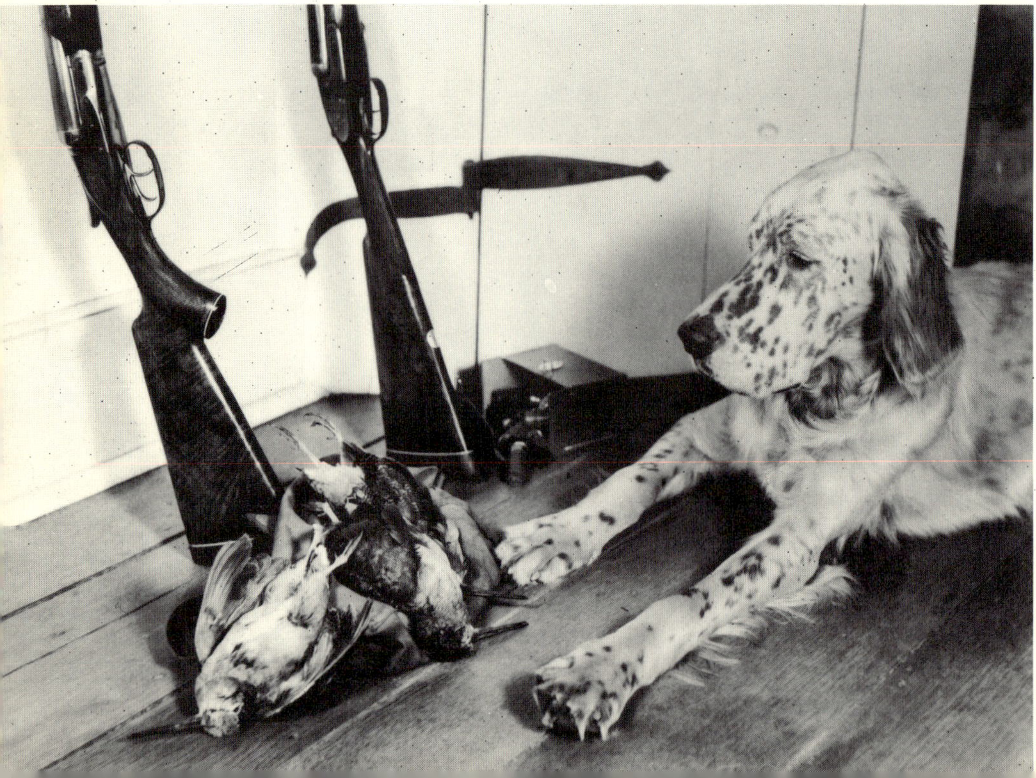

Grouse Shooting

grouse had fallen in a grassy glade, where I saw feathers but couldn't see the bird. Blue searched excitedly for a few moments but started on. I called him back, putting his nose to the feathers, commanding "Dead bird," but achieved nothing. When he again moved off, I started a mechanical search on my own, marking the spot of fall with my hat and working around it in widening circles. Still unsuccessful, I paused to see where Blue was. Far off through the trees he was coming toward me at his steady pace with the grouse in his mouth. I have no idea how far he trailed that runner— a long way, what with my interruptions each time he tried to take the trail—but setters are gentlemen, and when I accepted the grouse, a large cock, he grinned back to his ears and there was a special kind of wisdom in his blind old eyes.

A grouse hit only in the wing can make a fast getaway, once down. One afternoon when Ruff was eleven he pointed a grouse that went straight into the sun. All I could see was a blinding silvery ball with two wings, but at the shot a cloud of feathers drifted crosswise in the breeze. I sent Ruff to retrieve and hurried after him, unable to focus in that moment of visual readjustment. As I made out the grouse on the ground, it was running into blackberry briars. Then I saw Ruff pointing among some rocks. The grouse was in a crevice and, laying my unloaded gun aside, I reached for the bird but it moved beyond my grasp. Ruff, sniffing loudly, started digging and I worked from the other end, but after a quarter of an hour it seemed hopeless. Back at Ruff's diggings I tried again. This time my hand touched the grouse's tail and finally its feet. After pulling it out, I dispatched it and let Ruff retrieve it with great ceremony. It might appear unsporting to dig a bird out after it had tried so hard to escape, but not one such wing-broken bird out of a hundred will recover.

I have had other grouse go to ground. Ruff trailed one to a hole and, unable to reach it, I walked to a house far up the hollow. Finding no one home, I located a metal bar that I took back and worked with for over an hour, trying to dig the bird out without success. I shudder to think of places I've stuck my hand into, trying to reach grouse the dogs couldn't get to—places where I might have laid my hand on hibernating rattlesnakes or copperheads, not to mention antisocial groundhogs.

When shooting either a one-two flush or a true double, frequently one or both of the birds is not centered, owing to haste. One day in the Blackwater-Canaan in Dixie's second season, I shot a grouse that fell among rocks. As I snapped the double shut, a second grouse flushed left-quartering, dropping at my shot. I sent Dixie for the first bird and called to Kay to send Ruff for the second. Dixie retrieved hers, crawling under a shelving rock almost to her rump to get it. Ruff had gone down between large boulders, trying to reach the other grouse. When I saw he couldn't make it I pulled him back and, lying on my side in the crevice, put my arm under and groped in every direction. There were feathers but though we worked a long time we had to admit defeat.

In December of the following season when Dixie and I were hunting in deep snow, a grouse flushed from a hemlock I was under. This overhead-away shot is probably my most difficult. Swinging down blots out the bird and often results in a swing out of line. My bird was hit but not centered and I watched it slant out of view, guessing where it would go down. Dixie hunted eagerly but we reached the edge of the woods with no trace of our grouse. When you question whether you really hit the bird, it is wise to go back and re-estimate the direction of the fall. I found my shell under the hemlock, tried to recall the bird's action and started over, ending in a rhododendron thicket with rocks covered with snow. Dixie wove through it, paused, then pointed. In a moment she moved on and I saw her with her head down, tail wagging. Then she changed position and crawled into a crevice between rocks, going completely underground. She came out at once, with no bird or trace of feathers in her mouth. Twice more she entered but emerged without the grouse. When I peered in I saw the grouse's tail where it crouched beyond reach. Dixie went back in at command and I could hear her digging, then saw her backing out. At last she got turned and brought the bird to me—a nice bit of dog work.

Crippling birds is the result of imperfect shooting, yet no one centers all or even the larger portion of the birds he shoots at. It is a shooter's responsibility to have a retrieving dog that won't abandon crippled birds to a slow death. Regardless of time and fatigue, he should follow every bird shot at and hunt for it until it is reflushed or found, or until it is obvious that it is irretrievable. He may, as a bonus, be surprised at the number of birds he brings home.

The grouse that flinches at the shot may have been struck in

Grouse Shooting

the tail fan and thrown off balance but more often it has been hit in the body. The grouse that "towers" always indicates a hit. At the shot or a moment after, it begins to climb acutely. I have seen them go eighty feet straight up, then pitch steeply into cover. I have never seen one collapse at the peak of its climb and fall inert, although some men feel that a towering bird is always dead when found.

I shot a grouse on my birthday some years ago. Ruff was twelve, his daughter Dixie not quite two, and they were giving me one double-productive after another. On an edge of woods both pointed into greenbrier. The grouse came across a clear space and I shot too hurriedly, saw the bird falter, then climb, striking the branches of a tree. As it came free it remained airborne, flying in an unnatural upright position. I tried the left barrel and the bird suddenly towered. Running, I fumbled to reload and dropped a shell. In the moment it took me to pick it up I lost sight of the grouse. After a long search, I put the dogs into huge boulders on the brow of the ridge and scrambled after them. The eye recognizes some things faster than the brain and I was suddenly aware of the grouse flattened in leaves with fan spread, head raised but dazed. Dixie came in, struck the scent and retrieved. It was an adult cock with a head shot—not clean shooting but a lovely birthday gift.

Towering has long been thought to be the result of a head wound, often from a single pellet. In an unfinished manuscript on shooting, my friend the late Dr. Charles Norris suggested evidence to the contrary:

> Sometimes the bird flinches or it may for a time fly normally after the shot. Then it begins to rise with its wing action strong. The upward flight (tower) is at first vigorous, then the wings cease to function, the rise flattens and the bird plummets to earth with its wings closed. Based upon post-mortem and X-ray examinations, researchers came to the conclusion that towering results from massive hemorrhage. The towering bird faints from loss of blood and as a result suffers from what medical men term "air hunger." It gasps for air, elevates its head, opens its beak in an effort to secure oxygen and this causes the bird to tower.

Dr. Norris described the "false tower," which is often the result of a head wound or a grazing shot that merely stuns. Birds with such wounds are frequently still alive when found. He had observed towering only by bobwhites and ruffed grouse, never by pheasants or waterfowl, suggesting that towering may be a characteristic of certain species.

When towering, the grouse is responding to reflexes, at least partly unaware of its altitude or direction. One grouse that towered at my shot rocketed above the trees, turned and came back over me, turned again and, retaining altitude, flew straight away. I never found it. My guess would be that it was only stunned, possibly by a mandible wound. The bird that manages to keep flying after towering appears to travel farther than it actually does, because any high flight looks longer than a low one. It is important not to give up searching just because the bird seems to go too far to relocate. There is a chance your dog will find it where it came down. When a grouse towers, I try to drop it with the left barrel as it climbs. There is often time for such a shot if you are alert for it.

Grouse that tower are not the only birds that fly on after being hit. A grouse that drops a leg at the shot can almost certainly be found dead at the end of its flight. Appearances suggest a simple leg wound, but it is usually accompanied by pellets in the body. Curiously, I have no record of such a bird before 1947. When I walked into a grouse along a path, the surprise flush unnerved me and I got both barrels off before the grouse leveled. I thought I missed, but as the bird flew on I saw a leg dangling. A long grouse

flight ahead, the dogs found my grouse lying dead. It was shot in both legs, entrails and lower breast—a typical undershot rising bird. A hanging leg shows up as a bird flies off. Never ignore it.

Some grouse drop feathers at the shot but flush vigorously when relocated. During my early grouse hunting in Pennsylvania I dropped a grouse in a cloud of feathers and then stared open-mouthed at the second rise and flight over the trees. My setter Speck was not a retriever, though he would point fallen birds. He moved in and pointed at what I was certain was merely scent. Then to my delight I saw my dead grouse beside a log. It had fallen on a second grouse. This coincidence is treacherous, for under stress of the incredible thing that seems to be happening the gunner may believe his eyes and follow the flush, leaving a crippled or dead grouse.

In late November of 1940 I was gunning over Old Blue long before he was "Old." It was dense rhododendron-hemlock cover and though I had moved a number of grouse I had failed to get a shot. Finally I tried a right and left at a grouse that ignored both shots and flew over the treetops and out the ridge. I marked its flight by a snag and followed. Where I expected it, I saw Blue on point, headed toward me. As I waited for the rise that didn't come, Blue picked up the grouse, dead.

The next afternoon I joined my friend Art Thomas and, to give Blue a rest, we hunted over my father's setter Grouse. My first chance came on a long right-crossing bird well out over the trees. I fired, knowing I hadn't swung far enough ahead, and fired again, but the grouse continued over the ridge. I called to Art that I had missed, and climbed the hill in line with the bird's flight. I hadn't gone far when Grouse pointed, facing me. Steadying myself for the flush, I watched a duplication of Blue's performance the day before. Grouse lowered his head, picked up the bird, dead, and brought it to me. In dressing it, Kay found not one pellet—not even in the neck—but a pellet turned up when I took my last bite of breast. In flight, neither grouse had given evidence of being hit, each had been shot at with both barrels, both had flown a normal flight length.

I've had other such "misses" and in nearly every case the dog first pointed, then picked up the dead grouse without command. How does a stanch dog distinguish between a bird that is alive and one that is dead, holding his point on the former, breaking to retrieve on the latter? Some hunters think blood scent on dead birds is the clue, but these fly-on birds my dogs have found were not bleeding perceptibly.

There is question as to whether numerous grouse we think we have missed haven't been hit and therefore wasted. My dogs have brought me birds other gunners have failed to pick up, some of them still alive with festering wounds. A lot of time is spent humoring the optimistic companion who is sure he hits every bird he shoots at, but the bird should be followed, even if you suspect the "hit" was fantasy. Hit or not, there is a grouse out in front and it is better to follow every bird shot at than risk leaving a cripple.

In January '66 a group of five grouse flushed from dense greenbrier. I shot at one at about thirty-five yards and saw a float of feathers drift down but the bird flew on in normal flight. Marking it, I followed and carefully searched the area with no success. There was nothing to do but give up, hoping the bird was not hurt too badly. This is wishful thinking, for I believe most "feathered" birds eventually die. Ten days later while hunting the same covert, Shadows wheeled on a flash point and a grouse flushed, keeping a few feet above the ground. It dropped at my shot and Shadows delivered it, an extremely small hen, inexplicably lightweight, even for its small size. When it was dressed, we discovered a wound in one leg and a long yellow furrow on one side of the breast, making it necessary to discard the bird. I'm convinced that this was the grouse I had feathered. The bird's crop was jammed with greenbrier berries, implying no lack of ability to feed, but wasted muscles were apparently the result of the wounds.

A phenomenon that can contribute to losing a wounded bird is the manner in which a wing-broken grouse falls. The grouse that loses altitude gradually, settling to the ground with a slow fluttering action, is almost never winged but hit well back in the body. The bird with a broken wing may sideslip, going down on the side of the affected wing, but too frequently it will tumble over and over like a centered bird, giving the gunner the impression he has unlimited time before sending his dog to retrieve. By the time he does, the bird may have run to thick cover or crawled into rocks where it can't be reached.

Some men think a wing-broken grouse hits the ground running. While there is no time to waste, there is almost invariably a moment before the dazed bird rights itself and begins running or struggling to escape. If I can be sure of anything about grouse shooting, I can say that a crippled grouse never runs up a slope. It will occasionally move along the contour, but its progress is more often down.

After the disappointment of a miss has subsided and I look back on the day's shooting, I'm glad to know the birds I missed are there in the remoteness of their coverts, wiser but unhurt. But a bird that has dropped feathers and has not been found leaves an uneasiness in the back of my mind for days. Perhaps I make too much of this for my own good. Once the damage is done, provided every effort has been made to locate the bird, little else remains but to forget it. It is at least comforting to know that, with good retrievers, the situation doesn't occur too frequently.

PREDATORS

❧ / Bigger fleas have little fleas

Upon their backs to bite 'em

And little fleas have lesser fleas

And so ad infinitum.

MY FOX-HUNTING FRIENDS would have me think that foxes don't disturb grouse, pointing out with innocent sophism that where you find foxes you find grouse. I realize that rabbits and mice make up the larger portion of a fox's diet, but he still loves grouse flesh and grouse eggs when he can get them. In addition to Reynard, the deep *hoo hoo-hoo hoo hoo* of the great horned owl is too prevalent in these mountains to please me. Last season I found his work on two successive days in different coverts—a pile of grouse feathers with streaks of whitewash contemptuously splashed across them. More numerous than horned owls are Cooper's hawks, which flap-and-sail over most of our grouse coverts in pairs. In spite of theories of ecology, I begrudge all predators every grouse they destroy.

The authors of *The Ruffed Grouse* have done intensive study on grouse predation in New York. With the exception of the goshawk, most of those predators exert pressure in our Alleghenies. The authors lay a cooling hand on my brow and point out that eliminating predators would not solve the grouse scarcity problem

THE BIRDS

and that, without predators, rodents might increase until they had seriously damaged suitable grouse cover. They say: "Simple arithmetic will show that, without some check on their increase, one pair of grouse would produce a population of over 33,000 individuals in only six years. . . . Nature's system of checks is quite flexible. If one is removed, others 'take over' so that the ultimate result is essentially the same. . . . Thus a reduction in predators cannot be expected to bring about any lasting increase in grouse population, . . . except possibly in individual coverts."

Predators destroy around 35 percent of grouse nests and kill a number of young chicks during late summer and about 40 percent of the fall population of adult grouse during late winter and early spring. Grouse are preyed upon more heavily when the "buffers" (rabbits, squirrels, mice, etc.) decline in numbers. These buffers are taken before grouse, not because they are more tasty but because they are easier to catch. High limits on squirrels and rabbits "to let the hunter harvest the surplus that would go to predators" may, by depriving those predators, force them to take game birds they would normally pass up. However, rabbits and squirrels perform a buffer role with regard to hunter kill, taking a big load off bird shooting.

In a year-round study from 1930 to 1942 reported in *The Ruffed Grouse*, the predators responsible for dead adult grouse examined were:

Great horned owl	13.6%
Hawk or owl	44.3%
Some species of hawk	11.6%
Fox, red and gray	21.5%
Weasel	3.1%

During the same period, stomach content examination of predators revealed:

NUMBER EXAMINED		GROUSE	RABBIT	MOUSE	OTHER BIRDS
14	goshawk	9.1%	0	36.4%	36.4%
115	great horned owl	5.5%	30.8%	29.7%	20.9%
41	Cooper's hawk	4.5%	4.5%	31.8%	45.5%
134	red fox	3.9%	31.7%	44.6%	7.9%
20	gray fox	0	43.4%	26.4%	21.1%

Grouse Shooting

Examination of fox droppings and great horned owl pellets revealed:

	GROUSE	RABBIT	MOUSE	OTHER BIRDS	OTHER MAMMALS
Fox	4.5%	52.6%	40.4%	7.7%	11.0%
Great horned owl	4.5%	51.2%	37.8%	6.5%	16.7%

The authors say, "Predator control experiments have been effective in reducing nest losses, but have had less effect on mortality of adult grouse and little or none in respect to chicks." They point out that brood losses from June 1 to August 31 on wild study areas were similar to losses among chicks hatched from wild eggs in pens at the research center, though the latter were not subject to predation, suggesting that early-season losses are related to the age of the chicks and not due to predation, though in the wild predation may be the final executioner. After August 31, losses seemed more related to predation—on the game farm mortality is negligible after the birds are six weeks old; in the wild, moderate losses continue. Foxes and weasels are the chief predators during the nesting season, Cooper's and sharp-shinned hawks when the chicks become more independent of the mother, and the great horned owl and the fox among adult grouse.

To eliminate all birds and animals that have preyed upon grouse you would have to kill off foxes, house cats, bobcats, skunks, raccoons, opossums, groundhogs, red squirrels, chipmunks, mice, blacksnakes, and most species of hawks and owls, regardless of the clean record ornithologists accord them. However, when a predator kills a grouse, either adult or chick, it is impossible to say the victim was not weakened from disease.

Nearly every season I find a parasitic fly in the feathers of some of the grouse I shoot. About half an inch long, it abandons the retrieved bird and goes for my face or ears in a way that is less than endearing. The only way to kill it is to get hold of it with your fingernails and tear it apart. I rarely find more than one on a bird, though I have found three. Some seasons it does not appear, in others I have found it on 25 percent of the grouse I have shot. I have never heard another gunner mention this fly, though I can't imagine not noticing one if it got near you. In 1939 I sent a specimen to Dr. Arthur A.

Allen at Cornell, who identified it as a hippoboscid fly, *Lynchia americana*, "found not only on grouse but on many hawks, herons and especially on great horned owls. If the grouse were infected with any blood parasite, it is possible that this insect might become a carrier, but thus far we have no information that it transmits disease and in itself cannot be very destructive." *Lynchia americana* is also called "louse fly" and is found in New York, Ontario, and New England.

There is a predator I wish to condemn—the one who kills along highways from behind the wheel of a car, deliberately running down a grouse, even swerving to the edge of the road to do it. The driver who unavoidably kills wildlife that darts into the road feels bad enough; the man who drives too fast to stop could avoid it by moderating his speed through game cover. Both could cultivate the sportsman's eye for wildlife, learning to spot a bird or animal along the roadside and be prepared for any move it might make. It is the deliberate killer in a car who can't be appealed to as a human being. His kill is high in the spring when grouse are along roads, strutting or gathering gravel and greens.

Those of us who love the ruffed grouse find it difficult to resign ourselves to an ecology that seems to single it out to be a scarce species. Sixty years ago grouse were found in these mountains in large numbers. If today's low grouse populations can be explained only by "ecology" we should make it clear that it is *this* ecology, with pressures altered by man's own population spread and encroachments. That is not likely to become anything but worse. To fear to tamper with the "balance of Nature" is to imply that some Great White Father wants it the way it is, as of now. Interference shouldn't be attempted by irresponsible agencies—the present ecology is getting too much of that in the name of recreational development. But if a pair of grouse could, mathematically, produce thirty-three thousand birds at the end of six years if totally unchecked, I see nothing immoral, as a grouse hunter, in partially unleashing that kind of genie. Managing the ruffed grouse as a sporting bird is different from viewing it in its niche as a species. It is a large subject and a sticky one. I don't have an answer, but just because no one has come up with one, I see no reason not to ask questions.

Grouse Shooting

NOVEMBER SONG

MOST OF US HAVE memories of shooting grouse on Indian summer days when woods dripped with autumn smells, and many of us have known good sport in December after the snows have come, but over the seasons, it is in November when the leaves are down that grouse shooting and dog work are at their best. I can still hear, as a middle-of-the-head throb, at least four cock grouse drumming simultaneously on a high knob of Canaan Mountain in air you could inhale all the way to your belt. When grouse drum in November it is from simple joy of being alive and I always hope I won't come across the drummer and, by mistake, shoot him.

For years I bypassed an area above the house of a friend who had told me of a grouse that drummed on a rock there. This man is a gentle person who doesn't kill, other than occasional deer for meat, and the drumming grouse regularly lets him approach close enough to watch it. Returning from a hunt one November afternoon, Kay and I stopped to chat, and as we sat on his porch the grouse started to drum. I could see the gray boulder through the trees and took Kay's camera and began a stalk, moving up while the bird was drumming, stopping when it paused. As I drew closer the drumming seemed to come from further up the ridge, and when I reached the boulder it was empty. When I got back to the house, the drumming began again, as close-sounding as before. I can't decide if there were two cocks or if the sound was acoustically deceiving. A grouse drumming on that boulder had let our friend approach it in at least eight Novembers. There was no way to establish the identity of the bird but reason says it couldn't have been the same grouse.

Records indicate that the average wild adult grouse meets a violent death before it is three years old. One banded wild grouse lived to be five. Penned four-year-olds at the New York Conservation Research Center were numerous, five-year-olds not uncommon; all appeared vigorous and healthy and mated successfully. It is difficult to guess what age a wild grouse might reach if, by chance, it escaped the benevolent attention of predators.

It is a pleasant fantasy that grouse follow a rigid schedule in the

THE BIRDS

same places, day after day. I read that a hunter, having observed in August where grouse spent the day, feeding and loafing, could go back to those coverts in November and find the birds doing the same things. In my opinion, if he did, it would be a coincidence. Grouse don't consistently use the same coverts at the same time even on consecutive days, especially if they have been disturbed. Young grouse regather, possibly by using the *kwit-kwit* note or by a homing sense. But, unless the covert is small enough to hold them captive, it has often been my experience on visits a week apart that, instead of being in the exact spots as on former days, the birds can't be located at all.

Grouse reactions are altered where heavy gunning occurs. Though a grouse may lie tighter on the second flush after it has been shot at, repeated shooting makes grouse jumpy. Most of the grouse I shoot in heavily hunted terrain are yearlings, indicating a close killing-off, and this shows in the behavior of the birds. A season's bag of predominantly adult grouse indicates poor brood production for that year, but when I find numerous two- and three-year-olds, I know I am in country that hasn't been gunned hard.

It takes a close look to tell if your grouse is an adult or a yearling. Tail length can be a guide, especially on cocks. I've shot yearling cocks with center tail feathers (extracted) as long as $6^{13}/_{16}$ inches, and adult cocks with tail feathers as short as $6^{11}/_{16}$ inches. But generally, if the bird is a cock, a center feather less than $6\frac{3}{4}$ inches indicates a yearling; if longer, an adult. Adult cocks commonly have wider tail feathers than yearlings, but I've found yearling feathers as wide as $1\frac{3}{8}$ inches and an adult as narrow as $1\frac{3}{16}$ inches. It's possible this is influenced by nutrition and condition of the bird, like antlers on bucks.

Hens have shorter tails than cocks, with little difference in tail length between adult and yearling hens unless the young bird is from a late hatching, when it is smaller overall. Otherwise there is not much difference in size between adult and yearling hens, unlike adult and yearling cocks.

Any tail fan over $14\frac{3}{4}$ inches when spread to 180° is a large one. On the 17th of November in 1958 I shot a cock with a 15-inch fan and 24-inch wingspread. The first to exceed that was one on January 4, 1969, with a $15\frac{1}{4}$-inch fan. The largest cock I have taken was on November 27, 1970, with a wingspread of $25\frac{1}{4}$ inches and a fan that measured 15¾ inches. These large cocks are the old ones.

The best clue to age is in the outer wing feathers. During their first-year moult, young grouse replace all primaries *except the outer two on each wing* (No. 9 and No. 10). These two original primaries are normally retained until the second-year moult, when grouse replace *all* primaries. With the moult completed by the shooting season, it is possible to examine the outer two wing feathers to determine whether your grouse was hatched that year or some previous year. The two juvenile primaries retained by the young bird usually have tips more pointed than those of an adult, though occasional newly grown adult primaries will have pointed tips, which detracts from this method.

The more accurate method takes a moment longer and involves the same two primaries. When feathers erupt they are encased in a sheath. Portions of this sheath cling throughout the hunting season to primaries replaced during the moult. Take your knife blade or car key and turn back the short coverts at the base of the outer primaries on either wing. If a trace of cellophanelike membrane clings to the base of either of the outer two, frequently for half an inch from the skin line, it indicates that these have been newly grown. Normally, such a bird is an adult. If no remnant of sheath is present, your bird has not replaced these primaries and therefore was hatched that year. This sheath is gradually shed as the season progresses but it usually persists long enough on one or more of the feathers to identify an adult through January shooting.

There are exceptions. I shoot an occasional grouse that, judging from size or length of tail, is almost certainly a young bird but with membrane on one of the outer two primaries—usually the inside one (No. 9). Kermit T. Rinell, a West Virginia wildlife biologist, describes a more exact check on these primaries:

> Pull out primaries 8, 9 and 10 and examine the quill tips. If all are relatively soft it's an adult—if P. 8 is soft and P. 9 and 10 are hard it's an immature. If all are relatively hard then compare the color of the quill plug. As the feather ages this plug yellows. If P. 8 is white and P. 9 is yellowish the bird is immature. If both are about the same color the bird is an adult. I have two wings with very pointed, very immature Number 10 primaries and nicely rounded,

recently grown Number 9 primaries. I am sure these were immature birds that molted Number 9 primary. This occurs commonly in young turkeys.

Why anyone has difficulty distinguishing male from female ruffed grouse puzzles me, until I remember how long it took me to use my eyes. It is as simple as distinguishing a male bobwhite from a female; almost as easy—once you have them in your hand—as recognizing a cock or a hen pheasant, though more difficult when in flight.

One November day I descended a Pennsylvania mountainside to a hewn-log house and paused to chat with an old man squatting in the doorway. While my setter Blue sniffed acquaintance with a stiff-legged hound I reached into my shooting jacket and took out a grouse I had shot, still warm. The man stroked the black ruffs and spread the large fan with his bony fingers. "A big rooster," he pronounced quietly.

I had just read a book. "You have to dissect them to tell the cocks from the hens," I said. I could see he wasn't convinced but I didn't argue. "Mind if I eat my lunch here?" I asked. His eyes didn't leave the sandwich I was unwrapping. I offered him my other one and he attacked it ravenously.

"Git hungry for somethin' besides potatoes." He licked his fingers. "You git tired of boiled potatoes without salt."

I had no more food and I wondered if I should offer him my bird. But a mountaineer considers grouse far down the list below 'coons and groundhogs and, anyway, I dearly hate to give away a grouse. I left him sitting in the doorway, a breeze stirring the wispy hair, silvery as the weathered logs of his old house. Walking down the woods road I couldn't help thinking how right he was about boiled potatoes without salt. It took me years to learn that he was also right about how to recognize a cock grouse.

In *The Ruffed Grouse*, Bump and his associates suggest that you can judge the sex by the manner of flush: "Males tend to climb steeply for ten or a dozen feet before leveling off, while females more often fly off low." They point out that this "is most applicable on level ground without obstacles." In *American Game Birds*, Frank C. Edminster says: "The angle of flight in flushing from the ground is fairly dependable for sex identification; the male usually rises steeply and the female flies low."

In forty-five years of shooting grouse I have not noticed a pattern of flushing peculiar to either cock or hen. I checked my gun diary, which describes the flush of each grouse killed and sex determined when dressed. I selected the last 110 grouse shot. Nine flushed from trees; one gave no clue as to how it took off. That left 100 whose flushes I could be sure of. There were 40 hens and 60 cocks. Exactly 20 hens took off low, 20 rose in flushing; 28 cocks took off low, 32 rose in flushing. Disregarding sex, 48 took off low, 52 rose. Certainly, cover and situation affect the flush, but these cocks and hens performed astonishingly alike. In my 100 grouse there were 15 adult and 25 young hens; 41 adult and 19 young cocks with no relation of adult or young to low or rising flushes.

A popular method for distinguishing cocks from hens goes: a cock when the tail band is solid across the two center feathers; a hen when it is interrupted. The first is true; the second is only part-truth. Hens always have interrupted tailbands but so do about 40 percent of the cocks. There are varying degrees of interruption in the marking on these two center tail feathers. Of the 60 cocks, 35 had solid bands, 24 interrupted, and the center feathers on the remaining cock were lost in the retrieve.

A guide is the size of the fan. On cocks the tail is distinctly longer. Even young cocks have longer tails by October than adult hens. Grouse fans normally have 18 feathers but may vary from 16 to 20. One of the two center feathers pulled out of the tail is used when measuring. Some authorities give $5\frac{3}{4}$ inches or less as hens, and 6 inches plus as cocks. In February, 1969, I shot an exceptionally large hen with a $13\frac{3}{8}$-inch fan and $6\frac{1}{2}$-inch center feather, not more than eighty yards from where I shot a very big cock the following December.

The cock appears larger than the hen in every way. This has inspired legends about a strain of grouse, sometimes called "mountain birds," different from "regular" grouse. Near Davis, an old-timer directed me up Yellow Creek, where I would find "the big yellow grouse." In another Blackwater area the natives spoke of "the old German grouse, bigger than mountain pheasants." These were simply cock grouse, the extremely large ones being two or three years old.

Another accurate label of the cock is his ruff, larger and more showy than the hen's. This is conspicuous on a bird in hand; not so easy to see on a grouse beside a road unless he is strutting. The size of the bird can appear out of scale but the sex of grouse along a roadside can best be judged by length of tail. An erect crest means nothing, for both cocks and hens raise the crest when nervous.

One of the most reliable ways to tell a cock from a hen is by the throat and upper breast marking. It is not only infallible with the bird in hand but accurate at a moderate distance if the bird is on the ground. On the cock, the dark ruff feathers continue around in front to form a complete "necklace," while on the hen this is missing or broken. The hen's identifying marking is a rich burnt-orange on the upper breast, and beginning immediately below, her barred markings show distinctly dark. The cock has, instead, a golden upper breast and his barred markings are tan and faded-looking in this area, not becoming dark until well to the rear.

A subtle difference is that the light spots or "peacock" markings on the lower back are more distinct on the males. But the main labels are: (1) throat and breast, (2) ruffs, (3) size of fan, (4) overall size. When the bird is dressed, check your judgment by the ovaries (egg cluster) in the hen, or the two gray seed-like gonads in the male. You will soon be able to recognize a cock or hen grouse at a glance.

Almost every season I shoot a few grouse with red ruffs and tail band. Of my 100 grouse, 15 had red or semi-red ruffs—2 adult hens, 11 adult cocks, and 2 yearling cocks. This red pigmentation is most conspicuous in the cocks because of the more prominent ruffs and larger tail band. Some of these ruffs are a rich ginger with green highlights like the patina on copper, and I think of them as ginger-bronze. In some areas these are called "cherry grouse." The birds I call semi-red have chocolate-colored ruffs and tail bands.

The "red phase" as compared with the "gray phase," both of which biologists describe as occurring in all grouse subspecies, even in the same broods (as red and gray screech owls can occur in the same nest, or orange and blue belton setters in the same litter), refers to an overall rufous coloring and not the red-ruff and red-tail-band marking I have described. The red or gray color phases show up mostly in the tail fan, being more nearly tan or reddish-tan in one, gray or silver in the other.

Grouse Shooting

The terms "red-ruff" and "red phase" can be confusing. The red-ruff marking is shown on a gray phase silver-tail in a drawing in *The Ruffed Grouse*, Bump et al., and apparently occurs in both red-phase and gray-phase grouse. There is a gradual increase in the proportion of gray phase grouse as you go north. Conversely, the gray phase is almost nonexistent in our Allegheny *B. u. monticola*. I have shot only one gray-tailed grouse in our mountains—a young hen in the Intermediate Ridges on December 27, 1955. In late November of '59 I shot an immature cock on Canaan Mountain that, as Ruff retrieved it, appeared to have a gray tail, but with the fan spread it proved to be a tan tail with freak gray marking inside the black band, running up along the quills.

In the thirties I was in Eugene V. Connett's Derrydale Press office on East Thirty-fourth Street, discussing a grouse painting I had done. Be prepared for criticism if you show a sporting painting to a sportsman—they are the most exacting of all creatures. Mr. Connett's comment that my grouse didn't appear gray enough puzzled me, for I had never seen a gray grouse. Years later, it came to me—he knew New England's *togata*, I the *monticola*.

I shot a cock on November 13, 1940, with a wing spread of 24 inches. It had glossy black ruffs and unusual shading from grayish on the shoulders to a rich chestnut on the lower back, dotted with conspicuous peacock "eyes." The same year I shot a hen that had more melanistic tendency than any grouse I remember; the back feathers were predominantly black, the breast barring darker and more pronounced than usual, and the underside of the fan had a grayish cast with black bars.

To say that grouse use certain types of cover more at different periods of the shooting season is almost too obvious. A gunner could work out patterns of cover use, such as alders and aspen in October as compared with late November. But along comes an exceptionally wet season, or a low in grouse population, and the "rules" have to give way to a sixth sense that develops only with experience. I have hunted coverts that held grouse in November and appeared to be barren of birds in December. More frequently it is the reverse, with a covert that was unproductive in dry leafy early November providing good shooting later on.

I have learned that unbroken wilderness does not always offer the best shooting; that rhododendron and hemlock stands are "holding cover," not "shooting cover"; that small coverts may not contain as many birds as large ones, but what birds are there are often easier to locate. However, the small covert requires intelligent treatment to avoid overgunning. The man who takes the birds "while the taking is good" can show you numerous coverts in which the birds weren't there the following year, without knowing why it seems to happen particularly to him.

Reports of where grouse were seen are of supreme interest to the gunner, for grouse are often located through such channels, but unless you want to waste good hunting days, weigh these stories carefully. Rabbit and deer hunters bring back extravagant tales of grouse moved—meant to be helpful but usually out of scale. After the deer season I have hunted a covert where deer hunters "moved thirty-five grouse in one day" and with diligent dog work have succeeded in moving ten. During a drive they undoubtedly moved the ten birds, but they counted them several times. However, I listen with appreciation because deer hunters get around in large numbers in snowy weather and often move concentrations of grouse. Some of their reports have led me to rich coverts.

Deer and rabbit hunters are not concentrating on birds, but it is difficult to understand such discrepancies in grouse hunters—stories of a hundred grouse moved in one day. If some glowing tales are intended to impress, others are calculated to deceive.

Once in early fall, Kay and I were cruising unfamiliar terrain for new woodcock coverts. To inquire of a mountain man about woodcock is to become involved with description such as "about the size of a quail but with a long bill." They confuse "woodcock" with "wood hen," the local name for pileated woodpecker, and express understandable surprise that anyone would eat one. Even in areas where woodcock flights occur, the residents are seldom aware of the bird. And so I rely on my own eye for 'cock coverts and limit my inquiries to grouse. When we stopped the car to talk to a grizzled timberman working at the side of the road, I was interested to learn that he too was a "pheasant" hunter. He also turned out to be an awful liar, giving us directions to "the three best pheasant woods in the country." Our subsequent visits produced two grouse in the coverts. But logically, why should one grouse hunter disclose his best territory to another? I know that some of my grouse-hunting friends have sold certain coverts short, and again, why not? But

Grouse Shooting

this man did the opposite, charming me with promise of good shooting and simultaneously steering me a safe distance from his pet coverts, like the old trick of strewing empty shells in "woodcock coverts" never frequented by 'cock.

There is no reason for grouse hunters to miscount birds by a large margin. A man who can call himself a grouse hunter should, by its location and its action, come close to estimating whether the grouse he flushes is a new bird or a reflush. If he sees it, he should usually be able to tell whether it is a hen or a cock, which in some cases can distinguish it as a new bird. While it is not infallible, the direction the bird takes may be a clue, for a grouse seldom flushes back to the area from which it was just flushed. When there is doubt, I count a bird a reflush to avoid an overcount—which may be why I seem to move fewer grouse in a day than men with optimistic vision. I suspect if certain hunters had hit the first two or three birds they moved they would not have seen the other "ten or twelve" they thought they had up on a given day. But if they think they are finding a lot of grouse, who can ask for more?

In the grouse woods, I use my voice as little as possible. Whistle signals to my dog or a companion rarely disturb grouse, but conversation will make the birds wild as hawks. My dogs react adversely to continuous talking, as though they sense that the gunner isn't alert for shooting and dog work. If a companion doesn't take the hint from my monosyllabic answers, I don't hesitate to ask him to stop talking. It is a pleasure to shoot with a companion who moves silently, who keeps in touch and does not talk except during rest periods.

An even greater pleasure is to shoot alone with a dog with whom you have rapport. I had glorious afternoons with Ruff when I did not speak to him other than "Dead bird, go fetch," and to thank him for the retrieve or compliment him after each nice point. Communication was a clucking sound to give him my location on the rare occasion he didn't know, or a whistle to get his eye when I wanted to wave him to a definite place.

On the 21st of November, 1955, I took him out alone for the first time in over a month. I had been using him with his sons, Feathers and Shadows, or their mother Wilda, for it spread me thin to give them enough work without using them as braces or even three together.

THE BIRDS

Because of the fit of the new stock on my Fox, that grouse season had been a revelation of what shooting pleasure could be, but oddly I had gone through much of it with a deep sense of unhappiness. Ruff, who was past eight, had not worked well. He had handled a few grouse with his old flair but much of the time he was not out there where the birds were by the time the younger dogs got to them and I had to admit he was no longer the same.

And so, to see if I could discover what was wrong if it wasn't age, I took him alone to one of our old coverts—a valley in which the only trace of a house was an ancient cellar hole. The day was warming, with some snow on the ground—a beautiful day to hunt grouse. I was determined not to hack at him, for Ruff took criticism to heart, and after giving him the "All right, go on" I let him do everything on his own.

He made his first productive at the mouth of a little tributary. Further up, we moved two more birds and, following, got a nice point on the edge of a snow-covered field near a clump of hawthorns and greenbrier. As I approached, the grouse boiled up, rising and crossing to the left. Firing as I swung through a short lead, I could hear the pattern center, and the grouse fell on the unbroken snow, where Ruff zeroed in, picked it up and delivered.

We crossed to the ridge with the old cellar hole, where a late pear tree stood loaded with russet-green fruit against leaves like purple leather. Hunting along the unused lane with its hedgerows grown to trees, we had another productive but no shot. I had moved seven grouse for ten flushes by 3:30 when I stopped for lunch, leaning against the sunny side of a white oak. Ruff had been working beautifully—not wide, not fast, but hunting hard.

Veering away from the old lane, I followed him into second-growth hardwoods and hemlocks on a flat, moving a single, a trio, and a single. Ruff had his fourth productive but I failed to get a shot, through no fault of his. I came to grapevines heavy with fruit and began working around the steep brow of the hill.

In the Intermediate Ridges, even when land has reverted to woods as it had here, you can tell where once there were hilltop fields. As mountain farms were carved out of rocky forests, stones were hauled to the edge of the clearings and left, like a border of hair around a monk's pate. You find these bands of rocks in the forest floor at the top of nearly every ridge. There are further monuments

Grouse Shooting

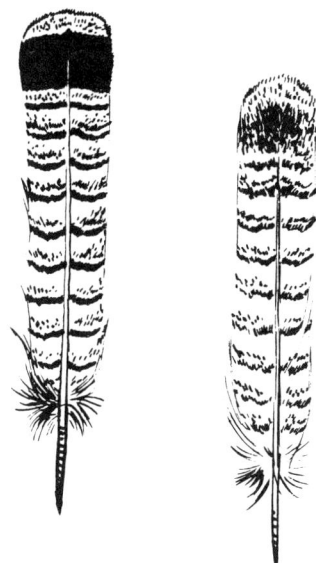

to the pioneers in the form of cairns—stones piled on boulders too large to do more than cultivate around. The determination to farm these mountains came close to exceeding human endurance, but the mountains won.

Tricky footing on the snow-covered stones turned me back to the flat and the old lane, and I followed it to the valley, where shadows were already deep. I could feel the cold as we descended but on we went, Ruff and I, the way we used to do when he was young and there was always energy for another mile.

Along the stream on a tramroad where I had never been before Ruff wheeled toward me and froze, pointing into the bank on my left. It wasn't the lonely setting or the bone-deep chill that raised goose pimples on my neck. Ruff's first four points had been lovely, but this was my old Ruff pointing now, not an aging setter who held a point because he knew his duty, but a superb grouse dog whose intensity said, "Right there, George, is your grouse." I'd have given the next two weeks of shooting to have been able to shoot that grouse but there was no way. Facing an unbroken wall of rhododendron, I used my voice and took several steps, hoping to put the bird up. It required climbing into the tangle to do it and of course the grouse went out the far side. But any way you looked at it—and I can still see it on my retina fifteen years afterward—Ruff's productive number five was a honey.

With the light failing and time running out it was foolish but we shoved deeper and deeper toward the Cheat, into that wild country, which that year was stiff with grouse. The next flush came up almost in my face and directly back over me. I turned, planning calmly how I would take it, fired too fast, and fired again as the bird bored away, and this time I saw it fall. As I hurried to it, fumbling with shells, the bird righted itself and fluttered into the tangle below the tramroad. Low rhododendron over old slashings snarled me knee deep when I plunged into it. I could see Ruff trying to locate the grouse too far out. At last I got him to the right place and his tail began to thrash excitedly, but each time he reached down he came up without the bird, which ran through the tangle past my feet like a trout darting between submerged branches. Just when I began to lose hope, I saw Ruff force his muzzle into an opening and come up dragging the grouse by the head. He changed his grip and carried the bird to a place where he could make the delivery properly—sitting.

We did a good bit of gloating before we started the long trek out of the darkening woods. On the way up the valley Ruff worked like a young dog, finding the fifteenth grouse. I wouldn't take the world for that day alone with him and the lesson I learned. I realized I'd been hunting him too much with the younger dogs; he needed to know that he was still essential to me for himself. Given the woods to work in his own way and at his own speed, he gave me grouse shooting at its highest level for six more wonderful years. In all the rest of my Novembers I suspect my thoughts of grouse will have Ruff in them.

Quail Shooting

❧ / *Size is no measure of a gentleman.*

THE OBLIGING MISTER BOB

NEXT TO WOODCOCK, the bobwhite lies for a dog better than any other game bird. More than that, he has the graciousness to present himself in coveys. Such gentility deserves the greatest respect.

My first wing shooting was on bobwhites in the foothills of southwestern Pennsylvania, where small farms provided the crop fields quail love. In those days there were coveys even on mountain farms, but change was already taking place. Now there are almost no quail in our mountains, and in the lowlands, which are still crop producing, the pheasant has taken over. In *American Game Birds*, Edminster says that the carrying capacity of habitat applies to the total of gallinaceous game birds present, not to separate species, and that pheasants usually displace quail.

I enjoyed some of the last of that quail shooting, when to find more than two coveys in an afternoon was exceptional. Before that, my father and a companion used to drive our horse Bird into nearby country—a setter and a pointer in the buggy at their feet—and have no trouble moving six to eight coveys in a day.

The last half of the 1800's was the golden age of quail. When the colonists arrived, the bobwhite was mostly limited to the Eastern Coast, the Gulf, and the Mississippi Valley, using forest/grass edges, burned clearings, and the edges of Indian settlements. To the Indian he was *Waquoit*, and if you've ever had a cock quail sit

THE BIRDS

on your shoulder and scream his call, you'll agree the Indian name came closer than our own.

As the forests were opened, the bobwhite followed the spread of agriculture as far west as New Mexico and north to South Dakota. For so long as cultivation remained inefficient, weeds sprang up with the crops and fence rows grew to hedges, making ideal quail habitat. With machinery, clean farming, and barbed wire, fortune turned against Mister Bob and extensive dairy farming and pasturing further transformed quail shooting in the North into a memory. Unlike the ruffed grouse, which benefited as mechanized farming put the small hill farmer out of business, the bobwhite could not do without farm crops, at least in the northern fringe of his range, in spite of wild foods and excellent protective cover on abandoned farms.

We saw this happen on Old Hemlock, where crop fields have grown to cover or have been planted to pines. Formerly, a few quail used our buckwheat or corn fields; now wild foods and perennial weeds are not adequate for quail, and the thousands of Natob lespedeza plants we set out have failed to produce seeds.

When we moved to West Virginia I came close to becoming *persona non grata* by hunting some of the bobwhites that were still to be found. I learned that mountain farmers almost never allowed quail to be shot and so, of course, I gave it up, but it took time for some of them to trust a man with bird dogs.

My neighbors blame the lack of quail on foxes and severe winters, but there were foxes and severe winters in these mountains when quail were here. As in all the northern fringe range, quail losses were always high during bitter weather but the birds were able to come back quickly when they had the ideal milieu of small producing farms.

The bobwhite's present range is south of a line beginning in Massachusetts and crossing southern Pennsylvania to southern Michigan, lower Wisconsin and Minnesota, and east of a line through Nebraska, Kansas, Oklahoma and Texas into Mexico. Populations fluctuate acutely in the fringes, affected by severe winters in the north and by droughts in the west. Twenty-two subspecies have been classified but gunners are most familiar with the Eastern bobwhite (*Colinus virginianus virginianus*), the Texas

Quail Shooting

bobwhite (*C. virginianus texanus*) and the Florida bobwhite (*C. virginianus floridanus*).

Even within better range there are some areas where few, if any, quail exist—the more intensive the farming, the poorer the range. Strip cropping plus protective cover could encourage a recovery, for the bobwhite can repopulate good habitat. Biologists, without knowing the reason, recognize a law of inversity that applies to quail: a high spring breeding population usually has a low reproduction rate, while a low breeding population often has a high rate of reproduction. This explains rapid recoveries after a year of low quail numbers.

Among hunters, a theory persists that thinning out a covey stimulates reproduction and that scattering birds by shooting prevents inbreeding. But to shoot a covey down to five or six birds allows no margin for predation. There are areas where quail have done well for generations without shooting. The classic argument for the benefits of shooting has been Ohio's lack of success with quail by protecting them. Edminister says that Ohio's effort was ineffective because hunting was not the reason for the bobwhite's decline in that state; what the bobwhite needed there, still needs, and will probably never get, is protection from improper land use and intensive farming.

A single bobwhite that fails to regather with its covey will join another covey if it can find one, and such mixture of breeding stock may be beneficial. But a stranded single is usually picked off by predators if cold nights don't kill it first, for quail require the body heat of a number of birds bunched together.

I've observed my training quail more closely than is possible with wild birds. A single bobwhite is an unhappy one, becoming uneasy the moment it is released alone. Its crest goes up and the bird begins to talk in low anxious tones. It may head for home at a run, or it may hide under the nearest cover—sometimes burrowing into fallen leaves—where some will remain until the sun is almost down before giving the covey call. The notion that scattering quail prevents inbreeding is unsound, for a covey will normally be back together by dark.

In a group, quail do well through cold weather. I've seen my birds coveyed in the most exposed part of their runway on a zero night, huddled tail-to-tail, so fluffed they looked like a large feather ball with pairs of beady eyes pointing outward, watching my flashlight. In a shelter, four quail can manage but it takes at least six to get through cold weather in the wild.

I once thought the same covey continued year after year, reassembling after each summer with their offspring, and that natural losses held this perennial body to a relative size. Many farmers think they have had the same covey on their land for years, without realizing that the covey breaks up at the mating season and that each pair, if successful, will comprise a new covey with their young. Occasionally, two or more of these family groups will join to form a bevy—one of the exceptionally large "coveys" hunters report. Normally this doesn't happen unless a covey has been drastically reduced, when it seems to sense the need for greater numbers to survive. In an overgunned covert this can be misleading, for the large group might appear to indicate plenty of birds when it is all that remains of several coveys.

Without natural losses, quail country would be alive with new coveys each year, but it almost never happens. Pressures reduce them or force them into other coverts. I've had training quail live to four years and I knew a pet quail that lived past seven, but in the wild it is rare that a quail lives much past its first birthday. Shooting reduces October populations by 20 to 50 percent. This is not a serious threat to breeding stock in good habitat, but losses from all causes may cut the population by as much as 80 percent in a year.

Biologists feel that repopulation by native birds is the only satisfactory answer to the quail problem, and that requires good habitat. Millions of game-farm quail have been released but have seldom established themselves, and Mexican imports have hardly been more successful.

Except for the mourning dove (more of which are shot than any other game bird) only the pheasant in its better years exceeds the bobwhite in number of birds shot. In '68–'69, ten million bobwhites were shot in Texas; three million in Kansas and Oklahoma; two million in Missouri, Florida, the Carolinas, Georgia, Illinois and Alabama; and over one million in Tennessee, Virginia, Mississippi and Kentucky. It has been estimated that, of all the shotgun shells sold, 14 percent are fired at quail as compared with 11 percent at waterfowl and 10 percent at pheasants.

On the big field-trial and shooting-preserve quail manors in the

Quail Shooting

deep South the bobwhite is the main crop, sustained by food plantings, weed strips and controlled burning in pine woods to create proper ground cover. Maintained for shooting in this way, quail respond in numbers never seen in their natural state as a bird of the fields and edges. In February, 1970, shooting on Al Rockwell's Pinebloom Plantation in south Georgia, my friend Jack Gates said they moved thirty and thirty-five coveys in a day—not uncommon on such places. It was surprising to learn, however, that on a well-managed preserve of that kind, the expected annual yield is only ten birds per hundred acres.

On those plantations where strictest ritual is observed, of the eight or ten gunners on horseback or riding the shooting wagon, only two approach the pointing dogs. Shooting is limited to the covey rise; singles are not pursued and the coveys are not disturbed for another few days. The bag is held to a safe limit, in contrast to uncontrolled, heavily-gunned terrain, where the birds may be killed off if they don't have the resourcefulness to escape. On plantations where singles are shot, the big-going covey dogs are rested and closer-working singles specialists are used; even the best of these are not infallible and if they find three-fourths of the singles they are doing well. Some plantations rely upon retriever breeds to pick up birds.

The nicest quail shooting I have had was in Virginia. Once they saw the setters in our station wagon, the colored porters in country inns would try to help me locate birds—Wiley at the Martha Washington in Abingdon, the man at Herring Hall, Cole at Thornhill in Winchester. I made the error of asking the waiter at Mrs. Bollinger's Corner Hall in Round Hill if there were quail nearby. He looked baffled until Mrs. Bollinger came to my aid and said, "John, he means *birds*."

In 1943 I was a shooting guest at Carl Covington's home in Culpeper County. At the Navy Department in Washington, Carl and I had talked of little else for days, and we were well out toward Warrenton by the time the sun came up huge and distorted through frosty mists. When we reached Carl's home we spent a few moments at the nice old house talking to his parents and sister and meeting the setters Jack and Duke, then took off on foot in the direction of Mount Pony.

It brought back scenes from Nash Buckingham's stories of

hunts at Brick House. In the service, opportunities to see birds were as hard to come by as shells to shoot with, and my shooting was ragged. Carl was an excellent shot and wonderful host. I remember the last point of the day with Duke backing Jack. Carl thought his fast shooting had "flustered" me and insisted that I take the shot alone. I refused and we both walked in. Carl hit his bird cleanly and I centered one with my right barrel and caught a second climbing for the treetops with the left. That double made the day beautiful for me and we trudged the miles back to the Covington house in a glow. Those coverts with more coveys than I had seen in one day, the soft-spoken warmth of Carl's family, the spoon bread at dinner, the house in its big trees "under the Blue Ridge, the side that is red in the sunrise" are memories that linger.

During that period I shot quail around Middleburg and Antioch, with the assistance of two understanding strangers—a young white-and-orange pointer bitch Queenie and a nice tattered old white-and-liver pointer Pete standing in for Blue, who was waiting out the war years in my father's kennel yard. Some of those honeysuckle coverts were as thick as anything I've tried to shoot in, and a bobwhite in such cover is as difficult to hit as a grouse. In those days I was shooting my 12-gauge Fox, its 28-inch barrels a little long and heavy for such work. If any gun can be called a quail gun, it is the 20-gauge double, though a nicely balanced light 12-gauge with one ounce of No. 8's or No. 9's is comfortable.

Like grouse hunting, early-morning quail hunting in heavy dew is not productive or pleasant, tiring the gunners and dogs before the optimum late shooting. In the coverts I used to hunt, if bobwhites weren't in ragweed, lespedeza, buckwheat stubble or cornfields in late afternoon you would do well to move to the next farm. In wet weather it is best to hunt the higher ground; in dry weather the birds prefer the bottom land and ditches.

A covey will fly to cover in spite of the gunner's position, flaring back over him if he tries to intercept them. Since quail lie so well under a point, it isn't necessary to walk in from the front or side, and doing this may put the gunner in the midst of the exploding covey—a poor place to shoot. It is important to let the bird get to good-pattern range, but the expert shot will drop his bird at the earliest opportunity. Something about waiting causes hesitation, which breeds misses.

Quail Shooting

More than any other bird, quail offer chances for doubles. With confidence, making a double on the covey rise is not difficult, but a "double" state of mind is detrimental unless you concentrate on the first bird. If you miss, stay with it and use the second barrel; don't switch for another bird as most novices do. As the covey lifts, select a bird on one side or in front, never in the center; to shoot into a rising covey, hoping to drop several birds, is stupid. And I can't refrain from saying I consider calling quail to be shot comparable to shooting them on the ground.

Quail shooters of my father's generation said bobwhites deliberately held their scent after landing, and gave single birds time to move about before following them. Deliberate or not, a frightened quail will sit with feathers tight against its body and little scent is released until the bird relaxes.

In 1962 I was invited to shoot on one of the historic estates in Virginia, but something had happened that put an end to my killing quail. Before he left for the South, Meade Foster had given me his training birds. Until you have lived intimately with four bobwhites you can have no idea what a delightful person each one is. Four strange birds became Mister Bob, Robert, Roberta and Little Miss. I got to know their language, from small chittering sounds at sight of favorite foods to their talk when they were insecure; I learned their covey calls and I even heard hens call, "bobwhite," always *sotto voce*. I've heard few sounds lovelier than quail coveyed late on a snowy afternoon, talking softly; had few surprises more pleasant than finding a wild hen in the pen with our birds, or a wild covey gathered outside.

Recovery pens for training quail have a re-entry tunnel. A calling bird is left in the pen while the others are flown out or carried in a cage and released where you want to work your dog. I could start them calling when they were scattered but at times they regathered without audible sounds. And there were evenings when, in spite of their strong homing instinct, one of them would not return, like the time with Mister Bob.

It was a mild afternoon at the beginning of March and we had released him on a knob three hundred yards from the pen. At the first flush he sailed over the far side and, rather than push him further, we stopped working. That night he did not return, but it wasn't cold and we felt no concern. Next day, Sunday, we failed to find him. On Monday a snow set in and for two days and nights it smothered us and weighed our big hemlocks down. By Tuesday night it was twenty-five inches deep. Wednesday, I shoveled a path to the three quail in the pen, pausing to give the covey call for the missing Mister Bob. When you do these hopeless things, you continue long after reason tells you it is over. By evening I gave up and came in to the fire. Before going to bed I went out one more time, walking the path to the quail pen with snow creaking under my boots. My flash beam picked out two hens and two cocks huddled in the runway. Eyes staring, I counted them again. When he had come I don't know, but Mister Bob was back. He had been alone four days in cold that should have killed him, in snow so deep he couldn't have fed. Yet something—the need for the other birds, perhaps my calling—guided him home.

In the wild, a hen quail will lay up to 18 eggs and then incubate them. That first summer Little Miss laid 125 eggs and Roberta 145. Both cocks and hens sat on the eggs sporadically, but it was not until we put two dozen under a bantam hen that any were hatched.

We took one of the young quail as a pet when it was three days old. At this age they will identify with humans and will spend a happy life away from other quail. Almost from the start, Bobbie spent every dinner hour inside my shirt, perched on my collarbone. He traveled with us, often inside my shirt, and never betrayed my confidence in him though he showed no restraint when at large on the floor. When he was seven months old, Bobbie died in an accident with one of the setters. Our next quail pet was Miss B., who was with us for two delightful years.

At hatching, little quail are the size of their mother's head—like bumblebees with two tan stripes down their backs. The sexes are identical in plumage to about five weeks, when the males begin to show white throats and black feathers on the head, but there is a subtle difference in shape of skull almost from the day of hatching. The male has a round-domed head compared with a sloping forehead on the female that gives her a pointed appearance. I selected Miss B. as a female on her sixth day.

During the shooting season, adult quail can be distinguished from yearlings by the outer two primaries, as in grouse—the tips being more pointed on the yearling. The primary coverts on year-

Quail Shooting

lings are spotted and have light tips and shafts, while adult coverts are gray.

Ratio of cocks to hens is even at hatching, changing with age to a predominance of males. This is more evident in the northern range, suggesting a greater ability among males to survive. Extremely dry or extremely wet weather may kill half the young birds during the summer. Normally, 80 percent of fall populations are young birds; fewer than 75 percent indicating a low quail year. The rise and fall of quail populations is not cyclic, as they appear to be with some game species, but such changes often follow cycles of severe winters. In less than ideal range, quail refuges help wild quail when gun pressure gets too intense; in good range, refuges aren't considered important.

On commercial preserves, quail shooting more nearly approaches the quality of wild shooting than pheasant shooting, because quail can be released and held for a longer time. A few feeding stations don't detract much from the illusion of natural cover and quail that have been on their own and have escaped some shooting soon behave like wild birds before a dog.

Now that quail are being offered on many preserves, I wouldn't have to go to Georgia to find bobwhites. Still, the journey to far places is a pleasant part of shooting and I know I am missing much by giving up quail. Bobwhite offers good, sporting shooting enhanced by grand dog work. If only I hadn't been a sucker for his winning ways.

Pheasant Shooting

> ❧ / ... *pheasants kukkered out of copse,*
> *Cracking the twigs down with their knockings*
> *And planing out of sight with cockings ...*
>
> —JOHN MASEFIELD, *Reynard the Fox*

PHEASANT SHOOTING CAME LATE in my shooting life, after years of quail and grouse and woodcock gunning, and the big showy birds were just too easy. The first pheasant I shot at rose in a clearing as open as a lawn, climbed with its long tail wriggling like pork rind on a spoon hook and leveled, still kukking. I let it go a few more yards, swung through and, finding myself too far ahead, waited for it and fired from stationary barrels. It didn't have the sense to fall so I held right on it and pulled the left barrel. The pheasant coasted on, like a cackling red-and-green circus wagon. I couldn't believe it.

My incredulity got a lot of wear that day. I learned that there are pheasants slow and pheasants fast and, finally, a little about how to handle them. But I have no ear for the person who says that pheasants are not sporting shooting.

Of my shooting friends, two qualify as exceptional pheasant shots. Less Crowl grew up on pheasants and I suppose he has missed a few but I haven't seen him do it. Dr. Charles Norris shot little else in his later years and on his last day afield missed three pheasants— with good reason. He was so ill he could scarcely walk.

I'm not a brilliant enough shot on pheasants to say how to do it but I did much thinking about it and a lot of worrying before I began to hit at all consistently. It is usually the poor shot who will tell you exactly how to shoot, and his fixed notion of what to do on every shot may be the reason for his poor shooting. Not many good shots can tell you, I suspect because they shoot instinctively.

Pheasant Shooting

Dr. Norris, when I appealed for suggestions, spoke vaguely of "seeing daylight between the bird and the muzzle," or of the white neck ring as "the place to hold on a rising cock." On the first, I know he meant to shoot from moving barrels, and on the second he no doubt meant to fire as you swing up through the white ring. The deliberate shot who "points them out" will make long shots fairly regularly, but no matter how slow they appear, you rarely drop a pheasant with stationary barrels.

Robert Churchill, the British gunmaker and shooting coach, warned against awareness of leading a bird and recommended that the gunner in a shooting slump try shooting the next pheasant "in the beak." Which means that the eyes of the gunner are then clearly focused on the bird and not at a blurred form. It helps to focus on a forward part and not on the big flowing tail—the empty two-thirds of the bird.

I shoot best on pheasants and all birds if I take each shot as it comes and forget everything but to see that bird clearly, then mount and overtake it. It produces a smooth swing timed to exceed the speed of the bird. On a fast pheasant in full glide, I try to pull as I go through a short lead (Dr. Norris's daylight ahead of the bird). I pass up long shots, for a bird the size of a pheasant is usually farther than it appears and could carry off pellets and die later. The going-away pheasant is notorious for its armor-plated bone and its capacity to carry shot, especially at a distance.

One of Kay's movies of a pheasant kill illustrates the sequence of the swing and follow-through on a left-crossing bird flying at moderate speed. It is in twenty-eight frames of 8-mm. film and when studied frame by frame shows what happened and how fast. Kay was standing behind me. During the first seven frames I am in the ready position, gunstock tucked under my arm against my ribs even before the bird appears. In frame No. 8 I begin to mount, continuing as the pheasant appears from the right in frame No. 10. Judging from the relation of muzzle to bird, I pulled the trigger in No. 13 but the puff of blue haze indicates that the gun fired in No. 15, demonstrating the delay between intent and discharge. From the bird's action, the pattern struck it in No. 16 with the gun muzzle well past the bird. Feathers stream behind the pheasant in No. 19 and it falls from No. 20 through No. 28 with the gun barrels still swinging far ahead in the follow-through. From frame No. 8, when

I began to mount, through No. 15, when the gun discharged, was eight frames or *one-half second*, giving an idea of the speed of the mount-and-overtake. Yet this was not a fast pheasant.

Number 6 shot is the most popular size for pheasants and most preserves insist upon nothing smaller. Some men claim an advantage with finer shot, with increased shock power from the greater number of pellet hits. I had good shooting on one trip using a 3 dram $1\frac{1}{16}$ ounce No. $7\frac{1}{2}$ load but I prefer the $3\frac{1}{4}$ dram $1\frac{1}{8}$ ounce No. 6 12-gauge load with plastic sleeve. The feathers on an old cock can reduce shot penetration—I have heard the impact of the pattern on heavily-quilled primaries sound like shot tearing through corn fodder—and a pheasant at thirty-five yards is not an easy bird to kill. Wounded pheasants have been known to strike when accepted from the dog, and a wing-tipped cock can punish a dog with its wings or spurs.

On an adult cock the spur will measure $\frac{3}{4}$ inch or more from the tip to the front of the leg, is hard, glossy and sharp. The shorter spur on a young cock is rough and blunt and can identify the yearling through the hunting season, though the plumage appears the same as the adult's. If held by the lower mandible, the $2\frac{1}{2}$-pound weight of a young cock will usually break the mandible; on an adult, the mandible will support the three-pound-plus bird. The average life span of cocks is about ten months, that of hens fifteen to twenty-four. While most pheasants die a violent death, they can live to a natural old age of eight to ten years. If toughness is a criterion, one cock I shot had reached his half score.

The pheasant population is a young one, with fall age ratio a good indicator of brood success. In good years, young pheasants make up 65 to 80 percent of the population; less than 65 percent is poor reproduction; if under 50 percent, the population is on the way down.

About half the fall pheasants are killed by gunning, including crippling losses, which are always high—a persuasive argument for the use of dogs. Of every hundred pheasants in early October, not over thirty will be alive by the end of the following September. This huge turnover is not drastic, provided enough survivors are hens. One cock will effectively mate with ten hens, and it is considered nearly impossible to overgun cocks in a healthy pheasant population. In 1950 more than 90 percent of the cocks on Lake Erie's Pelee Island were shot but egg fertility held at 86 percent.

In *American Game Birds*, Edminster suggests that sparing hens is wasteful; otherwise, where are all the hens that have been passed up for years? Not all hens are spared—in some places the illegal hen kill amounts to 37 percent of the cocks shot. Most biologists consider protection of the egg-laying hen vital to pheasant management. While the horned owl is admittedly the worst adult pheasant predator, surplus cocks are said to become fox meat if not shot. If Reynard's reputation is as bad as this, why wouldn't more leftover cocks take fox pressure off the essential hens? Immediately I am told that foxes don't kill many pheasants, adding to the confusion. To prove this, banded dead pheasants were scattered over a large study area; later, bands were found at every fox den, establishing that many fox "kills" are actually picked-up pheasant carrion—lost cripples, road and mowing-field casualties.

Pheasant nest losses are high—up to a third. During the first two weeks the chicks are vulnerable to cold wet weather, but after that, unlike grouse chicks, they are little affected by weather. The nides break up at about two months but only three-fifths of the young birds survive until the shooting season. Considering that gunners flush flocks of two hundred birds in the Northern Plains states, such pheasant country produces huge quantities of young chicks.

In less optimum range, stocking is necessary to maintain shooting. State agencies resist the idea, quoting costs up to $40 to put one pheasant before the gun. They should take lessons from an efficient commercial preserve manager who can show a profit on a fee of $6 per pheasant shot. Subsidized nonprofit game departments should do as well or better.

I would like to see a farmer free to breed pheasants without a game breeder's license; if he released these birds on his land and opened it to shooting—for a fee—he should be exempt from the commercial-shooting-preserve license he is currently required to buy. Such small preserves would create an enormous pheasant resource in pay-as-you-shoot sport and in free shooting on escaped birds. With no additional land overhead, the farmer could utilize his feed crops, and during low-work winter periods release pheasants on a bird-killed or bird-released basis, the latter as low as $2 or $3 per

The Birds

bird. A large pheasant spill-over in grouse terrain, though unlikely, might create adverse competition for grouse but should act as a buffer in grouse losses to predators.

Pen-reared pheasants are nearly as untamed as wild-hatched birds, unlike grouse, and lend themselves well to stocking. If both sexes are shot, a 50 percent return from stocking can be expected; if only cocks are shot, a 20 percent return is good. Stocking to increase the kill should be done at the beginning of and during the shooting season; stocking to increase breeders is most successful in early spring to late May.

There is little difference in pheasant kill between a one-week and a one-month season, for most cocks are shot during the first few days. A lot of hunters walk up, or try to walk up, pheasants without a dog. Like hunting any game bird without a dog, it seems as illogical to me as hunting with a club, but this doesn't alter the reality— most of the millions of pheasants killed are shot in this manner. Every pheasant shooter knows the pheasant as a runner. Wily old cocks wouldn't be old unless they were wily, and they soon learn to sneak off or run out of gunshot before rising. Hard-pushed for several days, they will take to lying in the middle of open pasture or a plowed field, far from the activity in the borders, sometimes in the shadow of a stump or plowed furrow. A man hunting without a dog may go home thinking pheasants were nonexistent in a covert that held numerous birds, not because the birds squatted and let him pass but because they legged it to the nearest ditch and exited without flushing. If he gets a shot and doesn't center it, with no dog his troubles have only begun. The appearance of a wounded pheasant on the ground may give a clue as to what to expect. If its feathers are held close to its body, it is probably wing-shot and it will run like a witch. If its feathers are ruffled, the bird is no doubt hit in the body and is not likely to run far.

Good pheasant dogs will consistently circle and head off pheasants that run out on their points. At less than a year old, Briar tried the circling tactic after a point on a pheasant in dense sorghum last season. The pheasant won, but for a young pup it showed thinking. My setters usually hit pheasants at full speed, pinning them in shock. A double point by a brace of dogs is especially efficient, the second dog blocking escape. Dr. Norris liked his dogs to work a pheasant cautiously, stopping on point if the bird held, moving up as

Pheasant Shooting

the pheasant moved but not too closely. Following such a dog, the gunner can get a shot even if the bird won't lie. Incidentally, to the purist—and Dr. Norris was one—a pheasant is *put up*, not flushed.

If two men, each with a dog, will keep a hundred yards apart they will find nearly twice as many pheasants as if they walked together. Aside from watching his dog, the gunner should not wander aimlessly through cover but should be alert for roosting and dusting sites, droppings and food. He should go around, not through clumps too dense to shoot in. Above all, he should not hunt in a straight line if he doesn't want to pass up birds.

If you've tried it, you've found it isn't wise to walk directly toward a pheasant seen on the ground. An approach a little to one side will get you closer, especially if you move casually. Often the first intimation that a pheasant is in the area is the *cock-up* call of a bird that has treed ahead of your dog. It's a poor chance for a shot, because if the bird doesn't take off before you get within range it may sit stupidly above you and refuse to flush. I rarely succeed in moving them and have to walk off with the bird glaring down at me from its perch. Noise seldom frightens tree perchers, yet nothing will clear a covert of pheasants so fast as the human voice. If they don't flush far ahead they go into a state of alarm and refuse to hold for a dog.

A wet day causes pheasants to lie tighter and make shorter, and lower, flights. Seeing a pheasant crouched ahead of a point can unnerve some gunners. The bird will often fly in the direction it is headed or it may turn about-face so fast the movement can't be seen, flushing away from the gun or rocketing up. An exceptionally high-headed point indicates a bird well out. If he can, the gunner should circle in on a point from in front to prevent the pheasant's sneaking out and flushing at long range. If you get close to the bird it may produce a perpendicular flush but it makes a nice shot if the bird reaches a good height before leveling. I've had some of these come directly back over my head. Turning and taking such a shot shouldn't be difficult if you remember to hold under the bird, but I miss it with regularity.

Any pinned pheasant may rise perpendicularly, especially among trees, but at times they take a run and fly off low. This often happens when they are flushed from a hillside to lower ground. These downhill gliders can embarrass the best of shots, for they seem to sail deceptively slowly. Pheasants don't fly truly level. A typical rise is a rapid vertical spring, then a leveling-off followed by a gradual descent, sailing on rigid wings. If it lands in sparse cover, the bird may run a long distance—usually in the direction of the flight. It is more difficult to locate a flushed wild pheasant the second time than any other game bird. If shot at, it may fly more than a mile. Many overhead pheasants are not shot at because they appear too high, yet, like any upland game bird, they are almost never high enough to be out of gunshot. It is a giant tree that is over thirty-five yards tall.

In 1955 we went on a pheasant-shooting trip near Dundee, Michigan, with Less Crowl. Lew Wilson, the dog breeder and trainer, was our host and guide. In that country each crop is laid out in flat eighty-acre pieces—alfalfa beside an equal spread of corn next to a similar stretch of soybeans, with stubble fields to match. There are few woodlots. Lew took us to land where shooting was limited but, even there, opening-day crowds detracted. Back roads teemed with carloads of cruising hunters. One jalopy passed where we were hunting, stopped, and a man got out. Standing in the road, he aimed a .22 rifle toward the bank, there was the crack of the report and he reached into the brush and lifted a big cock in the air, grinning at us. "That's the way to git 'em," he said, tossed the bird into the car and drove off.

Our first day was a frustrating one. In the early morning of the second day I had an opportunity to see how evasive a wounded cock pheasant can be. Lew, Less, Kay and I were in a large alfalfa field near Lew's kennels—ample cover for three guns, a movie camera and four dogs. I shot at a going-away cock, misjudging it as quartering right. It collapsed, hit in the right wing, and we sent the dogs to retrieve. To escape, it had to run between the legs of four good retrievers and four people but it wasn't found. At Lew's suggestion, I went back to his kennels for Buster, a little white-and-liver setter rated tops as a wounded pheasant finder. Buster was ugly as homemade sin but I opened his kennel gate and we were soon on the way. Ruff and young Shadows had accompanied me, and as we neared our waiting party Shadows went solidly on point, backed by Ruff. In the early-morning light it had everything Edmund Osthaus would have painted. I was disappointed when I put up a hen, but a moment later a cock flushed and gave me a crossing shot, folding in a gratifying manner. The deep alfalfa and a stiff breeze created mo-

Pheasant Shooting

mentary difficulty locating the bird. Buster got to it first but I was damned if I was going to have my first Michigan pheasant delivered by a stranger. I pulled him away and held him until Ruff hit the scent and picked up the bird, delivering it to hand. Poor Buster put me down for another crazy hunter—not far from right. In spite of his reputation and his reinforcement, we did not find my first cock and I've wondered if Buster might not, after all, have evened his score.

Crowds affect the behavior of pheasants. Less tells of droves of pheasants he has seen running half a mile ahead of hunters, abdicating before too many men and dogs. We found birds in the early mornings but within an hour they had covered up in standing corn or unharvested soybeans, which are out of bounds to hunters. There seems to be a feeling in most pheasant country, especially near cities, that few cocks remain in their original coverts after several days of shooting. It would take a foolish cock to show himself if he had a place to hide. But in a good pheasant year and with eighty-acre blocks of cover, enough cocks should dodge first-week hunters in Michigan to offer good sport to a man with a knowledgeable dog after the crowds have gone home. At any rate, I'd like to try it then.

Preserve Shooting

A BRASH YOUNG SHOOTING GUEST informed me over her second drink that preserve shooting was as artificial as patronizing a brothel. She hadn't shot on a preserve and I have never visited a brothel so neither of us were too well qualified to discuss it. I can say I've had a lot of fun on preserves.

Most men who reject the idea of shooting on commercial preserves would leap at the chance to shoot on a private preserve with game released in the same manner; others who object to preserve birds as pen-raised, shoot pen-raised birds released by state game departments. Preserve shooting appeals to me for several reasons. It is a pleasant way to reduce withdrawal symptoms at the end of the shooting season, prolonging gunning on occasional fine days through March, by which time spring is at hand and it is easier to stop. If a man's hunting life is not long enough, a dog's is even shorter and anything you can do to make that fuller is worthwhile. I like preserve shooting because I can be almost certain of getting action or at least know that birds are there—something that can't always be said for open pheasant shooting. Shooting in heavily gunned pheasant country turns into a where-is-everybody festival, and I prefer the privacy of a preserve. If it isn't managed to provide shooting without interference from other gunners it's not living up to what its name implies.

Most preserves offer pheasants, bobwhite quail, chukar partridge and ducks. I use them for partridge and pheasant shooting,

Preserve Shooting

often requesting hen pheasants because they lie tighter to a dog and rise and fly faster than cocks. Shooting both hen and cock pheasants leaves none of the uncertainty about taking the shot at a bird your dog is pointing. I don't pretend that preserve pheasants are superior to wild birds but they provide nice dog work.

A preserve is as good as its manager and its shooting grounds. Among men who have tried preserve shooting, those who denigrate it have often been to the wrong places. They may have been presented with birds dizzied and stuck under a corn shock or pile of pine boughs—birds that had to be booted out. This sickening practice is the only way some preserve managers will guarantee a given number of shots for a daily fee, usually over a dog from the preserve kennel steered to the planted bird by the guide who planted it. My first contact with this custom was on a preserve in every other way delightful. The pheasants were good birds but curiously hard to put up. When one flushed, climbing with its neck cricked at an angle from having its head tucked under its wing—an Anne Boleyn bird—the guide thought it strange that I refused to shoot.

Preserve dogs are often handled by boys not wise in dog work and they've learned they'd jolly well better work underfoot to avoid a flush out of gun range. I feel sorry for them. The man shooting over his own dogs knows preserve shooting at its best, if birds are properly presented. He can give each dog or brace of dogs separate turns; or introduce a young pup to the relation between gun and bird; or within a few hours give a partly finished youngster the equivalent of days of experience.

A preserve faces large bird losses. All gunners are not good shots and many birds fly beyond the boundaries. Game in quantity attracts predators; on every preserve I have gunned I have seen pheasant-wing leftovers from fox and hawk and owl meals, although some may have been picked up cripples. No matter how desirable it might be to hold a level of birds-out, pheasants won't stay put, and managers must operate to keep losses at a minimum.

High pheasant populations are maintained on British preserves but these are extensive tracts and management is at enormous cost. Back in 1958, Richard Waddington estimated the cost of driven grouse at £5 per brace shot; in Austria in 1970 it cost $4 to $6 per pheasant driven to the gun. Pheasant-stocking programs as carried out by our state game departments couldn't be successful on areas as small as most American commercial preserves. And so to present unnatural numbers of birds on a given area—the purpose of preserves—it has become a fact of preserve management that pheasants, at least, must be released just prior to a shoot, the ratio of return being in inverse proportion to the length of time the birds have been at large. Released quail that escape the gun will regroup and adapt to adequate cover, if only for a short time. Chukars are even more elusive than pheasants and are usually put out on a bird-released fee.

The man who shoots a preserve should do it with a bit of make-believe. He knows those aren't wild birds and that they had to come from somewhere. But, for what it amounts to, it can be exciting. It is the manager's job, in spite of limitations, to make it so. Since daily releases are necessary, birds should be taken to the shooting grounds an hour or more before the shooting party, not trucked out in front of them in crates. Ideally, they should be put out late the previous evening, for well-planned cover and food plots would hold them several days.

Too often artificial practices are followed because clients accept them. Instead of planted birds pushed under corn shocks, the gunner should insist upon normal releases. The bird need not be flown out—pheasants, especially, frequently keep going—but it can be put down gently and allowed to walk to cover. There is some loss this way but the fee should take care of that.

The daily fee on one of the preserves I shoot is $25 for three pheasants or five chukars or seven quail. Additional pheasants are $6, chukars $4, quail $3. This is about typical. The guarantee for this number of birds is with a guide, over the preserve's dog and, what is not spelled out, on planted birds. Most preserves are glad to have you use your dogs, provided they are well trained and that you do not insist upon a guaranteed minimum kill. I almost never use a guide and I pay for birds as released or, at a higher rate, as birds shot. When the management gets to know you regularly bring in birds, the latter makes a nice arrangement; otherwise, the former can mount up. I remember one pheasant that cost me $19.

By contrast, one preserve I shot was managed for the personnel of a corporation. To defray expenses it was open to other gunners by appointment. The daily fee of $6 included two pheasants; additional birds were $3 each. This wasn't planned to show a profit

Preserve Shooting

but it demonstrates how inexpensively preserve shooting can be produced.

A high proportion of preserve income derives from business entertainment and, like all expense-account spending, it affects the individual gunner adversely. A preserve manager prefers to have his spread used by a group on a shooting spree as guests of a corporation, when the kill may run to several hundred birds. While managers are hospitable to the single client, they encourage larger bags than I care to take. I don't feel the empathy for a preserve pheasant that I feel for a wild bird—it is raised for a purpose and if not put out to be shot by one man it will be put out for the next. Yet I don't have the stomach for unrestrained killing, and three or four pheasants shot over my dogs in an afternoon is enough.

If you approach preserve shooting with the proper state of mind, it will give you and your dogs extra-calendar shooting pleasure. For the older shooting man or the gunner limited by some disability, preserves are a welcome source of gunning. It isn't the equal of wild shooting but it may become a necessary substitute. With urban sprawl chewing up game cover, preserves can absorb gun pressure from an increasing number of gunners on a decreasing number of wild birds.

AMWELL

OF THE PRESERVES I have gunned, Amwell, Prairie Lane, and Nemacolin Trail stand out as exceptional.

Amwell is a limited-membership club with two thousand acres of rolling land on the New Jersey side of the Delaware River north of Lambertville. A substantial membership fee, plus dues, plus fee for birds shot, probably is the reason Amwell can present birds more naturally than most commercial preserves. My first visit there was in October, 1954, as the guest of Dr. Charles Norris. Parking near the clubhouse at the end of a long lane, we met Duncan Dunn, who manages the preserve. There were pheasant pens a short distance from the clubhouse and as we talked I could hear mallards chuckling and splashing beyond tall pines.

Dr. Norris's chauffeur Raymond, a burly Irishman with cropped iron-gray hair, acted as companion-sitter for whichever dog—Nellie or Charm—Dr. Norris wasn't using. He removed a canvas-covered trunk gun case from the car and Dr. Norris assembled a beautiful little double. It was the first time I had been that close to a Purdey.

We shot separately on that day and on all my visits to Amwell—a generous arrangement, for I had half the preserve to myself. Dr. Norris, wearing a British grouse helmet with a grouse tail feather in the band, started out with his pointer Nellie, and Kay and I used Ruff and Feathers, with Duncan Dunn as our guide. It was one of those October days when the foliage matched the color of the pheasants. There was not the overabundance of birds that can make preserve shooting seem false, but enough to provide sustained action. They hold spaniel trials at Amwell and there are plenty of birds out most of the time. The only releasing I was aware of was while hunting a wooded draw, when I heard the flap of wings. Swinging around, I saw half a dozen hens sailing down a hillside, then heard a truck drive off.

Kay was having a wonderful time with her movie camera, getting some nice dog work by Ruff and Feathers, but I was in trouble. No one is more wretched than the gunner who can't pull himself together. My unproductive rights-and-lefts were punctuated by crisp single reports from the Purdey on the far side of the preserve. Dunn was congratulatory on my few clean kills and tactfully commiserating about my misses, but I realize how painful it must have been for him to watch birds fly beyond the preserve.

Back at the cars we found that Dr. Norris had shot several pheasants over each of his dogs and was ready to return to Fairhill with Raymond. He insisted that Kay and I stay on and left us with a shooting lunch of pheasant sandwiches wrapped in large linen napkins.

By the time we arrived at Fairhill, Dr. Norris had already cleaned his gun and changed for dinner. Much of the pleasure of shooting is what accompanies it and sharing it all with a good friend. Dinner was roast pheasant with bread sauce, and Harvey's Amontillado. Nellie lay at one side of Dr. Norris's chair at table, the orange belton setter Charm on the other. Later, before the drawing-room fire, we talked of the day and discussed plans for tomorrow's shoot. I was ready enough when Dr. Norris suggested we retire, but I was overstimulated and lay long, missing every missed bird of the day all over again before I slept.

Preserve Shooting

Our second day at Amwell was in face of forecast for rain but the morning held at cloudy with bits of sun. Again we followed Dr. Norris's car through Bucks County, watching Nellie and Charm stiffly erect in the rear seat like obese dowagers glancing at landmarks too familiar to merit comment.

This time, leaving my gun and our setters in the station wagon at the clubhouse, Kay and I followed Dr. Norris in the field to try to learn how he handled these big slow birds that seemed so easy to miss. His first shot at a wild flush was a miss on bad footing—most probably because of spectators with a movie camera at his back. He missed no more. The second bird, over a point by Nellie, was dropped with a fast mount that was over before I could discern much about it.

Nellie's next point was a nice find and Dr. Norris flushed and dropped the cock, which she delivered to him. As he was pocketing the bird, Nellie returned to the site of the flush and froze again. A second cock rose with much kukking and leveled off. Dr. Norris made a quick recovery of his gun, which he had laid on the ground, and mounted, but the safety was still on and the bird sailed away.

I tried to study his swing but I could see only that he mounted rapidly and fired with no dwelling on the bird. At seventy-eight, his agility in the field was remarkable and he appeared to be at the peak of his shooting form. The guides at the club told me he almost never missed a bird and one of them recounted a double he had recently seen him make on two high incomers.

Kay and I spent the rest of the morning shooting over our two setters and I did better than on the first day. It began to sprinkle, scarcely audible on the dry leaves, but by the time we climbed into the station wagon it was pouring. We changed into dry clothes and ate our pheasant sandwiches while Ruff and Feathers licked their steaming coats in the rear.

At Fairhill during dinner I mentioned the guides' opinion of his shooting.

"I think I know where they got that notion." Dr. Norris chuckled. "One day I was standing talking to Dominic when two pheasants came flapping over our heads like angels—" he made appropriate gestures. "By some accident I dropped them both."

He wanted us to extend our stay for more shooting, but we were expected at State College to shoot grouse and woodcock and we left the following day.

My next shooting at Amwell was in February, 1956. Leaving our mountains under snow, we found weather in the East like early November. This time Amwell had the added charm of memories—the excellent coverts, the simple, comfortable clubhouse, the tombstone of a member's dog *Old Jack, 1921–1931* with the setter's profile incised in the marble. We had all four of our setters on this trip and Kay and I started with Ruff and Shadows. It was sprinkling and I expected good shooting, but we moved nothing on the first circle. Dr. Norris shot two pheasants and, as before, left for Fairhill early.

After lunch Kay and I used our other blue-orange brace, Wilda and her son Feathers. The rain had settled into a drizzle but we forgot it as we got into birds. My first shot was a good crossing pheasant that my newly restocked Fox dropped nicely—a hen, which Feathers snapped up and retrieved in a wide circle as if trying for a favorable angle in front of Kay's camera. The next bird was an incomer, which faltered at the first shot then folded as I turned and fired again. Once more Feathers, the ham, rushed to the camera with the pheasant while I ran to catch up with the retrieve.

We had two more days of shooting in beautiful weather. Kay's movies of this are fine: Amwell's fields of sedge, the winter-bare trees, dog work that still thrills me, with one point by Ruff that is perfection—Ruff rigid, orange belton in golden sedge, the hen pheasant walking under his nose and Ruff holding like a saint, the pheasant's left-quartering rise, the cloud of feathers filtering in sunlight. And Ruff's retrieve.

While Amwell is large, most releases are within half a mile of the clubhouse and, as at most preserves, the birds tend to work back toward the pens, attracted by the pheasants inside. But many pheasants move out, especially if shot at and missed, and I enjoyed gunning the outer reaches of the grounds. Some of the birds in those areas had been out long enough for it to be like wild shooting.

I remember a December day in one of those far fields. They had run a spaniel trial the weekend before, with a large release of pheasants, many of which had not been shot. Prospects for action looked good but there was a layer of clouds and a feel of impending snow. Ruff made the first point in a little draw, backed by young Shadows,

Preserve Shooting

but the bird—a large cock—moved out the far side like a Tennessee walking horse. Rather than follow it back the way we had come, we pushed on to the top of a ridge and over the crest to a field of sedge, where Ruff pointed. With both dogs solid I put up a hen. As it fell at my shot, a second hen rose, offering an easy chance, which I missed from overconfidence. As I reloaded and sent the dogs to retrieve the downed bird, a third hen flushed. It was a long shot but the pattern caught the bird at the far edge of the field. Ruff delivered the last bird first, then retrieved the first bird as if he considered it all a tall story.

We returned to the car to change dogs. After his long wait, Feathers began by plunging into the duck pond, giving two hundred mallards a stirring up. With the air full of clamoring ducks, he swam ashore, shook himself and set off. In his state of mind, I won't say he would have handled them carefully but if there had been pheasants present Feathers would have found them. With half a hundred at large somewhere on those shooting grounds, they were covered up, much like wild birds before a storm. We finally located a few and I shot one over Feathers. That evening at bedtime, Dr. Norris called us to come look out the door. Fairhill was being covered with snow, which by morning reached a depth of fourteen inches.

My last shooting at Amwell was, like the first, in October. It was Dixie's first season and, at eight months, she was being introduced to serious shooting. Amwell was beautiful but it was too hot for dogs and men. Age was overtaking more than one old sportsman but neither Dr. Norris at eighty-two nor Ruff at eleven and a half was to be deterred by eighty-degree heat.

When we met at the cars after the morning's shooting, we found that Dr. Norris had shot several pheasants in the two hours he had hunted. Gun cradled in elbow, he directed me to a covert, using a thrusting, wobbling motion with open palm that evoked the image of a low pheasant rising. There was a sparkle in his eye and I think he looked ten years younger when he was at Amwell. After he drove off with Raymond, Kay and the four setters and I ate a tailgate lunch in the shade of a pine while a wistful Labrador sat on his kennel near the pheasant pens and whined.

In spite of the heat, we had a fine afternoon over Ruff and Feathers and Shadows and Dixie in matched-color braces. It was

THE BIRDS

the kind of shooting you have after you fall asleep at night—the dogs worked beautifully, each bird fell solidly. In the last hazy hour, Dixie flashed into a point at my left. A cock boiled up directly into the lowering sun, but my luck was holding and I took it overhead-away. I know nothing more memorable than the first kill over your young puppy's point.

We had three days of shooting, all in excruciating heat, but we loved it. In late afternoon of the last day I missed my last bird after a run of ten. I'll always have pleasant memories of Amwell, thanks to Dr. Norris.

PRAIRIE LANE

SHORTLY AFTER New Year's Day in 1958 I was invited to shoot Prairie Lane Preserve near Wooster, Ohio, to use the several varieties of gun dogs in their kennels in a sort of bird-dog-fancier's smorgasbord.

The mountains were white when Kay and I and our three setters left Old Hemlock at noon but there was only snow in patches under the pines when our headlight beams swung up the drive to the cabin at Prairie Lane under stars so cold they seemed to blink. There were lights in the cabin and when the door opened we could see a blazing fire. A stocky man in a suede jacket stepped out and introduced himself in grits-and-pone overtones as Dutch Martin, the manager. He got us settled and left, telling us the shooting would begin at nine.

Next day was cold and cloudless. Prairie Lane, originally a private preserve of the Holmes Construction Company, was opened to the public in 1953. Ohio law limits a commercial preserve to 640 acres, but Prairie Lane lay within a 1,460-acre farm, giving it isolation. During the season from September to mid-March they liberated about 10,000 pheasants, most of them raised on the place.

Dutch Martin and his wife came from Kentucky and brought the Negro dog-handler guides with them. There was a kennel of around thirty dogs—German shorthairs, Weimaraners, English setters, Brittanies, and Labradors. Shooting was limited to three parties daily, each assigned its sector of the preserve. You could have your shooting for a straight daily gun fee, or you could stay in

Preserve Shooting

a cabin with catering service—breakfast and pheasant dinners served in front of the fire.

We found Dutch Martin talking to Mose, the major-domo of the kennels. They let me decide what dogs to start with and I chose a brace of German shorthairs, to the disgust of the Old Hemlock setters in the station wagon. Mose opened one of the runways and let out big handsome liver-ticked Dan and Queen, two-and-a-half-year-old litter mates.

As we started toward the shooting grounds, Dan cut to the pheasant pens and went on point. I was puzzled, for most dogs ignore penned birds; then I saw a hen running outside the pen. With docked tail oscillating, Dan moved up and worked the bird as intensely as if it had been a wild bird. It ran until blocked by a building, where it flushed and headed for open country.

Where my setters would have quartered the big flats in wide casts, the shorthairs trotted or walked within thirty yards, searching diligently. Cover appeared natural—weed fields, strips of sorghum, and a coarse tangled growth Mose called canary grass. Planted for bird cover, it breaks over into masses that make hiding places for pheasants. The unusual feature of Prairie Lane was the canals with weedy banks—gravel dredgings filled with water, dividing the preserve into rectangular areas connected by foot crossings.

Heads up in a stiff breeze, the shorthairs converged on a clump of canary grass with their stub tails frantic. Queen stopped but Dan pranced in a half circle and closed in from in front to about four feet from Queen's nose. Tail posture on docked-tailed gun dogs is often overlooked and points are sometimes credited when the dog is still flagging—a situation in which a dog with a full component is not considered pointing. Though otherwise immobile, the shorthairs' stub tails were like busy metronomes. Mose began kicking the tangle between the quivering dogs and a hen took off low and quartering. I shot and watched tail feathers float down as the bird melted into the landscape. Mose was tactfully quiet but I knew Kay had got the full shame of it on her movie film, and I asked myself why the hell you so often miss the first bird.

In the next field the dogs made another point but again I couldn't feel certain because of their tails, which were never still. I like a time bomb to stop ticking before the explosion. The explosion came—a cock, which I dropped on the far side of a frozen canal. Both dogs went for the retrieve and both came back across the ice, each grasping an end of the bird.

At mid-morning we returned to the kennels. Mose put Dan and Queen in their runway, where Queen fixed me with her sad gaze and bawled her grief in an absurd falsetto.

The next brace was a pair of Weimaraners. Rocky, at nineteen months, was a big pale-eyed spook, Susie a little busybody that couldn't bear to leave a square yard of cover uninvestigated. They moved at a lope, faster than the shorthairs, but not wide. We hunted new coverts, mostly weedy flats, and though a difficult wind had come up, the Weimaraners did well. Rocky's points were stylish with head and neck extended, and when working a bird he moved with the exaggerated mincing step of a welterweight, for all his sixty-five or seventy pounds. They didn't circle the bird like the shorthairs, but when they froze, they went rigid to the end of their stub tails.

We followed the flight of several pheasants to an old lane lined with trees, where Mose and the dogs worked the road on the inside while Kay and I moved through corn stubble beyond. Mose's dog handling was mostly vocal, ringing across the preserve like a *gone away*. I heard him call that he had a point and was going to flush. His "Heah come a cock!" merged into the *cock-kuk-kuk* of a pheasant climbing straight up between the trees, its long tail spinning like a streamer fly. It offered a nice shot as it reached the tree tops over my left shoulder and, centered, fell sixty feet with a thud. Rocky picked up my bird and paused for Kay's movie like a Hollywood star at a première, then delivered it to Mose (odd feeling, having my game retrieved to someone else).

As we worked along the tree-lined lane a hen flushed out my

Preserve Shooting

side, too far for a shot. Mose called, "You can git 'im!" but I hesitated—bad for wing shooting. The pheasant seemed determined to corroborate Mose, cutting back my way but still well out. I tried my full-choke left, then the open right and chalked up two misses as the bird banked into the hedgerow. Mose couldn't believe it and doubled back with the Weimaraners, soon walking out carrying my dead pheasant to show me the shattered legs dangling. The bird hadn't flinched nor had it dropped a feather.

The Weimaraners slithered through the silvery dead grass like gray Confederate ghosts, the only color the flash of the pink inner surface of their ears as they moved. With their strange pale eyes they have a peculiar beauty unlike other dogs and I wondered if I could ever get to know them. Mose reminded me we were due at the clubroom for lunch.

The clubroom had no frills—a rack for guns, a washroom and lockers if you cared to change, and a kitchen at one end, where Mrs. Dutch Martin and a Negro girl from Mississippi were preparing something with an irresistible aroma. Dutch joined us and I asked to shoot over his setters in the afternoon. They were an unregistered line that had belonged to Dutch's family in Kentucky "too far back to trace the breeding."

When I saw them at the kennels I regretted that they didn't have papers, for they were the old-fashioned type. We used Betsy, ten, and her two-and-a-half-year-old son Dash with black-and-white even-marked head. I appreciated Dutch's attitude toward the dogs; each was treated as a personality, not merely fed for the work it did. Stopping in the clubroom between hunts you might see Betsy taking her ease in a chair, opening one eye to smile with her tail before snoozing off again.

Right now, Betsy wasn't sleeping. Carrying her ten years like a youngster, she moved with Dash into a sorghum patch at command. Other than the dogs' names, Mose used only one command, "Ho!" bellowed with all stops out. Both arms waving with elbows at waist level, Mose operated with an unlighted cigar in a holder clamped between enormous teeth. The supply of cigars appeared unlimited but the mortality was high; one moment he had a fresh cigar at horizontal, seconds later after a dive between two eager retrievers it was a raveled ruin. Several times I saw him searching deep grass as if looking for a cripple before I noticed the empty cigar

THE BIRDS

holder, and I suspect there were as many of Mose's wrecked cigars as empty shells strewing Prairie Lane. At each flush, Mose would go into a low crouch and utter a hoarse, "Shoot 'im!" I got used to it but at first it tended to make me venturesome on long shots.

The setters Betsy and Dash moved wider than the shorthairs and Weimaraners but still what I call close. Like the shorthairs, they worked pheasants with the encircling tactic. We had good action over them, and I shot a couple of fast-flying dark birds with an overall greenish-bronze cast with no white neck band—birds that resembled the Japanese green pheasant. Mose said they were a melanistic cross, bred for additional speed.

In the middle of the afternoon we went back to the kennels where Mose introduced us to three Brittanies, Jocko two-and-a-half years, Billy fourteen months, and Babe six months old, and we started out again. I found them eager and very busy, as if they felt called upon to make up for their small size, but they were at a disadvantage in the high cover and couldn't be seen much of the time. They hunted close, but when they pointed, they did it with a high head and rigid stub tails.

That night after a shower, a glass of sherry and a good dinner we sat in front of the log fire in our cabin with Ruff, Feathers and Shadows stretched at our feet and listened to Dutch Martin tell about running Prairie Lane. Producing thousands of pheasants isn't easy. Predators converge on a place of this sort, and in the first year over five hundred hawks and owls were caught in pole traps at the pens. One female raccoon killed twenty-three hen pheasants and a cock in one night, eating only the corn from their crops and gizzards ripped out through the vent. When a pheasant flies off a preserve it is like a $5 bill taking wing. By game-warden reports, some of their banded birds had been shot ten miles from the preserve, proving that a game preserve is an asset to surrounding coverts. The previous year they had lost 1,034 pheasants but in general their recovery rate was high. Dutch gave credit to good dog work and guides willing to spend time looking for cripples. Re cripples, Dutch preferred to see gunners use a 12-gauge. On a shooting day they released up to one hundred pheasants, beginning at 6 A.M. If gun pressure required it, they made additional releases at noon while the gunners were at lunch in the clubroom with no view of the releases. The average daily kill was six pheasants per gun.

Preserve Shooting

When we began hunting the next morning it was even colder, with the remaining snow crunchy underfoot. This day was for the Old Hemlock setters. We started with Ruff and Shadows, quartering the middle and distant cover in that order, and had points pinned well out, the way I like them. Shadows hit his pheasants in mid-stride, his front end tilted over with brakes jammed on at full speed. Pointed in this manner, pheasants don't often sneak out.

After lunch I replaced Shadows with Feathers and took Ruff again, on the principle that an older dog should have every bit of living he can get. Overeager, Feathers was too wide at first but he came under control, making a spine-tingling point, clinging like a salamander to a steep bank. Again moving beyond Ruff, he went on point on the other side of a woven wire fence on the far bank of a frozen canal. The ice had supported Feathers but I couldn't risk crossing. I tossed some stones but the bird wouldn't budge, then I tried using my voice but the pheasant ignored it. Feathers was still red-hot, pointing through the fence toward me, and I hated to order him to break but I could think of no other way. My "All right, come here" brought him over the fence like a deer. He landed on four feet, pointing solidly, and a split second later a big cock came out from under his nose. At my shot, it fell on the ice and Feathers retrieved it, digging in with his toes for a foothold as he delivered the bird, its tail dangling to one side.

As the sun dropped lower, our fingers turned to frozen bones that bent both directions without sensation, and we headed toward the preserve buildings under cold pink sky. At the clubroom we warmed ourselves and chatted with some men who had been shooting old muzzle-loading shotguns loaded with black powder, which explained some strange *booms* I had been hearing. They regularly shot pheasants at Prairie Lane with those beautiful old pieces.

In the midst of my conversation Dutch Martin beckoned to me. The other parties had come in, he said, and the entire preserve was ours to use till dark. That suited Ruff and Feathers and Kay and we set off in a new direction, along a field of standing corn, with the dogs working an adjoining weed field as if they sensed this was the last crumb of shooting for the season.

On the brink of one of those wonderful canals Feathers wheeled and spread out like an ice skater set for the breakaway. The wind was cruel but loaded with meaning for the lanky orange belton with nostrils dilated and eyes bulging. As I drew off my right glove and walked in, I sensed Ruff in my peripheral vision, backing from where he stood on the frozen surface of the canal. There was the hum of Kay's camera during the moment of vacuum before the flush and from almost between my feet a hen bored out low—a straightaway that culminated in a puff of tan feathers. Feathers hit the ice once on his way across and came back proudly delivering the bird to hand, all in a rosy glow that might have been the setting sun or perhaps just the way I felt. I came out of my idyll to hear Kay saying that her movie camera had jammed from the cold.

I think of Prairie Lane, along with pleasant memories of shooting, with one image of Mose that doesn't fade. We had the German shorthairs and they had made a good point, pinning the bird under their muzzles. I had missed the previous bird and, seeing their bird squatting between them, Dan considered it my pheasant, crippled. Logically he reached down and grabbed it, its struggles to escape causing him to clamp down all the harder. Mose lunged in and with a warning, "Look out! He's gonna fly!" wrenched the pheasant from Dan's mouth and tossed it high in the air. Very dead, the pheasant turned a few cartwheels and came to earth with an indifferent thud. Mose looked as crestfallen as his wrecked cigar.

That's all right, Mose, you tried, and anybody who tries that hard to give me shooting is a friend of mine. I hope someday to hear once more your cry "You can git 'im!" ring out over Prairie Lane or wherever you may be.

NEMACOLIN TRAIL

MOST SPORTSMEN WHO own game lands think wistfully of insulation, like a nine-foot fence. Willard F. "Al" Rockwell, Jr., didn't just think about it; in the mountains in southwestern Pennsylvania he fenced in more than three hundred acres, a well-stocked trout stream, and a lake that holds waterfowl over winter. He has, on his dream place, wild turkeys, white-tailed deer, a few exotics like axis, red, spotted and white fallow deer, and some black buck antelope. There is a game breeding farm that produces thousands of bobwhites and pheasants.

In 1961 Rockwell made his place available to the public as the

Preserve Shooting

Nemacolin Trail Hunting Reserves for preserve deer hunting within the enclosed area, and for quail and pheasant shooting on an adjoining old mountain farm. A second reserve of over five thousand acres in Somerset County was set up for deer and grouse hunting during regular Pennsylvania seasons, with vehicle, guide and gun-dog services as well as camping facilities. Later a fenced seven-hundred-acre tract along Beaver Creek was opened for stream trout fishing, and bass and trout fishing is available in a series of lakes on the original estate. Pheasant, quail and chukar shooting is done on the more than four-hundred-acre shooting grounds in the Five Forks Glades.

At the nucleus around the original estate there is a small clubhouse for the use of guests, with an adjoining shop purveying such tidbits as Orvis rods, an automatic trap and skeet field, and a "quail walk" with thirty-five concealed traps. Since I began shooting the preserve, there has been continual expansion—a landing field, the four-story Nemacolin Inn and acquisition of more mountain land. It's a rather swanky place and the pet of Mr. Rockwell, who is a keen shooting man with a ten-thousand-acre plantation in south Georgia for quail shooting.

My first shooting on Nemacolin Trail was in February of 1962, when Ruff was fourteen and a half. He had hunted wonderfully during the long grouse season—his fifteenth—and I wanted to prolong his pleasure with some pheasant shooting. It was his last.

I expressed disappointment that they had only Reeves pheasants at that time, for I had hoped for fast-flying ringneck hens. Jack Alcot, the manager, implied that if I collected one out of the five Reeves cocks released I'd be lucky, considering I insisted upon using my own dogs instead of the preserve's. The Reeves pheasant has been stocked successfully on forest shooting preserves in Belgium and France. The birds I'd be shooting were pen-raised from those Continental wild strains.

We drove a dirt road to the shooting grounds that, to my delight, turned out to be the old Haas place I used to gun for grouse in the thirties. The hewn-log house with its view of Sugarloaf brought memories of a fine friend who once owned it, and of her nephew who had taken me hunting— both of them gone.

The weather was a sunny 50° with no snow. We started with Dixie and got our first point in a patch of millet. It seems incredible

THE BIRDS

that a bird the size and color of a Reeves pheasant can lie so covered up in low growth. It erupted like an oversized gold-plated ringneck with black scales, cleared Dixie's head and bored low, left-quartering, as fast as any normal pheasant. I was using my old Fox and the Reeves dropped in a shower of feathers—a bird nearly as long as Dixie. She made an effort to pick it up, tried again and gave it up as out of her class.

If a cock Reeves is large in the air, it is even larger in the hand. The black-and-white barred tail feathers are twenty-five inches long—a fourth again longer than a big ringneck's—and the bird is too big to carry comfortably in a game pocket. It is handsome, with an iridescent black head, a white collar, and jet-black scale markings on the golden breast that make it look more Oriental than a dragon.

I missed the next bird—a long flight across an open field—and we followed down a wooded slope. Through the trees I could see Dixie pointing, then trailing the running bird. Some preserves have low woven-wire or brush fences to hold running pheasants ahead of dogs. Our bird came to the high fence that encloses the original estate and this served the purpose. When I moved in to the point, the Reeves had no place to go but up, which it did, steeply. I caught it at its peak but it dropped with a thump in the middle of a jeep trail on the far side. It required a three-mile roundabout trip to get it.

While Jack Alcot drove off for my bird, Kay and I changed dogs. Shadows and Ruff moved out eagerly and Ruff soon had a point. The pheasant took a moment to gather itself, then went straight up, its long tail like a vapor trail. The cock Reeves weigh at least a pound more than a ringneck but they think they're rockets. This one fell, still kicking. Shadows went for the retrieve but a wicked cut on the muzzle from the sharp spurs drove him back. At my command he returned and, giving a *coup de grâce* across the back, made a nice delivery. From that day on, Shadows's birds were delivered dead.

Later, in some sedge and greenbrier I came to Shadows pointing toward me. I signaled to Kay and approached but no bird materialized. Then I saw a tail feather, apparently from a former kill. Looking closer, I saw the rest of the Reeves in a tight ball under the ripshins. At the touch of my probing boot, the bird ran out, hesitated, then took off. I shot and it fell almost on top of Shadows but struck out running. After his experience with the last bird, I doubted if he would tackle it but I needn't have worried. He caught it in a greenbrier tangle, dispatched and retrieved it, to complete the sequence for Kay's movie. On Jack Alcot's five Reeves pheasants, we had had five productives and four kills.

Since that first year, my shooting at Nemacolin Trail has been on ringneck pheasants and chukars. The chukar partridge as a sporting bird has a fine potential for preserve shooting if presented properly. Someone has made a rule that chukars must be "planted" in pairs to make them lie. They fly as fast as quail but having to actually kick them out of such an obvious site as a pile of fodder is not sporting. An alternative is to flush them from their planted site without shooting, then follow and hunt them in a normal manner. Their flights are low and, like quail's, not too long, and they handle well for a dog, once they stop running. Because of their reputation for elusiveness, chukars are usually charged for as released, so it is the gunner's loss if they provide no shots. They are a beautiful bird, with white throat, black bib and dove-gray body set off by vivid red-orange mandibles and feet, and are larger than you expect when retrieved. Chukars have earned their bad name for disappearing. In West Virginia the Department of Natural Resources released chukars in one area in the early fifties—the director's little bit of nonsense. The biologist in charge told him they were disappearing like water down a crab hole but the program was continued until it ran out of chukars.

To me the most appealing pheasant shooting on Nemacolin Trail is in the Five Forks Glades. I gunned it first on two consecutive days in November of '65. I had made a solemn decision never to work Bliss on pheasants, so we left her in the station wagon parked in an old field on a hill. The Glades spread out below us, typical mountain grouse cover, with an assortment of swamp, thorn thickets, pitch pines and old fields with game-food plantings. It was gray-cloudy and a cold wind hit us the moment we opened the door of the station wagon. In spite of this, Dixie struck scent immediately and pointed. When I walked in, three bobwhites flushed and pitched into the cover beyond the car. I don't shoot quail but dog work on these bobwhites is an additional pleasure on this preserve.

With difficulty I got Dixie and Shadows headed the other way and down the hill. At the bottom, I found Shadows pointing into brush on the far side of a mud road, with Dixie backing. At my approach a cock pheasant ran out and started up the hill. Putting up a pheasant that prefers running isn't easy. It finally flushed when I got close enough to rush it; it dropped to my shot and Dixie retrieved.

Once more at the foot of the hill, we had a choice of standing corn on the left and a field of matted kafir corn and canary grass on the right. Shadows made the decision, dashing down the long rows on the right, ignoring my blasts on the whistle. It must have been a running bird, for a hundred yards away he bumped a cock and chased it for a quarter of a mile like a puppy.

My scolding had no effect and he plowed through the planting, flushing another cock into the swamp. At the end of the row, he wheeled and pointed, then plunged into a tangle of greenbrier and disappeared. A cock kukkered as if to rise but failed to show and I ran up, yelling at Shadows until I was as hoarse as the pheasant. I longed for a bull whip but all I could lay my hands on were brittle sticks that crumbled at the touch. It ended with my giving Shadows a shaking and scolding, after which he went out of control again—a twelve-year-old dog who had worked pheasants most of his life. All I can think is that too little hunting week after week while I had used young Bliss on grouse had built up frustrations he couldn't curb. We took him to the station wagon, where we left him with Bliss.

Dixie is a comfortable dog to shoot over solo and she seemed to sense my need of her now. She made a gorgeous point in standing corn on a small covey of quail, which I flushed and watched as they sailed like a handful of tilted clay targets into cover. Circling in the big flat, she worked the waving swamp grass and suddenly was on point again. Moving in to flush what I thought would be more quail, I was surprised to see a pheasant wiggle out and run ahead of me. As with my first bird, I had to rush it up, using the left barrel as the bird went through the branches of a distant bare tree, but it kept going.

After a long tramp following the pheasant where Kay had marked it, Dixie paused, winding, and went stanch. I circled and saw the pheasant start out, change its mind and run back into the thicket. Dixie doubled to head it off, and when it came out it took off, giving me a right-crossing shot I managed to miss. I fired again and the bird made one more wingbeat and tumbled in an open field, where it lay with feathers paying out into the wind.

We walked to the station wagon under a sky spitting half rain and half snow and Kay decided to wait with Shadows and Dixie while I put Bliss down for a little exercise. The pheasants we hadn't shot we had thoroughly scattered, thanks to Shadows, and I felt safe in working Bliss on the bobwhites Dixie had found at the beginning.

In thick cover among briars where the quail had gone, I saw Bliss on point. None of Bliss's points were ordinary, but on this she was standing stiffly erect with her tail so high it looked as if it hurt. As I walked in I was thinking if it was a grouse it was lying mighty tight, and then a cock pheasant was going straight up out of the briars, streaming whitewash. I took it with a fast swing up and through and it fell into a tangle in front of Bliss. She found the bird but refused the retrieve, crawling back as if she had committed a sin. As a grouse dog, I continued to avoid working her on pheasants, but what points I renounced.

Next afternoon we were back in the Glades for another go at pheasants. The weather was still cool but sunny with no wind. Warned by yesterday's fiasco, we left Shadows in the station wagon with Bliss.

Dixie's first point was in standing corn—a pheasant. I took too much time and saw only a puff of feathers drop from the bird's rear, then watched it glide to the swamp and settle—the old story of a pheasant that seemed to rise so slowly.

We failed to locate it but later Dixie made an odd point in kafir corn with her head cocked toward her toes, and I saw the body of a pheasant. I hadn't seen a dead bird here yesterday and I gave it a touch with my boot. Something made me prod the stiff form again and suddenly it was coming out of the tangle, rising in a perfect open shot. I swung through and pulled, feeling myself lean into recoil that wasn't there, and by the time I'd fumbled my safety off, the bird was too far out.

Walking up the long field, I saw a cock, standing tall, watching us from a hundred yards off. We moved toward it with Dixie at heel, losing sight of it only to regain view of the white neck ring in another place. At last I waved Dixie ahead. She circled and pointed.

The cock gave me a close, right-crossing shot and fell solidly, and Dixie retrieved.

We carried our bird to the station wagon and ate lunch, where Shadows went to work on me with his big dark eyes. I gave in, knowing what to expect, but when we set out it was evident that he had been doing some serious thinking. After yesterday's spectacle, sweet religion had entered Shadows and I'll always think of this second afternoon in the Glades as his day.

Working the edge of corn in ideal range, he promptly went on point. I moved in to flush and stepped on a big cock pheasant that went up, I think, straighter and faster than any pheasant I can remember. It should have been simple to take it at the top of its rise, but I was so close under the bird I had to shoot directly up. I missed and as it leveled I bent over sidewise to get ahead and below, with barrels canted, and missed again. These high overhead shots should be made by turning and waiting for the bird to get well out, then shooting, holding below. The closer the shot, the greater the chance of a miss.

With Shadows back in form, we moved into the swamp to try to locate the bird I had feathered earlier. In some greenbrier, Shadows swung to my left and stopped, his tail ramrod straight, his belton coat like dappled shade. It was a pheasant and it went up kukkering but far from wounded. My shot stopped it near the treetops, fighting to maintain altitude but coming down. Shadows was there when it hit and retrieved, sitting to deliver and grinning from ear to ear.

At sunset, Dixie made a point in some pitch pines—a pheasant that went down at my shot. It was a runner that gave the dogs trouble, but they cornered it in some brush, where our hunt ended.

During March of 1971 in slushy snow, I gunned this Five Forks Glades in dense marsh cover, working pheasants that had gone wild from former releases. When you can get preserve shooting in natural cover such as this, there is little that is wrong with it. With good dogs the gunner can make it about as sporting as he cares to. As for the dogs, old and young—they love it. And frankly, so do I.

PART FOUR

The Men Who Shoot

❦ / FOR A MAN WHO'S BRED TO HUNTING

MUST FOREVER BE THAT WAY.

—ARCHIBALD RUTLEDGE, "Rain on the Marsh"

Profiles

THE STRAIGHT-BRED SHOOTING MAN keeps his shooting clothes laid out throughout the season. In the South he shoots bobwhites; in the North the greatest number of upland bird hunters shoot pheasants; in the Appalachians, New England, and the northwoods of Michigan, Wisconsin and Minnesota the better wing shots are grouse gunners. And there is that group of fanatics who shoot woodcock seriously. I omit dove shooters because, for me, nothing constitutes shooting unless it is over a dog. By its emphasis on stalking, turkey hunting—beyond its lack of dog work—belongs in the category of big game.

Upland bird hunters have never been easily catalogued. When you read of a pioneer fox hunter you get a picture of a man with a large tract of land, a pack of Walker hounds, a horse or two, and God help the soul who killed one of his foxes. Tales of Meshach Browning, a frontier bear hunter in our mountains, evoke an image with a Pennsylvania rifle, long knife, long hair. But when you hear that someone was a grouse hunter in the late 1800's you face a choice. Was he a gentleman sportsman, or a market hunter? Did he live far enough south to call his birds "pheasants" or was he a Yankee who called them "partridges"? There is the part-time quail hunter, and there is the aficionado who is impatient about wasting time on other birds and who heads south the moment quail season opens. There are degrees of pheasant hunters from men who put them up with beagles to the dedicated gunner who prefers pheasants over an expert pheasant dog to any other shooting.

Woodcock gunners have always been a special breed. For years I heard, "John Lambert is a woodcock hunter." John Lambert is long dead but I remember sitting on the porch of his old mountain house—he was boarding a setter for my father—and thinking *John Lambert is a woodcock hunter.* Because of his legend, the Fawcett

Bottom where he lived fascinated me as probably fabulous 'cock cover, but I've never gone back. Woodcock gunners, of course, are often grouse gunners and the dementias overlap.

Being the sort he was, Oscar Wilde couldn't have had a shooting man's point of view, but he came close to something pertinent with that business about each man killing the thing he loves. Certainly the bird puts its mark upon the man in the way it characterizes the dog, but shooting is so much what each man makes it. The term "sportsman" has no qualifiers "good" or "bad"; as a shooting man you are a sportsman or you are nothing.

I describe some shooting men by name, for there can be only one Riley Worden or one Cliff Springer; if I speak of others as the Long-Shot Addict, or the Purist you may feel you've seen them, perhaps know them well. Here, then, are some of the men who shoot.

THE OLD-TIMERS

AT SOME TIME almost every grouse hunter staying in Davis had a consultation with Riley Worden. Riley at eighty-four was living in the glories of the past, a chubby little man with china-blue eyes and the face of a small boy about to cry, only Riley was always about to smile. As much a fixture of the Worden's Hotel as the creaky stairs, it was like taking away a part of it when Riley had to be moved to a convalescent home in another town.

Sitting in his sidewalk chair in the pale sunshine, Riley and Indian summer seemed to go together. "I've seen this sidewalk," he would motion with his cane, "filled with deer laying on it." How long ago? "Fourteen or fifteen years." Riley's past, like the town's, was recent.

"Grouse?" He would aim his cane across the bridge. "I used to find them over there across from the pulp mill. I've moved a hundred in a day—in coveys." When Riley said it, I believed it.

"Yes, Riley," I would interrupt, "but that was years ago. Where can I find birds tomorrow?"

"If they're anyplace, you'll find them up on Stony River." His eyes went to my station wagon at the curb. "That's a nice-looking dog you've got. Is he a good one?" I usually had three but Riley always singled out shadows, and we established Shadows's qualifications each time Riley saw him.

The last time I talked to Riley Worden was more than three years ago, in his third-floor-rear bedroom at the Worden's. At my knock his voice came strong and gay, "Come in!"

The room was just able to hold a single bed, a lavatory, a chest and the chair by the window where Riley sat in jersey and shorts with a blanket over his knees, crippled by arthritis. I squeezed around the bed and sat on the edge. "How are you, Riley?" I asked, wishing I didn't have to use those words.

"I'm fine." The blue eyes had the old sparkle and I've never heard anyone sound more as though they meant it.

"We missed you in the dining room," I said. "They tell me you take your meals in your room now, like a gentleman of leisure."

"Oh, I go down every other night," he said. They told me in the dining room he hadn't been downstairs for more than a month.

I looked at the walls pressing in, covered with photographs and cutout reproductions of paintings. There were two subjects—grouse and very unclothed females. He saw my grin.

"The maids put those up." His face got redder. "It makes me feel good."

When I got Riley talking about grouse, time turned back. "Fourteen or fifteen years ago I was hunting across the river and this grouse came right at me. It was so close I just held my gun straight up, like this—" Riley sat erect holding the imaginary gun. "The grouse flew into it and just dropped and laid there without a flutter."

We talked of places I had tried that season. Before I was aware of it we were back across the river and the grouse was flying right at Riley. "I just held my gun straight up, like this. The grouse flew into it and dropped and laid there without a flutter. They usually flutter."

I liked hearing it again and seeing the excitement in Riley's eyes.

"Grouse die off in *sipuls*," Riley was saying, "but they come back—thick everywhere. There's lots of birds yet."

"You've shot a lot of them," I said, "when the birds were really here."

"You ought to try across the river. There was this one grouse." Riley held his gun straight up and the grouse flew into it again. "He just dropped and laid there. I thought that was unusual for him not to flutter."

I shook hands with him and said I had to go and his grip was firm and strong like his voice. "Now you come back," he said. "I was glad to see you."

While Riley was in the nursing home I wondered if anyone would talk to him about grouse. I meant to visit him but something made me put it off, though I should have known he would be cheerful. But now Riley is back across the river and there are grouse—a hundred in a day, in coveys.

It has been more than ten years since Kay and I came out of the Worden's where we'd had dinner after shooting and I first saw Mel Heath—a bulky figure in a red-and-black Woolrich shirt moving out of the shadows. He mumbled something about birds and for an unworthy moment I thought we were being offered some grouse for sale, a reaction I've been ashamed of ever since. All this man wanted to know was whether we'd had any luck.

Now that Mel is eighty-three, I see no change in his appearance since that first night, even to the shirt. I've come to know him as a singularly kind and rugged person, a remnant of that breed who lived when game was abundant and life in our mountains more primitive. As a young buck, Mel worked in the Blackwater lumber camps when giant hemlocks and spruce were cut by sheer heart and muscle, not by power saws. One icy February evening in 1924 he and a companion were starting to walk the long miles back to Davis from the Stony River camps when Fred Viering gave them a ride down Cabin Mountain on a flatcar. The Shay locomotive went out of control on ice-glazed rails and Mel and his friend leaped free, as did the fireman. Viering, caught in the cab, couldn't stop the engine and it jumped the rails, burying him in a bog.

Mel lives alone in Davis but it isn't difficult to locate him. One day I inquired at the barbershop and was told they had "heard him over in the other part of town." His guffaw at his own jokes starts off like the old Shay locomotives, accelerating with momentum and carrying a quarter of a mile. Some people find it disturbing but anything that good-natured appeals to me and, like muzzle blast, if it doesn't happen too close I can take it.

Mel loves to go along as a quasi guide and has shown me a lot of the Blackwater country. A few seasons ago he took a bow hunter to a stand where the man killed a buck. Out of gratitude, the hunter gave Mel a nice old English hammer double with the name James Webley on the locks. In spite of its Damascus barrels, Mel shot modern field loads in it. One afternoon he took it along when he was showing us a new covert. We parked and walked a woods road to the bottom of the mountain, where we left Mel to mosey around while we hunted the base of the ridge, having arranged to meet at the station wagon. We had a nice turn, I shot a grouse, and when I had run out of cover I suggested to Kay that we drive to a woodcock covert for the late shooting. At the station wagon I whistled and called but Mel was nowhere about. It was getting late so we left a note under a stone saying Kay would return for him.

Kay told me the story when she came for me at dark. She found Mel waiting at the side of the road and drove him back to Davis. When he was getting out at his house he exclaimed, "My God, where's my gun?" Recalling where he laid it while he waited on the mountain, he began worrying the thought that the car had run over it or that someone had come along and stolen it. Kay promised to drive directly to the place before going for me. She found the gun where Mel had left it and she had it in the station wagon when she picked me up.

Mel was waiting at his gate when we put his gun in his hands. He was immensely proud of it and referred to it as "my double-barreled gun made in London, England." Shortly after this happy ending, some kind soul stole the gun. I hope whoever did it tried to use magnum loads in it and got a faceful of Damascus twist.

"Wright and his friends will never make grouse hunters." Cliff Springer was speaking of his son. "They're not killers like you and me." I have never been a "killer," but when Cliff looked at you over his half-lens glasses like gun barrels, there wasn't much to be gained by arguing. And no one can say that Cliff, himself, was not a killer.

Cliff hunted grouse from the time he was a young man until he was past eighty-four. On his last hunt he fell and hobbled back on an improvised crutch. That winter he slipped on ice while feeding his seventeen dogs, mostly strays, and broke a leg. The surgeon, after reducing the fracture, said Cliff had leg muscles of a forty-year-old man. If any single factor contributed to his excellent condition I would guess it had been grouse hunting, for Cliff probably shot more grouse than any other man I've known.

I first saw Cliff Springer on fishing trips with my father when we stayed at his old stone Youghiogheny House in Somerfield, Pennsylvania. Cliff ran the hotel from a rocking chair on the veranda, where he sat with his feet on the railing and watched a leisurely 30-mph world go by on the old National Pike. The floor of that veranda was alternate cherry and ash boards, scrubbed gleaming clean, and there was a one-story wing I wasn't allowed to enter, which emited pleasant beery smells. It was on the bar, according to Cliff's son Wright, that grouse were laid out to be counted after a day's shooting.

Over the mantel in the musty-smelling lobby there was an enlarged photograph of three white-and-orange setters, progenitors of Cliff's setter Bud. The dining room was quiet and redolent of chicken dinners, and there was a parlor with a square grand and a lithograph of Edmund Osthaus's painting of 1898 National Champion Tony's Gale. Upstairs the bedrooms had creaky mattresses and the straw matting on the floor felt cool to my bare feet, and there was fog outside the windows when we got up in the mornings to go fishing.

Until I got to know him, Cliff seemed taciturn, rarely speaking other than to keep Wright stepping with orders given in the tone he used for Bud when Bud ventured too far off the flagstones onto the Pike. Wright, who seemed much younger than I, scalded chickens for the chicken-and-waffle dinners and at the other end of the line scraped chicken bones into a bucket for Bud, who must have had a special kind of setter intestines, for in spite of this diet he lived to be seventeen. It is Bud's bell that Dixie wears.

The Youghiogheny House, a stage tavern built in 1816, was headquarters for Cliff's shooting cronies Marshall Bell, Cliff Budd and Joel Stoneroad of Pittsburgh, Jake Cromer of Greensburg, and Dr. McKennan from "little" Washington. All of them are gone, like the old hotel and the stone bridge and Somerfield—gone or under the Youghiogheny Dam. During low water the old bridge shows itself like an apparition. Cliff moved up on the ridge to Addison and maintained solitary quarters, which became a sort of gun club when Wright and his friends arrived for the grouse season. His stories of "hunter's back" from climbing river hills with eleven grouse in his coat, of coveys of thirty grouse on "Puzzly Run" and Negro Mountain, of birds feeding on "sink field" (cinquefoil) and getting tipsy from crops full of fermenting grapes, were part of the color of the man. He didn't care to eat grouse—"I've cleaned too many and it spoiled my taste."

I knew Cliff Springer best when I shot with him one season. He refused to hunt early in the fall when most of us develop frustrations, waiting until leaves were down and cold weather had set in. There was no use hunting if the wind was blowing a certain way or if snow had not begun to "break up." The grouse was an adversary and you "guarded" for the dog while it investigated every brush pile. Cliff advised getting to a point promptly—a good axiom—but he hunted leisurely, eyes sweeping the cover from side to side without turning his head, gun cradled across his left elbow. Cliff hunted the hollows and ravines, working to the ridge on contour. When a grouse flushed he wasn't winded and when his double cracked it usually meant a bird. He told me he liked to swing with the bird and "give a little jerk ahead just as you fire"—a variation of the fast swing-through. In spite of legends, the man has not lived who never missed a grouse but I suspect Cliff missed as few as any gunner. He shot a Parker 20-gauge chambered for 3-inch shells.

There is reason why the old-timers were good shots, for the way to be a brilliant shot is to shoot a lot of birds. Waterfowlers were notorious for unreasonable bags; old men tell me about shooting four turkeys at a time, of killing forty quail in a day. One gunner described a day on Allegheny Mountain early in the century when he shot fourteen grouse, explaining, "There was no bag limit in those days." They are survivors from another age and I would miss their quirks and positive notions, like scars on an old gun from years of use in rough cover. Yet it is beyond my understanding how anyone who loved shooting could so lose sight of what shooting is about. There may not have been a law and the game certainly was there for the taking, but along with their skillful gun handling and devotion to the sport, where was the individual sense of enough?

Those hunts with Cliff are good memories—the Yough in a

sweeping curve below us, the hills across the river a pattern of diagonal tree shadows, the grapevines that always seemed to hold a grouse. Without qualifying as a "killer" I would like to emulate Cliff Springer and hunt grouse until my mid-eighties. Blessed with large-bore arteries, lean and tough, Cliff made it beyond ninety-three and knowing him was a privilege, like living a little in the past.

Opening a book by Nash Buckingham is like standing beside him on a hill, looking back over magnificent bird country with bird dogs casting below. No matter how splendid those dogs, how abundant the birds, you see them as your dog handling bobwhites that you shoot. Peering from a blind at Canadas and greenheads and "cans" with Nash Buckingham, you are looking at the geese or mallards or canvasbacks you see over your gun barrels on a cold and blustery present day. Wildfowlers remember him as Director of Game for Western Cartridge and as Executive Director of American Wildfowlers; field trial disciples know him as a judge of the National Championship Trials from 1934 to 1951. Shooting men of my generation looked up to him as a beautiful wing shot who held principles of conservation above the size of the bag.

Nash Buckingham first came through to me in his pieces in *Field & Stream* and as the author of *De Shootinest Gent'man and Other Tales* and *Mark Right!* His stories of bird shooting at "Brick House" and "Solitude" seemed, even then, to give background to my own shooting. As co-author of the first volume of *National Field Trial Champions*, he put his mark on every word he wrote in it, for Nash wrote, the way he lived, with flair. His description of an old Parker hammer gun—"Betsy's locks sang like harp strings"—is the sort of color he gave to everything he touched. He knew the famous Llewellin setter, Gladstone, literally as a neighbor, and told me how, as a youngster in Memphis, he would sit astride the back-yard fence and divide cookies impartially between the gun dogs in his father's kennel and Gladstone in Mr. Bryson's kennel next door.

Nash Buckingham's letters to me during the last year and a half of his life, letters rich with reminiscences, brought him very close.

August 10, 1969. "I began seeing the Nationals at Ames Plantation in '02. Mrs. Buckingham's great-grandfather, John Walker Jones, acquired the lands and built 'Cedar Grove' in 1847. Hobart

Profiles

Ames told me how, while considering a preserve near New Albany, Mississippi, he received a telegram from the celebrated dog handler and breeder, Jim Avent, inviting him and Mrs. Ames for a week's quail shooting and to see the Jones home and lands at Grand Junction, Tennessee that might be acquired. They went, saw superb bird land, and Mr. Ames took over and settled at Cedar Grove. Thus we see one telegram changing the fate of a nation's field trials."

September 28, 1970. "From the vantage point of 90, God be praised for my being able to enjoy wildfowling and bird shooting in scenes of my youth protected by unchanging ownerships. Today, merciless pollution of air, water, land and, alas, sportsmanship have done the grisly business. I am thru with the so-called 'club' duck shooting life and do mine at the old Beaver Dam, which is privately owned by one family—12,000 acres of plantation and eight miles around the lake. If I want to go quailing or for doves, my cousin Hugh has a big farm on the outskirts of Memphis, and John Bailey at Coffeeville, Mississippi has 2,000 acres he's been tending since he was eleven and has a show place. I like to go along these days, take a shot now and then and keep in shape as to paddling and walking a bit. I had the cataract job in 1963 and for a season or so you have to readjust as to magnifications, but you get the hang of it. It's a great life."

On October 16, 1970, he wrote: "Dear Br'er Evans: Going through old pictures I came across some I thought you'd like to have. One is of A. G. C. Sage, the pointer fancier and breeder, with Saturn, Ariel, and Luminary and their famous handler, Clyde Morton at Shuqualak (pronounced Sugar-lock), Mississippi in 1944. Henry P. Davis and I judged the Free-For-All there that year, which Ariel won. A strange thing happened in the Derby race; we were along a road by a high stone bluff and the dog pointed on a bit of levee ahead. The gallery halted and Clyde Morton hastened up with his gun (the season was open and you could shoot). As a single flushed and whisked back at Henry and me, Clyde whirled and swung on the quail headed straight between us. Henry went over his horse on one side, I over mine on the other. Clyde fired and by some miracle we escaped. I have never seen a chap so broken up as poor Clyde. He was always keyed up but a fine and Godly lad."

Among the old photographs was one of Mrs. Buckingham in boots and velveteen skirt and broad-brimmed hat, holding her gun and a kill of mallards at Beaver Dam in 1913. On June 6, 1970, Nash wrote of her:

"Few men equal my luck in celebrating their 90th birthday, and the next day their 60th wedding day with 'the glorious and unquenchable star at evening.' My Irma was a skilled equestrienne, gaited or aboard the rough broncs of our ranching days. She was a trout, bass or bream rod handler from who-laid-the-rail. She was the best woman shot and hunter at any game I've ever seen, drove an ambulance in WW I, and held her own with the early golf sharks. We were married June 1st, 1910 so she's known many a National Field Trial Champion. Now she's in a nursing home and fighting as gamely as a pebble to get back on her feet."

In the same letter he wrote: "Not long ago, my dear old friend Bob Stoner, who owned and handled and campaigned the great Eugene's Ghost, and I drove out to visit with the now-retired Reuben Scott at the Ames Place. As we got out of the car at the Ames gate an old colored man came up to us, last old family retainer and still going. He put his arms around us and we all three enjoyed a good cry. It made the day, and Reub joined us. That is the spirit of field trials."

Nash Buckingham was a shooting man's man, a bird hunter to his finger tips. His last letter, on January 22, 1971, was to thank Kay and me for a photograph of our setter Briar on point:

"We do so hope you had and are still enjoying good sport over that grand dog. Do you intend visiting the National Championship? I wish I could attend the drawing evening of Sunday, Feb. 15, but I just can't leave my lovely mate. She has filled my whole life. Good luck and God bless you both through the years.

Irma & Nash Buckingham"

On March 10, 1971, at nearly ninety-one, he died peacefully in his sleep. It had been a full life and a good end for one of the most gentlemanly of shootinest gent'men. The one note of sadness is that he had, at last, to leave his Irma—the sun setting before the evening star.

Profiles

THE SOCIAL OR GREGARIOUS HUNTER

MEN HUNT IN GROUPS for a variety of reasons. Some enjoy the company of other gunners more than the actual shooting. Some are afraid to go into the woods alone; many hunt with others to learn how-to-do-it, or for the opportunity to shoot over a good dog. Some, and these have included Presidents, do it because it is the thing to do, especially in the South, where quail shooting has been liturgy for generations. But I am convinced that most men hunt with others to find out where to go.

At its finest level, the Combination-of-Two is a relationship as delicately balanced as a marriage, occasionally lasting longer. The loss of a shooting friend can be deeply felt, and I know a man who gave up gunning after the death of his shooting companion. Although large groups may kill a greater number, if two men know what to expect of each other and their dog they usually account for more birds per gun. Two-man shooting encourages gracious shooting manners—calling your companion to the point and making sure he gets his share of shots, not shooting at the same bird. It entails consideration for physical limitations the other may have, awareness of where he is at all times, responsibility to turn up when and where you have planned, restraint in talking, yet communication by signals that have become habit between you.

Some kinds of game may be shot sportingly by groups but I feel that woodcock and grouse should not be gunned by more than two men. Not that nasty little tricks aren't employed by some twosomes on the excuse that these birds don't give the gunner any breaks and deserve none, but two men can be counted on more frequently than large groups to show deference to 'cock and grouse.

I've enjoyed splendid shooting friendships with several men— Less Crowl, the late Dr. Charles Norris, more recently Obie Conaway. And I can't mention shooting companions without including Art Thomas. His loves are horses and foxhounds, but we usually shoot grouse together once each season and his reverence for these mountains where he has spent his life makes sharing a day with him an experience.

THE MEN WHO SHOOT

I share my finest shooting pleasures with Kay. She is game as hell, going through cover where I couldn't take most men, and though her gun is a movie camera her involvement is intense. Most precious to me is her sense of the beauty and ethics of the sport. The companion who enriches a day is one who, after you've brought off a good shot, will say that it was good, or make an intelligent comment when the dogs handle a bird well. Kay does these things. Most of all she is aware of a November sunset, of a colored leaf lodged on a rail fence. She can pick up the sound of a grouse flush with uncanny keenness, quick to drop when a bird flushes her way and to mark its flight. Kay shares everything I love about the birds and the dogs and gunning and this, in part, explains why I'd rather shoot with my wife than with anyone else I know.

One of the famous social-shooters combinations is the Old Regulars—a sort of skeet club gone afield. They often have no bonds other than love of dogs and shooting but on the gala annual trip they are brothers. We know one such group who hunt grouse in southwestern Pennsylvania and they find no other form of hunting satisfactory. They drive over to see us yearly. Certain threadbare jokes persist and I note small frictions as to opinions of dogs and ways to hunt, but these things are part of their friendship and without them the week together wouldn't be as good. Group hunters of this sort characteristically take pleasure in group results, speaking of the birds "we" shot, and some of these men would never hunt if not to "get out with the boys."

Quail shooting is probably the most pleasantly social form of shooting when done on a plantation in style, with a midday shooting lunch and after-dinner conversation in good company in a mellow old house. Group shooting ranges from the Continental form with beaters driving partridge or pheasants or red grouse over guns in butts or stands, to cornfield ringneck shooting with two dozen men driving huge acreages. These have tradition or at least function behind them. Conversely, grouse or woodcock hunters operating in groups of eight or ten behind dogs are carrying social hunting to absurdity. It detracts from dog work and from the quality of sport for each gun, multiplying the limitations and the hazards. Most important, it puts too much gun pressure on game, for legal limits taken by several men can clean out a covert. Shooting with friends can be a wonderfully satisfying experience, but it is at its best if each gunner is a perceptive person with something to give and not out simply to take something away.

THE LONER

I'M CERTAIN THE SOCIAL HUNTER thinks the Loner is an incomprehensible eccentric who shoots alone for selfish reasons, content to forgo companionship because he doesn't want to be annoyed by other people's idiosyncrasies, But at the same time I suspect he envies the Loner his freedom to hunt as he pleases. There have to be times when the most gregarious of hunters yearns to miss a bird without unsolicited comments, to hunt without having to keep track of other men, to feel that the glorious wilderness is there just for him and his dog. It is this undiluted immersion in beauty and tension and action that places lone shooting above other forms for those who have experienced it.

I understand the Loner pretty well because much of the time I have hunted alone. Beyond the basic need to be in big country with no one near, it is the best way to develop a gun dog. The man hunting alone risks a fall or twisted ankle miles from his car, but avoiding this is part of knowing how to handle himself in the woods. He should leave word where he is going so help can be sent if he doesn't return within reasonable time. A man in good physical condition is not in danger hunting alone, and provided he knows how to handle his gun he is in less danger from shooting accidents than with a companion.

A child first knows experiences as related to himself, not as influenced by the opinions of others. Later he learns that by recounting his experience he elicits approbation or at least attention from friends and even strangers. The extrovert finds these responses in others as rewarding as his experience and eventually comes to seek experiences for the sake of reaction in others. You find this type among shooters who must have someone to shoot with—the greater the audience, the greater the pleasure.

The Loner, by contrast, is the introverted type, who has retained the less-complicated viewpoint. For him, shooting—no matter how unextraordinary—is richest when unspoiled by what someone less appreciative might think or say. Where the extrovert finds need

THE MEN WHO SHOOT

for ever greater and more exceptional experiences to share, the Loner finds pleasure in less spectacular and more commonplace happenings and enjoys his shooting because these occur more frequently. New and exciting coverts become personally significant, and if he remains secretive about them it is less from selfishness than from a desire to keep something unchanged. The Loner with integrity shoots no more game and in no different manner than if he were with a companion whose opinion he valued highly. He is, in a manner, at a disadvantage in that no companion is moving grouse toward him, but I think he shoots under more sporting conditions as a result.

THE FAIR SHOT

LIKE THE WOMAN WHO RIDES, the woman who shoots has always been attractive to men—something about the clothes, the sporting attitude, a flair. One evening at dusk a mountain man, rough around the edges, walked up to where Kay and I were cooking out after shooting. After a few comments about birds, he said, "I wish my woman would go with me like that. All she knows is ladies aid an' feed the preacher." There's something in what he said. However, it isn't always the woman's idea to be left at home with a batch of babies while her man goes off, perhaps with an attractive bit in shooting pants. Plenty of girls love the shooting life when given the chance.

Some even go it alone. I once met a girl bumping her car down a rocky road with only her gun and an Irish setter on the seat beside her. She'd been grouse hunting. She confessed she'd never shot a grouse but she was hoping. Kay and I gave a setter to a girl, who used to train him, about as alone as you can get, in a graveyard. A covey of quail used there and she described Jubal "pointing, indistinguishable from the tombstones."

The woman who shoots should not accept undue deference in the field. If she's going to share the sport, she should observe sporting ethics, taking no more shots than if she were a man, covering her area of the terrain independently. If she goes out season after season without hitting a bird, she is to be admired for holding her shooting standards high. There is nothing more false than the

Profiles

woman who takes her birds off a branch or on the ground and considers herself shooting.

Good women shots aren't common, though some become expert, especially at skeet and trap. Most girls try to "get away" from the recoil, pulling the face back instead of leaning into the gun. A girl should shoot light loads in a small gauge and use a recoil pad, but light gun weight is less desirable than good gun fit. She should start her shooting on pheasants, after a good foundation on clays—certainly not on grouse or woodcock. A shooting preserve is probably the best place to begin.

The true sporting woman isn't interested in only the tweeds and the *après ski* aspect of shooting. She's out because she loves the setting, the exercise in good air, the dogs. If she should learn that she doesn't really enjoy shooting a gun, it doesn't deter her. Kay went with me for years without carrying a gun before she discovered that, for her, upland bird hunting was most fun when shooting a movie camera. Her take is on film instead of in a game bag, and on it she encapsulates our days and the dog work and the shots. Whatever her participation, the woman who shares the shooting and the dogs knows one of the finest relationships between a woman and a man.

THE LONG-SHOT ADDICT

THE MAN WHO MAKES a practice of taking excessively long shots is not on my list of people I admire, for he shows no consideration for what he may be doing to the birds. Many times he leaves the covert thinking he missed, with his bird huddled under a grapevine dying from a single pellet.

Most Long-Shot Addicts have heard that the killing range of a shotgun is forty yards, without realizing the statement doesn't apply to all chokes. If they have lucked a bird at fifty yards, they think they can do it regularly. One flaw in their thinking is lack of judgment of distance. The Long-Shot Addict is especially hard on grouse and pheasants, which can appear closer than they are and which have vitality to carry off one or two pellets at reduced velocity. The worst offender "shoots anyway, just to make them lie" or proudly reports that he "stung that bird as it went out of sight." A novice can be put straight. The hardened case is difficult to cure—possibly pattern him at fifty yards to prove that it does more than "sting"?

THE GADGETEER

SHOOTING MEN HAVE ALWAYS had a soft spot for field clothes that are more than what is indispensable to keep the weather off, guns beyond the simplest form of firing a load of shot, and dogs considerably above a pot licker. But for generations, a shooting coat, a gun and a dog were about all a man took afield with him to shoot birds.

With the end of World War II this began to change. Servicemen brought home new ideas, enterprising merchandisers caught the smell of money and hunters were soon being sold many of the accouterments they had been using in the services, from Korean cold-weather boots to Jeeps. Since then the cult of gadgetry has spread. Shooting is more comfortable because of insulated and rainproof garments but I'm not sure all gadgets have made it more sporting. Doing without the four-wheel-drive vehicle would immobilize some men. It will get you over roads too rough for the conventional chassis, but to Jeep through the cover itself rather than get out and hunt on foot suggests something lacking in the man.

Progress is hard to resist when it offers an advantage over the game—walkie-talkies, electronic calls. If you doubt that hunting gadgetry has become big business, turn to the mail-order pages of the sporting magazines. You can purchase anything from kennel yards to sonic or electric dog-training devices; trick shotgun sights for wing shooting, remedies for hernias or hemorrhoids. You can buy motorbikes, snowmobiles or transportation by helicopter or floatplane to "get there"—meaning the very center of a wilderness covert or lake. You can even buy the place to go.

I observed a Gadgeteer at close range on a grouse hunt. He got out of his four-wheel-drive, hung what looked like a transistor radio around his neck, then strapped a collar with a receiver box on his pointer and adjusted a foot-long antenna, giving the dog an out-in-space appearance. His gun was a beautiful drilling, the third barrel

Profiles

carrying a rifle cartridge "just in case" of I don't know what, the open shotgun tube rifled to throw a 50-inch spread at seventeen yards.

Gadgetry, I think, is a state of mind, a seeking for happiness through mechanical devices. Just as the M16 no longer resembles a rifle so much as something the plumber left behind, complex mechanical trappings detract from, rather than add to, the color of shooting. Doubtfully, gadgets may make the hunter more efficient, but some of them keep him sitting on his fat foam-rubber cushion instead of walking. The move might well be toward simplification. With more gunners and less game, it would seem more sporting to handicap ourselves with muzzle loaders, until I remember that man and dog festooned with gear. Perhaps gadgets have a purpose.

THE REPORTER

I STRIVE FOR a better label for this missionary type but I keep coming back to this one. Unlike those of us who cherish certain coverts and hope to keep them private, the Reporter has an urge to tell the world. On first thought this appears a nice thing for him to do and I have occasionally enjoyed his generosity—until I discover he has told a dozen other hunters. This is especially irritating when the covert he has "reported" is a favorite you have been nursing for years.

He is usually a novice who has learned he is accepted by experienced gunners because he directs them to birds. If, in his new-found glory, he notices that his companions (there are usually a lot of them) just never happen to have any place in mind, it doesn't worry him.

One subspecies of Reporter requires a little time to classify—the man blessed with exceptional luck in finding birds, except the day he takes you. Hearing impressive reports of birds moved, I thought for a period Lady Luck smiled on everyone but me. After serious research in the coverts reported, I have come up with the conclusion that men who move forty grouse in a day are congenital liars.

On a face that attracts drunks I evidently wear a credulous expression that draws the Reporter type with tales they think I want to hear about doubles, and triples, and even two grouse dropped with one shot. Many Reporters think they see all those birds, some think they seldom miss a shot. To these happy fellows each flush is a separate bird, and they remember only their hits—with a memory that grows with time.

THE PURIST

THE PURIST IS LIKELY to be a subspecies of the type form Loner. I know, because I tend to be one. He is on a cloud when things go well; when things don't happen according to his standards —his dog's work, his shooting—he would best be let alone, for no one is a deeper griever. If the Purist were any more exacting he wouldn't hunt at all, yet all this raises his enjoyment of shooting to a plane perhaps higher than the average gunner's, simply because when events occur in such rare combination as to satisfy him, angels hum softly.

It may be so simple as waiting to take shots only over points, something most men may consider no more thrilling than shooting a bird with no dog work. The Purist may insist upon near perfection in his dog, to the way it carries its tail or uses the wind, or sits when delivering a bird. Most gunners won't argue with luck, but if the Purist pulls the trigger before he gets his face into the stock and happens to hit the bird, he will fret because he didn't make the shot in his orthodox manner.

Making sense out of a Purist is like trying to understand an Englishman—the more serious he is, the more unbelievable he appears. The Purist is found more frequently, I think, among grouse and woodcock gunners, though quail shooters have their share. He is almost always an above-mediocre shot, shoots a double—side-by-side or superposed—and he never guns unless over a dog whose bloodlines will have been arrived at with deliberation. In the extreme form he breeds his own. He may be of the shell-vest Pendleton-shirt persuasion or he may wear a fine shooting coat, but he'll wear them until they fall apart or are ripped off by thorns. And he is tight-mouthed as a tombstone about his pet coverts.

For the bone-deep Purist there is almost no other game bird but the one he guns for, though if a grouse Purist he may shoot wood-

Profiles

cock in the early season when leaves are dense, but his eye is keyed for that larger, faster form that can materialize even there. Outwardly calm and benign when there is the pleasant plumpness of a bird in his game pocket, he changes into a worrier after a miss. A string of three missed birds will undo him. Mountaineers dismiss grouse shooting with "Cain't hit the bastards." Not the Purist. I'm convinced the Purist is born this way. He knows what Thoreau meant when he spoke of a different drummer and he is certain it was a grouse.

The Smell of Powder

Shooting friendships—probably residual from tribal hunting—are at their best when sharing the failures as well as the successes. Most of us feel identity with the man who missed the shot, and some of the best tales we tell are of human, and dog, frailty. Scent of frost-nipped fern, the click of a breech lever, the tang of wet leather are as much a part of shooting memories as a string of birds. When I asked a few of my shooting friends to give me a brief glimpse of a memorable experience the responses varied. Some recalled the frustrations; others remembered a day of outstanding gun performance; still others dwelled on how they managed it, or the setting, or the beauty of the bird; some remembered most the dogs.

I listen to their stories with vicarious enjoyment, frequently stories of a type of gunning I haven't experienced, and some of these take me to a time or place outside my scope. Sitting before the fire at Fairhill on wonderful after-shooting evenings, I listened to Dr. Charles Norris tell of dove shooting as he had done it in the South—invitation affairs preceeded by luncheon and often followed with a dove supper. As a superlative shot, he dwelt on loads and guns. "In your fence-corner blind you could hear their wings before the birds appeared—singles, pairs or small broken flocks, usually upwind and not too high. High doves require a fast swing or they'll twist out of the pattern. I consider 40 percent excellent shooting and 20 to 30 percent not far below average for even good shots. A third of the fallen birds are lost without a retriever. In the old days Negro youngsters loved to mark and pick up birds and some were expert." But always Dr. Norris was aware of the bird. "Did you know that the male dove 'drives' the female when courting, in the manner of pigeons? Lovely birds, with their black spot behind the eye and the white-edged diamond-shaped tail flared when flushing."

The Smell of Powder

Bob Wingard's letter describing Susquehanna River duck boats gave me as much sense of participation as almost anything I have read:

"When a chill down-river breeze sweeps through river birch and a string of ducks hooks over the water, duck hunters get feathers in their eyes. I can't pinpoint when ducks became a part of my life but I've had a quarter-century of wildfowling traditions and experiences which befall men when they mix guns, boats, boots and decoys. My pleasures were shared with Roy T. 'Biff' Rutter, who stood alone as a wildfowler. He knew ducks and decoys and how to get the best from the duck boats unique to the Susquehanna from Sunbury to below Harrisburg. 'Roll-over' duck boats were originated in the late 1800's by local craftsmen who constructed the stubby pointed-at-both-ends, ribbed, cedar-planked canvas-covered boats. Unlike the Merrymeeting boat, Connecticut sculler, Long Island scooter, Barnegat sneak boat, or Aluma-craft ducker, the roll-over duck boat is, to the best of my knowledge, used only on the Susquehanna.

"In September 1930, Biff's invitation to hunt graduated me out of the gum-boot duck hunter class and started our hunting relationship that continued through his last season. We set out our decoys well ahead and were on the river before daylight for that opening day. Waiting for the legal shooting hour, I heard disturbed ducks winnowing overhead in the dark and a few mallards, as tense as I, exchanged quacks. Biff tuned his duck call a time or two and ended with a coarse feeding chatter. A pair of mallard drakes circled the decoys, hooked their wings, and through binoculars we watched them back-paddle and ski to a stop. Biff insisted that I shoot from the front. Balance and coordination are needed by two men using a roll-over. I steadied down when I found that these round-bottomed boats were so carefully designed that they could be safely tipped at a 45° angle with the right side to the water while the left or high side rode out, hiding the paddler and shooter.

"Down-river we headed for the greenheads which were far outside our decoys. We were seated on the bottom of the boat, hunched over to keep hidden. Stubby paddles produced short meaningful strokes and aching arms. Biff got us within fifty yards and tapped me on the rump with his foot—signal to stop paddling and get my Parker. He maneuvered the boat with the blind side to the ducks

THE MEN WHO SHOOT

until I could count the tail curls. When he tapped again I knew he was going to swing the front around so I would be exposed. From jump shooting on the islands I thought I was set for the way mallards leap out of the water. I was off on my first shot and winged the far drake, but the second was a clean kill. With the boat in open water it was no problem to retrieve the winged duck. Our caps carried drake curls for the rest of the season."

I was in Walt Lesser's gun room, examining a pretty 12-guage English percussion muzzle-loading double with side locks bearing the name *W. Greenfell*. Walt was describing the load he used in it for woodcock—2¾ drams of FFg black powder with 1¼ ounces of No. 9 shot.

"Normally I use a .135 nitro card over-shot wad, but one day I tried some extremely thin 'B' card wads a friend gave me. Tinker was about a year old, and just coming into her capabilities, and I took this little gun for I wanted it to be special." Tinker is his orange belton setter bitch. "She soon pointed—beautiful—and the woodcock gave me an easy straightaway shot. Engulfed in a cloud of blue smoke, I gave Tinker the order to fetch but there was no bird. She made seven more points on woodcock that afternoon and I had shots at all of them but neither she nor I could find a dead bird. I was as worried about spoiling Tinker with orders to retrieve nonexistent birds as I was about my shooting. The fault might lie in the gun fit, or in my follow-through, which is especially important with slow-burning black powder, but once you've trained a young dog, you don't like to let her down. I reloaded and was trudging back to the Jeep when I heard the fine shot trickling down the gun barrels. At the river I tried test shots with each barrel, firing at a sycamore leaf floating on the water. This time a breeze dispersed the smoke enough for me to see that nothing but wads struck the water. While crawling through the thickets with my gun barrels pointed down, the thin over-shot wads had let the fine No. 9 shot pour out and I'd been firing blank loads at all eight of Tinker's woodcock!"

There is a curious something in every shooting man that gives him comfort if he can assure himself that an empty game pocket is not the fault of his shooting; sometimes there is bitter satisfaction in knowing that Lady Luck played all the nasty tricks she knew. Luch Scala says they get around the latter in Italy by never wishing a hunter good luck.

The Smell of Powder

"Italians love shooting," Luch said. "You see them riding a bicycle with a gun slung over their shoulders and a dog in a basket behind them. They shoot larks from pits dug in fields, attracting the birds with lures with mirror-covered metal wings whirled by a string, first one direction, then the other. Larks are a delicacy spitted between bacon and a slice of bread and roasted as they were in Roman times." He described duck shooting from barrel blinds sunk in the mud in the Comacchio swamps south of Venice, and in the Tuscan region between Florence and the Mediterranean near Grosseto jump shooting standing in the bow of a narrow *barchino* poled along canals. "Partridges, quails and pheasants are shot in preserves, and there are boars and mouflon in Sardinia and chamois hunting in the Alps."

"But what about this no-luck thing?" I asked.

"Rather than wishing good luck you must instead say *in bocca al lupo*, which means 'in the mouth of the wolf.' This started long ago when a bitter winter drove hungry wolves into the valleys to prey on the farmers' flocks. Hunter after hunter left the village, climbing the snowy mountains to hunt down the wolves. Fearful villagers gathered in the square to wish each hunter good luck but none came back. The lupine raids continued and desperation grew. Finally the local wise woman was consulted. Her judgment was that, since wishing good luck had failed, wishing the opposite would bear fruit. To make it more effective, wish that the hunter would find himself between the jaws of the wolf, eliminating anything more to fear. So it was done. The hunters who were wished a miserable death all came back carrying wolf pelts. From that time on it became custom, for hunting or any sporting enterprise, to say *in bocca al lupo*."

Obie Conaway recommends blaming the gun but adds that it is best to let someone else do it.

"Back in the fifties my hunting companion, Dan Chapman, then with Fish and Wildlife Service, and I left Washington for two days' quail shooting in central West Virginia. We anticipated good shooting on abandoned farms but mostly we looked forward to shooting the Model 21 Winchesters we had each acquired. Dan's setter found the birds in those narrow valleys but despite the Model 21's, we left all but one or two to other fates. Finally we stopped at a farmhouse where an old man allowed there were lots of quail in his overgrown fields and was glad to let us 'try' them, asking if he could come along and 'watch the show.' The show didn't proceed as expected. The setter pointed and at the covey rise four shots rang out but not a bird fell, which seemed to puzzle the old fellow. While hunting singles we found a second covey. With four shots we pulled about three feathers. I saw our host draw close and peer at our guns but he was silent. At last we found a third covey. There were four shots and all the covey members settled safely on another hillside as two dejected young men watched, too depressed to follow. It was then I heard the kindest words ever spoken to me while hunting. 'Boys,' the old man stepped to my side, 'is there somethin' wrong with them guns you've got?' "

In 1954 Less Crowl arrived for a grouse-shooting visit bearing what appeared to be a baby swaddled in a blanket. It was a Canada goose he had shot the week before in southern Illinois. Roast goose is not enough; I insisted upon the details.

"I was with Harold Kinsey of Springfield, Ohio, and Walter Sheaffer II of Fort Madison, Iowa, in a goose pit in a harvested soybean field." He described a typical pit, surrounded by silhouette decoys. "We were facing east toward Horseshoe Lake goose sanctuary below the horizon and about two hundred and fifty yards in front of us a gravel road formed the boundary of the field. It was a cold, gray November Saturday and the air was filled with the cries of high-flying geese moving toward the Mississippi a mile to our backs. Walter Sheaffer had a Greener side-by-side and Kinsey and I had Winchester Model 12's, each taking turns on the lookout for geese within range.

"It was my turn and, doubting my eyes, I saw six black shapes flying low, headed our direction. I blew two longs on my call, followed by two shorts in goose cadence. As I gave Kinsey and Sheaffer

The Smell of Powder

whispered reports, the geese came on in wing-tip formation. A few motorists had parked along the road, hoping to see action, and when the geese saw the cars they flared for altitude. At my call they reassembled, locked their wings and entered a long descending glide straight for our pit. They were within twenty yards and half that distance from the ground when I said, 'Now!' At point-blank range it was point and shoot, point and shoot and within three seconds six geese, our combined limit, were lying on the ground."

Charles Westerman's first turkey, shot on Beech Mountain in West Virginia, was the excitement that comes only once—the long stalking in the rain, the response to his homemade caller, a "gobbler running toward me cherking like a giant chipmunk each time his foot hit the ground. Eighty yards away he turned and disappeared. The sun had come out, splashing color from wet leaves, and I tried my call again. This time there were several answers from up the slope. After a long silence I started to rise and saw motion in one of the brilliant sunny spots on the ridge. Caught in a kneeling position, I eased my Fox to my shoulder and over the gun barrels watched those birds flash across the sunny areas and disappear, working always towards me. I had muscle cramps, one foot was numb, my eyes were watering and I itched all over but I remember the incredible beauty of sunlight on bronze feathers. When the first bird came in range I was in such misery I couldn't wait for the gobbler. At my shot the mountainside exploded with turkeys running past or flying over me. My bird was flopping on the wet leaves with a head and neck shot—a thirteen-pound hen."

Among disappearing native game, the prairie grouse—pinnated (prairie chicken) and sharp-tailed—are species gunners will have increasingly fewer opportunities to hunt. Ward Sharp, now retired from U.S. Fish and Wildlife Service, knew this shooting from 1954 to 1962 over one of our setters, Old Hemlock Dram.

"In the sparsely settled grassland of north-central Nebraska, pinnated grouse require the true-prairie, tall-grass association of the eastern half, while sharp-tails extend westward into the dry sandhills, though both do best in a combination of sandhills and prairie meadows. Because of grass fires from car exhaust pipes, many ranchers won't permit hunters to drive over their range, and where hunting is allowed it is important to keep dogs away from cows with calves. Most days winds are above 15 mph, making scenting difficult. I remember Dram quartering one swale with head high. After 410 yards (I paced it) he went stanch and I flushed a mixed covey of sharp-tails and pinnates twenty feet in front of him. In the prairies a fast point meant sharp-tails, an unproductive heralded prairie chicken, which lay a lingering trail hot enough to provoke a point two hundred yards downwind. One cloudy afternoon, hunting a wet edge of willow marsh, Dram pointed in cover that seemed too sparse to conceal a grouse. But as I walked in a sharp-tail flushed almost out of the sod, dropping at my shot—as did a second bird that had flushed without my seeing it, flying into the pattern.

"I find No. 6 shot best for prairie grouse, for they are strong flyers, quickly getting out of range. Their flight is as fast into a high wind as when it is calm—an adaptive characteristic to windy environment. Once hunted, they may flush far ahead of a dog, flying to the sandhills where sentinels watch from the highest hill. When the dog and gunner approach, the sentinels fly off clucking, flushing all the birds in the area. Coveys vary from five to twelve birds, often both species. The ratio of sharp-tails to pinnates is about eight to one. Grazing is not adverse to prairie grouse but summer droughts make the difference between a huntable population and almost none. The points Dram made and his finds on difficult cripples, the behavior of the grouse, the big unspoiled prairie landscape make those days in Nebraska live on in my mind."

During his tours of duty in the Foreign Service, Meade Foster has shot in many parts of the world. Like me, he values shooting because of dog work, and of all the shooting men I know I believe he is the only one who gives as much time and attention to his dog as I do to mine. I've known his present Brittany, Tess, since she was a puppy. On a hike during the past summer, he described a nice bit of work by Tess during his most recent season in southwest Georgia, where he shoots, not on the big plantations, but afoot in quail coverts most gunners from the North never know.

"One morning last February we had a forecast of clearing and warmer, with afternoon temperatures in the high seventies. This called for a morning hunt, not only for comfort for man and dog but to avoid diamondback rattlesnakes that would emerge from gopher holes to bask in the sunshine later on. We started at ten o'clock in a lifting fog and Tess was soon on point, but I saw her relax and back away and swing wide to head off the running birds. The covey

The Smell of Powder

flushed out of the thin cover and pitched in a field of wire grass and briars, where we were soon on singles and had three birds over solid points. Circling toward a cornfield, Tess located another covey, which also produced three birds over points. We had been out our usual two hours and had as many birds as we like to take but Tess was full of hunt. Each time she failed to return from a cast I found her on point and, to honor her, I decided to fire once over each point. Perhaps it was Tess's enthusiasm that enabled me to bag four additional birds.

"I had never taken the Georgia limit of twelve birds, but on her final point I promised Tess that if there was more than a single I would go for the limit. Four brown bombs blasted away and two were stopped in a shower of feathers. Tess found the left-barrel bird and delivered it but neither she nor I could locate the first one. Then Betty, my wife and spotter, discovered it hanging in a small live-oak tree. For us, this would be a memorable three-hour shoot any time. I cherish it beyond that, not because of numbers but because Tess, my companion since she was seven weeks old and whom I have trained, gave me the full measure of her skills and joy in doing what she was born to do."

In some dogs there is character that reaches out to you, often in an individual you have never seen before. There is poignancy in these encounters, especially if you don't see him again other than in your mind. Dr. A. E. Wright told me of such a dog he met on a woodcock shooting trip to Maine. He and Tom Whyel, M. T. Balling, Jr., and Emmet Martin, who has Friendship Hill, the historic Albert Gallatin place, were shooting at Gene Moriarity's camp on Pocomoonshine Lake in Maine's Washington County.

"He followed our guide into our cabin the first evening—a grizzled pointer with a small bell attached to his collar that sounded gently as he moved. Politely, he stayed in the background, allowing his companion to regale us with the adventures awaiting us the next morning.

"At daybreak, after a light rain, we were in the alder clumps. Not until the pointer was working ahead did we realize that he was deaf. When his bell ceased tinkling, a point was to be expected. That morning we appreciated many beautiful points, followed by as many fusillades and all too few birds in the coat. In an afternoon drizzle we floundered through the thickets and finally gathered with the guide on a hummock of drier ground—all of us except the pointer Jake. We listened for his bell, our guide using his whistle to no avail. Someone said he subconsciously remembered the bell stopping some time ago. We separated and cast back. After a long period of beating the alders I came upon the fine old dog on stanch point under a tamarack and I could count his ribs as they heaved. The fruits of his efforts are inconsequential, but by my reckoning Old Jake must have been on point nearly half an hour. Such devotion to duty can only be the result of breeding combined with training and love of work. As I left the area with the pointer I remember thinking how little I could accomplish if I were unable to hear. Man has ceased to use his sense of smell; on many occasions he refuses to believe what he sees. These two senses offered this dog the tools for success.

"I'll never forget the whistling, erratic flights of those woodcock, the rain, that point under the tamarack and Old Jake on his last hunt. Gene Moriarity wrote us later that Jake had been run down and killed while ambling across the road a few days after we returned home."

The following, from Wayne Bailey, former West Virginia wildlife biologist, now at Chapel Hill, North Carolina, shows a wild-turkey expert at work:

"Five factors—luck, knowledge of the terrain, knowledge of turkey habits, skill with a caller, patience—enable a turkey hunter to be successful. The West Virginia season opened with twenty-five shots at the head of a long hollow up which I was threading my way but no turkey sailed over my head, no yelping could be heard. By mid-morning I had made a semicircle to the mountaintop, where I moved slowly from cove to cove, keeping just under the summit. While resting I noticed movement in dense shrubs to my left. Three turkeys—all young males—emerged from the thicket. I fired. The nearest fell, lay inert, then fluttered violently in sudden death. Plain, 'dumb luck.'

"A few weeks later, guest at the camp of Frank Piper in central Pennsylvania, I found fresh droppings in an outcrop of rocks in an extensive thicket. Outside in the open woods there were fresh scratchings—a set-up for turkeys. If disturbed when feeding, a short dash would put the birds in cover. The next day I would lie in wait for the turkeys to come out to feed.

The Smell of Powder

"It was a long wait and by nine o'clock I was restless and occasionally yelped on my caller. Unexpectedly a gobbler answered from my left. I called again; he replied, closer. Startlingly, from *behind* the turkey, a rifle shot! Two birds flushed uphill into the thicket, a third cleared the trees and sailed for the valley below, a fourth bird flushed and headed my way. 'Lead him six feet, lead him six feet,' I repeated without moving my lips. Barely clearing the tall oaks, straight overhead he came. At the shot he collapsed and fell amid the rocks with a thud. Luck, combined with a little patience.

"That same season in Bath County, Virginia, I decided to try a cove that had yielded Virginia's two-gobbler limit to my friend Frank Dugan the two previous days. Entering the area just before dawn, I unfortunately flushed a gobbler from the roost and he headed for the mountaintop. I concluded he would return at dusk to the cove where his two pals had met an untimely end, to attempt a reunion. In late afternoon I found a nice stand, but there was another hunter in the cove, banging away at squirrels. I would have to intercept the gobbler on his way. I knew the area and the behavior of turkeys in it when pursued by hunters. The tom would have loitered till mid-day on the mountain peak, then would have descended a ravine to the foothills, and before sundown would follow a foothill contour back into the cove from which he had been flushed that morning. Carefully, I followed the contour to meet him, the squirrel hunter's rifle becoming fainter behind me. In a ravine ahead I heard scratching in the dry leaves—a squirrel perhaps? As I listened the rustle became louder and presently a gobbler appeared. Nearer and nearer he came, headed straight for the cove. I was on the correct contour and to have missed him would have been inexcusable. Knowledge of the terrain and of the habits of a lonesome tom paid off.

"The succeeding Saturday the mountains of western Virginia were shrouded in fog so dense that a turkey would have been visible only within shotgun range. I found much fresh sign but no turkeys until mid-afternoon, when I flushed two gobblers, one descending one side of a ridge, one the other. I was sure they would attempt a reunion before dusk. Selecting a stand, I waited twenty minutes and yelped loudly a couple of times. No answer. A quarter hour later I yelped twice more. Still no answer. It was getting late and I had left my stand when I heard one turkey call from under the ridge. I re-

The Men Who Shoot

turned to my hiding place, got out my caller and yelped cautiously. He wanted to 'talk' and I talked just enough to let him know I was waiting for *him* to come to *me*. Seeing him come through the fog, his head held high, looking for me in every direction, was an unforgettable experience. As I said, the fog was so thick you could see a turkey only in good range. The key to success in this case was a good yelper judiciously used."

These then, are men who shoot. Whether or not they know each other, or love dogs, or even pursue the same game, they share one thing when they share their experiences—a quickening of the senses at the smell of powder.

Passing of a Sportsman

🌼 / *My dog and I are old, too old for roving.*
—JOHN MASEFIELD, *On Growing Old*

ON THE DAY I WAS BORN, Dr. Charles C. Norris was on a Christmas-season quail shoot at Rutherfordton, North Carolina. Thirty years apart in age, our friendship, almost half a century later, lasted the final nine years of his long, full life of sport.

My first contact with him was a response to an ad in which we offered a litter of setter puppies for sale. Dated August 18, 1952, under the letterhead *Dr. Charles C. Norris, Fairhill, Bryn Mawr, Pa.*, the note said he wanted "a handsome, blue or orange belton that is well trained, moderate range, stanch & that will retrieve." My reply that we had no mature setters available would normally have terminated the correspondence but something kept us writing.

Here on the table are the ninety letters Dr. Norris wrote me. Gradually a picture of this man emerged—no longer young, a man who lived primarily for gunning.

"I have been fooling with setters & pointers for 50 odd years. Last summer Nininger sent me an untrained 18 mo. orange belton bitch. I bought her for my wife not thinking ever to use her. In despair of getting a decent shooting dog I bought a 3 yr. pointer bitch, untrained. I started to train her and also gave the setter a chance. Charm, the setter, now has a slashing range of 100 yards, proved to have a good nose. Two weeks ago & without having seen a bird brought in, she started retrieving & has brought in her last 11 pheasants.

"Both young dogs are coming along finely. I am 76. I give each dog 2 hours & that is enough for their handler. Don't forget our latchstring if you are in Philadelphia. Excuse scrawl and haste."

In July of '53 Ruff and Wilda presented us with another litter and I wrote Dr. Norris, remarking that if he was an M.D. he could have been useful throughout the night while Kay and I attended. His reply was characteristic:

"Glad to hear of your fine puppies. I doubt if I could have done as good a job as you did when your bitch whelped though until I retired eleven years ago I was Professor of Obstetrics and Gynecology at the U. of P. Med. School. I ceased practice at the time I retired from teaching and live on 100 acres out here. After quitting I wrote *Eastern Upland Shooting*. It was good fun and curiously the book had a bigger sale than any of my six medical efforts. If I can find a copy of *E.U.S.* I will send it to you."

When my copy of *Eastern Upland Shooting* (Lippincott, 1946) arrived, the description on the dust jacket gave us a further glimpse into the background of this man:

> Born in 1876 in Philadelphia, Dr. Norris has been interested in shooting and fishing since boyhood days, and has been fortunate in possessing the means to follow both through the seasons. He has made eighteen fishing and hunting trips to Newfoundland and Labrador, twenty-seven trips to the South during quail season, and many expeditions to Nova Scotia and New Brunswick for woodcock.

In October, 1954, we accepted his invitation to come over to shoot at his pheasant club. It was twilight when we located Fairhill on a back lane in Delaware County near Bryn Mawr. Autumn was at its throbbing height and this unfamiliar land with its impressive country houses was lovely.

I had suspected Fairhill would be unusual. Ivy-covered stone, huge in the dusk, it was something short of a small castle, commanding wooded grounds—I am tempted to say park—sloping on both sides and the end of the ridge. A wing, blind with ivy, bore a Tudor stained-glass window at the near end. There were no lights visible as we pulled our station wagon into the turning circle. A little numb from the long drive, we mounted the steps and pushed the bell button. Indoors a dog barked.

An elderly maid let us into a hall that reached to the ceiling of

Passing of a Sportsman

the second floor. Caribou and moose heads peered down from dim walls and a lamp revealed a carved stone mantelpiece. Upstairs the dog barked again and then someone was coming down the stairs.

I had pictured him, the way you do, as tall and lean. He was not over five and a half feet and I would guess he weighed 160—quick moving, pink complexioned, with thin white hair and blue eyes behind round steel-framed glasses. He had the sensitive mouth and nose of his early Norris ancestors—the ones who came to look after Penn's Woods—and the same intelligent brow. An incredibly fat white-and-liver pointer and an equally fat orange belton setter waddled from the shadows and sniffed me.

As I patted them, the phrase "slashing range" in his letter came to mind. He read my thoughts but addressed the pointer: "Yes, my dear, you're much too fat. You too, sweetie girl," he turned to Charm. "And so's your boss." He pulled the tweed jacket together and got the lower button fastened. "Well now, how many dogs did you bring and have they eaten?"

The thin maid reappeared with a pan of cooked meat in each hand.

"Two," I said, appreciating the maid's appraisal. "Ruff and Feathers."

"Fine. Mary—" he turned—"show Mrs. Evans to their rooms. We'll have dinner at six-thirty."

It gave me twelve minutes to feed my dogs, unpack and dress.

Mary served the roast pheasant, stepping expertly over Charm and Nellie. Six tall candles in silver candelabra burned low as we sat on at table, Dr. Norris talking around the pipe held in the center of his teeth. Nellie came over and laid her head in my lap. Dr. Norris suggested we take care of our dogs and turn in. I fell asleep half dreaming I was a guest in an English country house. Tomorrow I would be shooting pheasants.

The shooting and the after-gunning mood of this visit were the first of many such experiences with Dr. Norris. I thought about this man, a widower, living alone with two obese dogs and with three house servants and a chauffeur to look after him—a carryover from an age when men of means traveled great distances in pursuit of sport and shot thousands of shells each season, men who fished wilderness salmon rivers and waters of famous trout clubs. His two closest shooting and fishing friends had been Dr. Williams Biddle

Cadwalader and Lynford Biddle, with whom he shot woodcock in Nova Scotia and New Brunswick and grouse in the Poconos and around Ellsworth, Maine. Dr. Cadwalader and Dr. Norris had shared a suite of offices at Thirty-sixth and Walnut in Philadelphia, where a certain aura of stream and field existed. Now I seemed transported to that earlier period to share it with him.

His gun room was steeped in the bouquet of Hoppe's No. 9, the uncarpeted floor saturated with gun oil. There were photographs that appeared in *Eastern Upland Shooting*, and part of his sporting library was in the adjoining study. I got to know this library on one visit when a fourteen-inch snow isolated us at Fairhill. Fairhill, with its eighteenth-century portraits looking down on an overflow of books, its great hall with the rack of walking sticks, the aroma of good pipe tobacco and the click of dog feet on hardwood floors, was a good place to weather out a storm.

Dr. Norris, aside from his niche in the Main Line pattern, was a figure in the medical world. But if he could return now for one day of life, I'd wager he would spend it with the Purdey in a good covert behind Nellie and Charm, and not at the Philadelphia Club or in the operating theater of the University Hospital.

In October of '57 he wrote me:

> Thank you for your nice article on gun fitting. My own experience is somewhat like yours. I have just read it a second time. I think you were right about straightaway birds.
> Sincerely,
Charles C. Norris
>
> P.S. Think of me sometime when you kill an old cock grouse. My word! I would like to be with you. There is no good thinking of it for I can't walk much anymore. Tame pheasants all I can manage.

Our 1958 October visit gave Dixie her first taste of shooting. The sport was good and the finest part was seeing Dr. Norris at past eighty-two in such splendid spirits. As we drove off for home his parting words were, "You can leave that little Dixie here with me any time you want." He was standing in the open doorway, flanked by his two plump bitches, and the upraised hand waving a farewell seemed to beckon us to return.

I enjoyed a curiously warm friendship with this man who did

not give himself easily to friendships. It may have been attitudes we shared without mentioning them—a ritual sense that a gun should be cleaned each time it has been handled, a conviction that there are ways things should be done, from a code of shooting to acknowledging amenities. And, as Dr. Norris put it, both of us were "fools about our dogs." There was the night we were walking the dogs along the lane at Fairhill when he confided that he had made provision in his will to have his dogs put to sleep if they survived him, rather than face the uncertainty of what might become of them. I discussed it with Kay and when we returned home I wrote that we would see that Nellie and Charm lived out their days in proper circumstances. His responding letter was grateful—he called it "baring my soul." Neither of us mentioned it afterward.

In January of '59 we had one of his cheery letters.

> Dear George and Kay,
>
> Glad your Dixie is doing so well. To me training is one of the most interesting sidelines of upland shooting. My congratulations on your shooting on grouse. Years ago I or my dog moved 57 grouse in one day in Penna. Had 3 shots, killed one in the ordinary manner, got another with an extra long crossing shot (sheer luck) & missed the easiest shot of the lot.

One month later a note:

> Last Sat. a week I slipped on icy steps. Broken leg. I am in a cast in the Bryn Mawr Hospital & will be here for at least 2 weeks more. Little Nellie takes it hard. Sorry to write such a letter but the latchstring will be out later. Have missed a lot of nice days shooting. You and I will have some real sport next fall.

We went over to Fairhill in June and found Dr. Norris looking fairly normal aside from the cane. We spent the time mostly talking dogs and guns and viewing Kay's movies taken on our former shooting trips.

> November 11, '59. Managed to miss 3 cock pheasants yesterday & that after killing the first 9 this season with 9 shells. A bum shot always has an excuse. Mine was I was sick all over the preserve. Am O.K. this A.M. Be sure to keep a date open for your visit here. Do not make your stay too short.

That day was Dr. Norris's last gunning. In our letters we continued to pretend we would be shooting together again but Anno Domini would not relent, even for the finest shooting man I have known.

> Feb. 16, '60. The grave M.D.'s keep telling me "go slow" which I do not like much. Except to clean, oil etc. have not had a gun in my hands for months.

When we visited him in June of 1960 Dr. Norris was obviously not well but his spirit was unchanged. He insisted that we all drive to a field trial, stopping off at the University Veterinary School, where I met his friend, Dr. Mark Allam, the Dean.

We tarried over our final breakfast at Fairhill while Dr. Norris fed his scrambled eggs to Nellie and Charm in turn, from his fork. As we drove off he waved good-bye to us from the window of the small front parlor instead of his usual position in the entrance.

On Sunday, February 26, 1961 his nurse phoned to tell us that Dr. Norris had died. When I inquired about Nellie and Charm, she said Charm had died two weeks before. Nellie lasted a month, moving only to the door when someone came and, when she saw it wasn't Dr. Norris, returning to her spot in the hall.

Dr. Norris paid me two high compliments—to want me as a friend and to want me to have one of his Purdeys. I think of him each time I "kill an old cock grouse"; or when the woodcock flight is in; he is beside me when I open *Eastern Upland Shooting* and each time I touch the little Purdey; we think of him when one of us calls Dixie "Sweetie Girl." And in his letters he is on every gray-threaded page.

He is very much in the pages of his gun diary, which I had the privilege of examining in his study at Fairhill two years after his death. Sitting at his desk where he had written all those letters to me, I knew as I closed the heavy covers of his diary that I was closing them on a way of life. With the passing of Dr. Norris an era had ended.

PART FIVE

The Dogs

❦ / Proud-headed dogs that hunt

GAME BIRDS IN AUTUMN—

Gentlemen and Ladies in My Life

❧ / *Old pups with their souls in their eyes,*
Own me for their lord and master.

—Percy Blogg, *There Are No Dull Dark Days*

IF IN SOME STRANGE rearranged world I would have to choose between possessing gun dogs and seeing people, my choice would be unhesitating, provided I could keep Kay. To exist without having setters always near enough to run my hand over a sensitive head, to not have a cold nose sniff my ear and to know the clean country-ham smell of setters' ears as I sniff back, to forgo the tolerance and loyalty that indulge my foibles, would be like trying to exist without my heart.

Kay calls this old house the most elegant kennel south of the Mason-Dixon Line. It bears marks of five generations of Old Hemlock setters—grooves Feathers clawed on the studio door the night he wanted out but didn't want to disturb us, the woodwork chewed by Shadows, who adored gunfire but got nervous when it thundered, Dixie's puppy tooth marks in the arm of a settle. Keeping gun dogs in the house made old-time dog men shudder, but it has no ill effects on a dog's nose. And if gunning over an intelligent handsome setter enriches my sport, certainly a heartful of them on a winter evening or speckled faces peering out of our station wagon are things to value.

My first beautiful friendship with a setter began probably as early as my father thought the dog and the baby would not give each other germs. I have a photograph dated 1908, which looks like one Mathew Brady might have taken, showing me at thirteen months sitting beside Ted, a sensible-looking setter with black head

[213]

markings—both of us gazing into a future of birds and guns. Ted came from Conneaut Lake and won my father's esteem by plunging through the ice into Seaton's Lake to retrieve a mallard my father had shot the first time he had Ted out.

My father's office was hung with framed pedigrees and FDSB registration certificates. There I first thumbed through the *American Field*. Before I was old enough to shoot I lived with a succession of, first, Ryman setters of the Sir Roger de Coverly line, and then Mohawk dogs—all with old-fashioned setter type. Lady, one of the little Llewellins, permitted no one but my father or me to enter the yard, and I used to have to haul her away from the board fence where a workman, triple the combined size of Lady and me, perched high and for good reason. There was a Eugene M. bitch, Peggy, who had puppies in the stable; my father assisted while I remained outside, and I remember my bewilderment and asking why she cried. There was Millie who, like Peggy, died of distemper in those days before inoculations. And then, in the early twenties there was Nat, line-bred to Count Noble.

I learned to shoot quail over Nat, who circled a field first to determine if birds had worked out to feed. Nat, who didn't tolerate point stealing. Nat who, above all, was a grouse dog. His son Speck, when he was two, found my first grouse hours after we had given it up as lost. Speck and I shared the wonder of grouse shooting for ten more years. After he was gone I carried his collar in my shooting coat until the scent of him had disappeared.

Speck's son, Nat 2nd, was born in 1934. In contrast to Speck, who had trained me, young Nat was the first dog I trained. A big fellow with a heavily marked, beautiful head, he was coming into his capabilities as a grouse dog when distemper killed him—the last of the Count Noble Llewellins in my life.

For a while, living in New York, I had few contacts with dogs. My father's health curtailed his shooting and he turned to field trials. I wasn't enchanted with his little new dogs with heads so unlike those of the setters he used to have. They were equally dissatisfied with me and wanted only to get far away on their own. When my father purchased a son of Sport's Peerless—a bit to my liking—I nearly weaned that dog away. I even named him Grouse. Then his half brother Sport's Peerless Pride won the National Field Trial Championship.

Gentlemen and Ladies in My Life

If Father could have resisted, the pressure of friends would have been too great, and Sport's Peerless Grouse was sent off to a field trial trainer. He had attached himself to me and this did something to his soul. Each day a stranger on horseback drove him to move wider. He was run in small trials and proved a bolter. Another stranger took over but by then Grouse had lost faith. I tried to discourage all this but I feel I let Grouse down. I paid my price when I saw his eyes look straight through me as if there had never been the old thing between us.

When in 1939 Kay and I moved to Old Hemlock and could keep a gun dog, I was unable to find the type of setter I wanted. The prospect of breeding one to our taste, like custom-building a gun, was a challenge. Private shooting lines had been bred for centuries —various country places and castles in Britain developed their own strains long before Laverack and Llewellin, strains such as Lord Anglesey's Beaudesert, the Edmund Castle dogs, the Duke of Gordon's. Statter, Field and Armstrong bred the Duke-Rhoebe cross with Laverack blood, which gave Llewellin his best strain.

To breed a grouse and woodcock dog you must know what you want. To handle in woodcock cover a dog should shorten his range, but on grouse I prefer a moderately wide dog, provided he is stanch. Whatever his range or breed, he must hunt for and check with the gun. Grouse trial champions have been used for shooting but the usual wide trial performance is not comfortable to gun over. Try following each brace on foot for half a day at a grouse trial and picture yourself carrying a gun at that speed. The *Field Dog Stud Book* registers around twenty-four thousand English setters and pointers every year. The average gunner shoots grouse and woodcock over one of these dogs with predominantly field-trial bloodlines, which may be the reason gunners see so little of their dogs in the woods. Some older trial dogs are recommended as gun dogs but a dog slowed down by age leaves you only three or four years' shooting. There used to be grouse dogs whose consideration was for the gun, not racing. They are rare today.

In the 1800's a mix of imported setters had produced good grouse and 'cock dogs known as "American Natives," strains like the Campbells, with a lacing of Irish blood, Ethan Allens of Connecticut, Davidsons, Morfords of New Jersey, Gildersleeves of Maryland. Currier & Ives prints show them working grouse, usually

The Dogs

in brace with a pointer or a Gordon or an Irish—big white-and-orange or white-and-liver setters with astonished expressions. The first field trial in America in 1874 brought an influx of Llewellins, and specialized breeding for speed and "class" evolved a smaller setter with a wider head and the twelve-o'clock tail. It didn't happen immediately—there were the early champions we see in Edmund Osthaus's portraits—but it happened.

I find that the ground-eating speed that makes a field-trial winner presents an obstacle in a grouse-gunning dog in the problem of control. I like a dog sensitive but not high-strung. Field-trial men can rightly say I was behind the times in that I was looking for a setter more like the American Natives than a National Grouse Champion, a dog that would more nearly go with a Joseph Manton than a modern automatic. This satisfaction with the past, when it was good enough, is what makes a gun like the Purdey great. I think it makes a great grouse dog.

The urge to shoot over dogs with the deep muzzles and sensitive skulls of the better old-time grouse and woodcock dogs might seem to have no basis in function, but head formation is related to type of brain. If the fleet modern trial dog, bred for competitive drive, has changed in appearance it may be that the calm, easy-to-handle grouse dog of former years looked the way he did for a reason.

With this in mind, I set out to breed our line of setters. The first step was to select foundation stock. Earl Twombley had bred grouse and woodcock setters in Vermont, one strain of which Corey Ford kept active until his death. Mrs. C. P. Hunt of New Hartford, New York, was breeding belton-type setter gun dogs. And there was George Ryman, who was still breeding setters up at Shohola, Pennsylvania, from bloodlines of early bench champions that were shooting dogs, crossed with Gladstone, Count Noble and Nugym blood. In September '39 we purchased our stud dog from him—a sixteen-month-old blue belton, half Ryman and half old-style gun-dog bloodlines, an ideal combination for our plans. Part of the experience of buying a Ryman setter was correspondence with George Ryman. I have a sheaf of his letters typed on a ribbon that shifted impulsively from black to red. Ryman was a positive man who aroused no half-way responses. I remember his advice: "Don't hunt him with other dogs. Just shoot grouse over him; he'll do the rest." He did.

Gentlemen and Ladies in My Life

Blue spent the lonely war years in my father's kennel, separated from me. We saw him on short leaves, arriving late at night at Old Hemlock, where my parents would have him waiting before a fire. At first there was joy in reunion and certainly it was going to be good again; then just when it had begun it was over and Kay and I were leaving and Blue once more found himself in a kennel yard in town. Each time I could see the doubt grow until, when finally we were back to stay, Blue could never be sure we would not be leaving him. He had aged and I discovered he was going blind. He hunted three more years, doing remarkable work, but on opening day of his twelfth season his hind parts gave out. Handing my Fox to Kay, I shouldered him like a fur neckpiece and carried him the long miles back. He lived to be nearly fourteen, feeling he was hunting with us by waiting in the station wagon. People around here remember "Old Blue" when they can't remember the names of our other setters.

As a mate for Blue to contribute head refinement, we selected Dawn, an orange belton granddaughter of a bench and field winner in England. She also carried Mohawk and Prince Rodney blood and her parents were working gun dogs. Blue was eight and a half but the honeymoon was passionate and much of what books call love play went on in our studio.

There is a breeders' theory that mates with similar bloodlines throw uniform litters seldom superior to the parents, and that mates with unlike bloodlines produce uneven litters that occasionally contain an outstanding individual better than either parent. By the latter genetic phenomenon we got Ruff in that Blue-Dawn litter.

I selected him at five weeks—early for accurate judgment. Unlike a field-trial prospect, the aggressive pup doesn't make the best gun dog. Primitive strains of bird dogs were selected for crouching (for net hunting) and later pointing, not attacking; for ease in handling and restraint from a distance; for retrieving with a soft mouth, not devouring the bird—all opposites of aggressive behavior. Inhibiting aggressive impulses may have contributed to the nervous temperament of bird dogs but it is still a pointing dog we are after, not a pursuit dog.

I pick a puppy for refinement of head bone because I find it related to intelligence, sensitiveness and nose. I show young puppies a recently shot grouse and watch their reaction. I have not found that females are birdier than males but they often seem more precocious and easier to train. The drawback to giving your heart to a female bird dog is their vulnerability to mammary tumors.

After Ruff's first season on grouse I knew he was what I wanted. Orange belton, with a head like something chiseled, when I looked into his dark eyes I saw all the way to his brain and he saw into mine. From his first point on grouse the day he was seven months old, until his last point more than fourteen years later, Ruff made 547 productives on grouse for me during actual gunning, 114 of them within thirty-six days in his fifth season. I promised myself this book would not contain phrases like "the best dog I have ever seen"—Ruff and I were not the only dog and man who lived in each other, but it was an experience I didn't expect to know again.

In fifteen years Ruff was never ill; his muzzle grew silvery and his vision clouded—the price of living long—but his hearing remained sharp and his teeth were like those of a young dog. He hunted twenty-nine times on grouse his last season at fourteen and a half. His hind parts had stiffened but Ruff savored life to the end. I hope I'm correct in thinking he did not anticipate such a thing as death, though he had seen death many times in the field and had carried it in his mouth. He was working our training quail ten days before he died. During his last two weeks he began to fail. On a May night four weeks after his fifteenth birthday, he grew suddenly uncomfortable with an anxiety that became more uncontrollable until, just before dawn, I sedated him with Nembutal. I'll not forget the long drive to the vet's with Ruff, quiet on the seat between us, and that terribly beautiful sunrise over the Brieries. In his office, without waking Ruff, our vet completed what I had begun. *As still as death.* When you see it there is nothing quite so still.

It was Ruff who shaped our Old Hemlock line. Having achieved what we were striving for in our Blue-Dawn litter, we could either repeat the mating or we could line-breed to Ruff to fix his characteristics in our strain. Since we didn't want another dog so near Ruff's age we did the latter. Line breeding, even as close as inbreeding, is the tool to establish a superior progenitor's qualities in the bloodline. Because a few excessively high-strung dogs have resulted, it has been condemned. If instead of simply talking about "a pedigree that long" owners will study their dogs' pedigrees, they will learn that good bird dogs invariably have ancestors appearing more than once, especially in the early generations. This is line breeding. The characteristics that evolve are as good or as bad as the characteristics bred from. One of Laverack's pedigrees had litter mates, Pilot and Moll 2nd, as nineteen of the thirty-two ancestors in the 5th generation; eight of the others were the grandparents of these two individuals, three were their parents, and the remaining two were their pups.

The easiest characteristic to predict is color, often varying with pups in the litter. Blue is dominant, orange recessive. If one parent contributes a blue gene and the other an orange gene, the puppy will be blue even though it carries both blue and orange genes. The resultant blue dog mated to a similar blue will throw orange pups when both contribute orange genes. If both contribute blue genes, the resulting pup will be a genetic blue carrying no orange genes. Therefore, breeding to a genetic blue will result in only blue puppies even if the other parent is orange. An orange dog carries only orange genes, for it would not be orange if a blue gene were present. Two orange parents can have only orange puppies.

Our Old Hemlock setters are occasionally referred to as belton setters, as if it were a breed, like Irish. Belton is an allover speckled marking with no solid patches; even the ears are a mix of dark and light hairs. The term applies only to English setters and the color is usually blue or orange, rarely liver, sometimes tricolor. Beltons, more common in certain bloodlines, are associated with a typical head conformation and coat, but belton is a marking, not a breed. Because patch markings persist, perfect beltons are not easy to produce.

In his *American Game Bird Shooting*, George Bird Grinnell said that Edward Laverack was the first to use the term "belton" for that marking, after a village in Northumberland County. Ponto was a dark-blue belton, Old Moll a light-blue belton; both were supposedly the result of a pure strain belonging to the Reverend Harrison from whom Laverack obtained them in 1825. Laverack inbred from Ponto and Moll for generations but ended with some patch markings.

The earliest mention of the marking I can find was in *Of Englishe Dogges*, by Johannes Caius (pronounced *Keys*), published in Latin in 1570 and in English in 1576:

There is also at this day among vs a newe kinde of dogge

The Dogs

brought out of Fraunce . . . speckled all ouer with white and black, which mingled colours incline to a marble blewe, which bewtifyeth their skinnes and affordeth a seemely show of comlynesse.

Caius, who was Royal Physician to Elizabeth I, stressed that hunting was reserved for the nobility in dogs as well as in people. He speaks of "The Dogge called the Setter, in Latine *Index*" as

> making no noise either with foote or with tounge, whiles they followe the game. These attend diligently vpon theyr Master and frame their conditions to such beckes, motions, and gestures as it shall please him to exhibite. . . . (In making mencion of fowles my meaning is of the Partridge and the Quaile) when he hath founde the byrde, he . . . stayeth his steppes and wil proceede no further, and with a close, couert, watching eye, layeth his belly to the grounde and so creepeth forward like a worme. . . . neere to the place where the birde is, he layes him downe, and with a marke of his pawes, betrayeth the place of the byrdes last abode.

If all desirable qualities could be produced with as much regularity as color, bird-dog breeding would be simple. Conformation can be foreseen but I know of no formula for producing nose, style and pointing instinct other than to breed from parents with those qualities or, preferably, to line-breed. Even then, results depend upon the prepotency of individuals or the strain, and within the litter there will be one or two pups with superior qualities.

To line-breed to Ruff required breeding litters by him out of different dams. To maintain type, when he was five we bred him to a female we bought from a leading bench kennel. I don't consider it probable that a straight bench-bred setter today will make a fine gun dog, though some early bench setters such as Rummy Stagboro were gun dogs. Wilda (like wildflower) was a blue belton beauty, with eyes made more sad that first day from car sickness. Upchucking in the square at Gettysburg and again on Sideling Hill, she regained her poise after the long ride from the kennels and made her entrance at Old Hemlock, sashaying past Ruff and Blue like a hussy. Blue tried to rise, following her with his nose, but Ruff growled once and took over. It was love between Ruff and Wilda for as long as she lived.

Wilda had a burning desire to find birds, but, once cast, I might see her ten minutes later when she sailed past, her tail a bloody banner, and I don't think she gave me a thought until she happened onto me. This drive was all I could ask for in show blood but what pointing instinct was in her handsome puppies was put there by Ruff.

Kay and I assist with delivery, taking each puppy as it is born, severing the umbilical cord after clamping it with artery forceps, then tying it with thread an inch from the puppy's belly. This prevents umbilical hernia, common when the mother is allowed to bite off the cord too close to the belly. Wilda wanted none of my interference with her puppies but I managed with all but one. Feathers, the lone male in the litter, entered this world in trouble and left it in the same manner. Delivered from a standing position and dropped to the floor, his umbilical cord was torn and the resultant hernia required four inches of steel suturing, which he carried the rest of his life. He grew into a handsome sixty-pound orange belton. We had lost Old Blue and when Ruff and Wilda gave us a blue belton male, Shadows, the following year, we decided to let Feathers go to a shooting man who was eager for him. The night before he was to leave, Feathers stood proudly while I groomed him. When I called him to me to clean his ears, he sat between my knees giving me that look of his. That did it. Feathers remained at Old Hemlock.

Any dog would be better for being the only one, but you don't develop a bloodline by keeping a single dog. Feathers and Shadows were too near the same age. Mutually corruptible, self-hunting became the evil the moment they could slip away together. The ordeal came when they were nine and eight. Without warning they took off and we immediately started searching. The next day we learned that thirty minutes after leaving home they got into a flock of chickens. A woman considered two handsome well-bred setters the price of two chickens and shot them. When Shadows was reported, covered with blood, dragging himself from the area, I set out on his trail, leaving Kay at home to take calls. She intercepted me by phone to tell me Shadows had reached home thirty hours after the shooting, a bullet furrow plowed through his back, grazing his spine. Our vet managed to save him. For five days and nights we followed reports of Feathers. People try to help, but a "big orange hunting dog" described on the phone would turn out to be a tan-and-white mongrel or a collie. When on the fifth day, exhausted from worry and lack of sleep, I found where he had been buried, it was a relief

THE DOGS

to Kay and me to know he wasn't wandering half dead down some strange road trying to get home.

Shadows did not come of age until Ruff's death. During his first season, he had to watch Ruff and Feathers bring in birds, but in his second season he began to retrieve and became my most indefatigable retriever. His integrity as a backpointer was touching; he wavered only when failing vision prevented his seeing the pointing dog. When he made his own productives he did them with drama. I can think of no dog who more eagerly lived life, but his intensity gave us some bad moments.

Shadows had the lives of a cat. There was the December day he and Ruff crossed a roaring stream in flood before I could stop them, balancing on the remaining beam of an old bridge. Kay and I had to watch them teeter back, knowing a false step would plunge them beyond assistance. The rifle wound that nearly killed him affected his nervous system. One summer afternoon when I was patterning my Purdey, I left him in the station wagon with the windows partly down. After the first shot I found him at my side, awaiting orders to retrieve. Returning him to the car where he had squeezed through the seven-inch opening, I closed the glass to within two inches of the top. Back at my pattern sheets, I fired again. This time it took him a few seconds longer but he got there, his mouth streaming blood and several teeth broken. When I managed to stop the hemorrhaging, I found he had eaten his way through the car window glass as if it had been peanut brittle. One snowy night he strayed, bringing back memories of the search for Feathers. It was foggy and we lost his tracks. Next morning he was found wandering down a highway, miles from home. The nervous disorder became more acute as he aged, though his basic health was excellent and we had many wonderful shooting days together. When he died at not quite fourteen, Old Hemlock, became very empty, but by keeping Shadows that long we had outwitted Fate.

For his next litter we bred Ruff with a Ryman bitch carrying Sport's Peerless blood. Dixie from this litter is an exceptionally comfortable dog to shoot over, with intelligence to a degree that borders on neurotic. With her fine-boned sensitive head she closely resembles early pictures of Laverack's females. "Laverack" and "Llewellin" are labels used inaccurately to describe current bench and trial setters, which are not only more unlike each other than the Laveracks

Gentlemen and Ladies in My Life

and Llewellins were, but are unlike the prototypes they are named for.

We bred Dixie to her half brother Shell from the second Ruff-Wilda litter. As sire of both parents, Ruff was the double grandsire of the litter. Dixie gave birth to three puppies with more difficulty than Wilda had with ten. The first one, Bliss, was partially presented in our station wagon in front of our vet's office, where we awaited results of pituitrin injection to stimulate labor. She was a large pup and when I saw her head, purple from engorged blood, I was certain she was being strangled. I carried Dixie inside to the operating table, where Dr. Kotchek managed to deliver Bliss. I didn't know it then but it was Ruff coming back to me. Although blue instead of orange, she had his type, his nose, his style on point and his magic way with grouse.

No man is quite objective about his favorite dog and for a time I didn't want Bliss to be as good as Ruff, perhaps didn't recognize it when it was happening. In her five seasons Bliss hunted 276 days on grouse, made 250 productives with 27 of her 81 kills shot over points. At the end of his fifth season Ruff, with shorter seasons, had hunted 139 days, made 256 productives, with 25 of his 100 kills shot over points. Ruff was trained exclusively on grouse; Bliss on quail, woodcock and grouse. Both were given, as nearly as it is possible with additional dogs, the feeling that they were my most important dog; both were certain of it. To shoot over two such dogs as Ruff and Bliss is almost more than any man should know.

Abruptly and incredibly we lost Bliss in surgery the summer after she was five. Along with the bleakness without her was the knowledge that our bloodline was close to drying up and that I was without a grouse dog. By a happy chance a friend had bred Bliss's litter brother and offered me an orange belton male puppy, a double great-grandson of Ruff. We brought Briar home in mid-August, nearly adult size at seven months, achingly beautiful like Bliss with a typical Old Hemlock head. With Dixie still handling woodcock expertly at nearly thirteen but not enough dog for the strenuous gunning I do on grouse, Briar is now the orange-belton hope of Old Hemlock.

Other Old Hemlock setters entwined themselves in our lives in the short time they were here—the puppies that rapidly grew from small fungi-looking things in their natal membrane into irrepressible little rowdies that swarmed over us after each feeding, trying to tear our clothes off. All too soon it was time to see them leave, suddenly sober and clinging, and a little of us went with each.

The man who breeds his own gun dogs not only risks extinction of his line but evolves its characteristics slowly. With limited numbers, he must place each pup where it will be developed to the finished stage to prove his progress. Over the years my taste in gun dogs has changed, shaped by what I have found makes the best grouse and woodcock dog for me. In our Old Hemlock line we have developed a handsome belton type averaging fifty-five pounds in the males, under fifty in the females, with a deep muzzle, a typical long, fine-boned head. They hunt almost daily through our long grouse seasons in roughest cover, and they are natural gun dogs, with nose and style.

Each setter in my life has been a privilege to know, from my hazy remembering memories of Ted all the way to Briar. Each has been, superbly, a gentleman or a lady. If I add the years each of them gave me, I have had more than ninety years of gun dogs during the past five decades. You can't do better than that.

Scent and the Gun Dog

❧ / *Their noses exquisitely wise,*
  Their minds being memories of smells;

—JOHN MASEFIELD, *Reynard the Fox*

BLISS RETRIEVED THE GROUSE, its fan spread and head dangling, then sat and relinquished the limp form to my hand. I put my nose to the warm breast and with my inadequate human sense of smell tried to capture a trace of the elusive thing my dogs respond to feverishly. All I got was a dry feathery smell combined with the musty odor of leaf humus.

My setters can detect bird scent thirty yards away, three times that far if the wind is right, yet there are days when they have failed to scent a grouse within feet. There has to be a reason, for it will happen to a dog with the keenest of noses who couldn't be pushed into a grouse. A stylish dog covering a useful amount of terrain will flush an occasional bird involuntarily—it is the dog that potters underfoot that never does—but I'm convinced that most off-days are due to the vagaries of scent.

Some dogs that have difficulty with grouse scent can locate and point pheasants in rank weeds. Pheasants give off stronger scent than grouse, woodcock or single quail and it is this that spoils a dog for grouse, even more than the pheasant's trick of running. Accustomed to the strong stream of pheasant scent, the dog comes to expect an equal volume of scent from grouse and pushes closer until he flushes. By contrast to single bobwhites and woodcock, which emit no more scent than a grouse but permit closer approach, a grouse has a proximity fuse set for a respectable distance, and the sooner a dog learns this, the sooner he may become a grouse dog.

The Dogs

From their manner on point my setters show that they get a different scent from woodcock, quail, pheasants and grouse. They ignore training quail in the pens but point them a few yards outside. Dogs often notice the man smell on planted birds at trials and on preserves and may not handle them as stylishly as wild birds. Some men think dogs can distinguish cock from hen pheasants. Usually it is because cocks are more apt to run than hens, and dogs behave differently on a running bird.

Experience plays a part in interpretation of scent. Two dogs with approximately equal noses will perform differently depending upon how each has learned to use his nose. After years of work, an old dog will handle birds more brilliantly with the scenting equipment he was born with than he did as a yearling, and though he may lose his vision and hearing, he is not likely to lose his wonderful nose. I once thought that all well-bred gun dogs were born with equally good noses. I still don't discount brains but I'm convinced that a fine nose is the product of combinations of genes. Among litter mates with the same ancestors, only one or two may possess the gift. Just possessing it is not enough; some dogs are wasted for lack of development.

Scent has been described as taste operating from a distance. Like taste, it is a chemical process. The odor floats from the bird as tiny particles that must come in contact with cells in the nasal passage of the dog to be identified. The mucous membrane must be wet for the particles of scent to be dissolved, which is why scenting is poor in dry air.

We speak of body and foot scent as different odors, though no one is certain which portion of the bird produces scent. The source may be the anal glands or the skin glands, but all parts of the bird are permeated, even the feathers. Body and foot scent are often mingled. If foot scent is strong, some of it spreads to the air; if body scent is strong, the ground and vegetation may be impregnated.

True body scent floats like a cloud around the bird, agitated by the slightest movement of air. The smoke from a smoldering cigarette on a nearly windless day illustrates the movement of scent, except that scent spreads more horizontally. A light breeze can carry it to the dog for an impressive distance but heavy winds dissipate it almost immediately. If the air is still, scent will be strongest at the

Scent and the Gun Dog

point of origin—the bird in the center of the cloud—becoming gradually fainter toward the perimeter until it is undetectable. The better the dog's nose, the bigger, in effect, is the cloud. He must detect the cloud and judge the distance from the bird by the intensity, then work in the direction from which the scent becomes stronger. If scent says *grouse* he must, by his "exquisitely wise" nose, know exactly when to stop; if it says *pheasant* and is diminishing, he must realize that the bird is running and must move up or, better yet, circle to head it off.

If you picture scent as the smoke from a campfire, continually changing direction, you can learn a lot by watching experienced dogs utilize the slightest air currents. Some raise their heads to catch stronger scent and then advance toward it, others make short casts, and still others drop their noses and try to work nearer from foot scent. A good pointing dog uses the cloud of body scent and goes boldly to the bird. When in full lope he lands pointing, he has encountered a heavy cloud of scent; when he draws slowly to his bird he has usually met the edge of the cloud. The dog that trails like a hound is inclined to potter and may fail to recognize increasing body scent in time to stop before flushing the bird. Avoid working this kind of dog downwind, for body scent is carried away, leaving foot scent to be encountered first. Running pheasants are bad medicine for the ground trailer.

Dogs work best on cool damp days because high humidity retards evaporation of scent and of moisture in the dog's nasal passage. I've had good points in a downpour, but a light drizzle or hanging mist—even a fog so dense you can scarcely see your dog—creates ideal scenting conditions. Scenting is especially good in the 35° to 45° range, as if thermal variation between the bird's body and the air causes scent to rise like vapor from the bird. At 60°, evaporation is too rapid unless the atmosphere is damp; below freezing, the air tends toward dryness. A fox-hunting friend tells me his hounds find scenting difficult in falling temperatures.

Scenting conditions change from hour to hour. Some men say scenting is bad when the breeze is from the south, others say from the east. Dusty foliage is detrimental. Rank or rotting vegetation detracts from early-season scenting and conditions are not at their best until there has been a killing frost. Heavy snow is unfavorable, yet a melting snow makes for good scenting. Imperceptible air currents can efface scent; a bird over the brow of a hill or behind a boulder may be in a dead pocket out of the air flow.

Each time a bird moves or fluffs its feathers it involuntarily liberates its scent. The bird that drops to the ground and freezes instantly gives off almost none; it is air washed and even its faint trail in the air is soon gone. A bird killed outright, particularly if high in the air, is harder for a dog to locate than one that flutters and releases a cloud of scent. The pheasant with a wing broken near the body that flaps during its effort to escape is easier for a dog to follow than one that is wing-tipped and runs with the wing held close.

When you smell a flower, the fragrance is strongest with the first whiff and is sensed more acutely in short inhalations than in one long intake. Observe the way your dog breathes when he is on point. Instead of inhaling scent in a prolonged draught, you will see him taking a series of short, rapid sniffs followed by a long exhalation, the sequence repeated all the while he holds the point. Each short sniff duplicates the impact of the first whiff, giving him pulses of scent at high intensity. On a hot day when he has been running hard and gasps for breath, your dog can't detect scent by breathing through his mouth any more than you can. In quail hunting, a dog will occasionally stop in the midst of a retrieve to point another bird. It might seem that the scent of the bird in the dog's mouth would drown out the more distant scent of the unshot bird. The smell of blood may separate the two, but more probably it is the impact of the fresh whiff of additional scent that comes through and says *bird*.

Fox hunters say that many times hounds cannot "own the line" when they have been put on a fox that has just been "viewed." While I have had nice points after waving my setters to a bird I have seen, there are situations when they get no scent at all, especially on a bird that has sailed in, though it seems it must be under their noses. The bird, being frightened, may hold its feathers tight. A dog will do better on a bird that has not just landed.

The fact that pointing dogs find the birds they do is a miracle of sensory perception. To the unappreciative a point may seem only to be expected, for isn't the bird dog a pointing strain bred to do that? But the more you grasp the problems of scenting, the more you marvel that any point is made.

A bird dog has a fantastic ability to separate and analyze scents.

Scent and the Gun Dog

Drenched with skunk odor, he can point a bird. I have seen one of my females in heat, with the strong odor of a male-repellent spray on her, point a grouse. I don't know if it is a trait of setters, but those with the best noses have loved to roll in foul matter; plastered with cow manure or worse, they can point birds as if in the purest air.

Certain medications blunt a dog's sense of smell and perhaps his mental responses. One day I gave Shadows one quarter grain of phenobarbital. Instead of acting as a mild sedation, the drug whipped him into a frenzy. Trailing froth, he dashed through the woods running into grouse as though they didn't exist. I learned that dogs fight the effects of phenobarbital unless administered in large doses. Young Briar, as young dogs will, got too intimate with a bee. The sting not only caused enormous swelling on his nose but obliterated his capacity to scent pheasants for a day. Gasoline fumes impair a dog's ability to smell—one more reason not to transport a dog in a car trunk. Smokers can't imagine tobacco smoke being unpleasant, but it can temporarily reduce a dog's keenness of scent after he has been riding in a smoke-filled car.

Fatigue may affect a dog's scenting capacity, and pollen or dust will irritate the mucous membrane of his nose, so don't be hasty in criticizing your dog if his performance is occasionally below normal. There are reasons why he may have off-days, like the men who shoot.

No perceptive shooting man needs to be told to cherish a dog with the gift of a good nose, for dog work, together with the mysteries of scent, add up to enchantment on an autumn afternoon.

Education of a Grouse and Woodcock Dog

> ❧ / *And strains to be gone with briars tearing his coat*
> *And burrs in his ears and heaven's long wind*
> *at his heels—*
>
> —NANCY BYRD TURNER, *Old Game Dog in November*

RUFFED GROUSE AND WOODCOCK are not the exclusive property of the purist, but in a sense this is achieved by the manner in which the purist takes them—a ritual only the discerning can appreciate. If you have roots in tradition, if you need to be part of this bird/dog/gun obsession, you won't be completely happy until you shoot over a stylish dog of your own. It won't come easily, for, especially with a grouse dog, the gunner must give himself to his dog with the devotion of a falconer to his hawk.

I barely remember "Irish" and "Gordon" in the shady side yard at my Grandfather Hunt's home—old citizens with counterparts in many small-town households of that era. Today Irish and Gordon setter gun dogs would seem exotic, at a time shooting men seek new breeds in hope of finding the perfect dog.

". . . . men are marvelous greedy gaping gluttons after novelties, and covetous cormorants of things that be seldom, rare, strange, and hard to get." Toned down a bit, that comment by Caius four centuries ago could apply to men and dogs today. It was suggested that the "new" Continental breeds—Brittanies, Weimaraners, Vizslas, German short-haired pointers—were uniformly brilliant. There are no brilliant breeds; there are only brilliant individuals. Springers have a place in pheasant shooting and on woodcock, but I question their value on those grouse that won't wait for a man to approach within gun range. Even Labradors are used as bird finders, which reveals what some men think a bird dog is supposed to do. If you can generalize, Continentals are easier to train, work close and seem good dogs for men unused to pointers and setters, which I am convinced require an accredited psychiatrist to deal with them. In fairness to any breed, when a dog proves unsatisfactory there is the likelihood that the fault was with the man and not the dog. There have been excellent setters and pointers since 1800. If it were entirely in the breeding there would be more good shooting dogs than there are today. Some gunners buy well-bred dogs but never get one to suit them; others, willing to spend time with their dogs, seem almost regularly to have good ones.

Dog training is most effective when kept simple. Training is showing the dog what you want him to do and making him eager to do it; breaking, which must not be traumatic, is correcting him of bad habits. The best "cure" for bad habits is prevention before they are formed. Each dog is a separate case, the finest material often offering the most delicate problems.

Professional trainers rarely start until the pup is eight months old, although there is a theory that the puppy's brain is sufficiently developed to respond at seven weeks. I commence the moment he is born. As I dry him off and tie the umbilical cord, the warm, squirming puppy in my hands is imprinted with my scent when most pups know only the scent of their mother and their litter mates.

Bliss had grouse shot over her *in utero* when her mother, Dixie, heavy with puppies, was working and retrieving birds. On the day she was two weeks old, Bliss smelled her first grouse, brought in

still warm thirty minutes after being shot. Her eyes were no more than slits but she raised her little head and eagerly sniffed the wonderful scent.

During the first two weeks, before the puppies' ears open with their eyes, I begin precautions against gun-shyness by slapping the whelping box to give them vibrations. After their ears have opened I clap my hands and slap a folded newspaper against my palm at feeding time, accustoming them to noise associated with pleasure, not fear. A dog can be made gun-shy even after this—by children snapping cap pistols at him, by taking him to a skeet range "to get him used to shooting," by shooting pigeons in front of him without the excitement of game-bird scent, and by what is probably the most common error of too much shooting the first time the dog is hunted. Like "blinking," gun-shyness is man-made but it requires endless patience to cure and the cure is doubtful. Prevention by regular association with loud noise at meals—a slapped newspaper or blank cartridges—is better than treatment.

Retrieving can be begun as early as the puppy will carry things. Toss out an object that does not resemble a bird—your glove is good—and as the pup picks it up order, "Fetch." If he wants to carry it away, work him on a long cord or in a narrow passage with no choice but to go toward you. I don't use force training because our setters are natural retrievers. Using a mock-up grouse with wings and tail produces enthusiastic retrievers but gives some of them ideas about going for the bird while pointing. Save the mock-up until after the dog is stanchly holding points. Wrapping it with heavy wire to discourage chewing develops a gentle mouth. Using a mock-up made with both grouse and woodcock wings, later gradually removing the grouse wings, often overcomes the distaste some dogs have for retrieving woodcock. Tossing out the feathered mock-up can encourage chasing birds; it should be planted in grass or brush and the dog sent for it with *dead bird, go fetch*. In the finished stage the dog delivers the bird from a sitting position.

The sooner I get a dog to pointing seriously, the sooner it becomes a gun dog. Before pointing I taught Bliss the commands necessary for control—*lie down, hold, stay, come here, heel, go on, sit* and *no*. To the puppy it is a serious experience and a daily game to be anticipated. It should begin at twelve weeks and be done with no one but the teacher and pupil present.

Education of a Grouse and Woodcock Dog

You teach *stay* by placing the puppy's food before him and making him stay until the command *go on* is given. Our setters enjoy this drill at every meal during their lifetime and go into a trance as on point. Another effective pointing drill is to toss out a biscuit and make the dog stand with *stay* until sent on, stopping him occasionally and letting him draw to it as on a bird. I prefer "stay" instead of "whoa," which sounds like "no."

No is a way of explaining, not necessarily a reprimand. Properly spoken, it carries meaning. When the offense is serious, a smack on the bottom is in order but no rougher than the puppy is used to in play. Never slap with a folded newspaper; the shooting breeds must associate any sound like gunfire with nothing but fun. Shaking by the scruff of the neck is punishment without pain, and the upraised finger is always a reminder of the switch. Distinguish between a mistake and a sin—the latter is when the dog knows it is wrong and does it anyway. Some dogs have higher moral principles than others but doubt should be in the dog's favor.

I'm not convinced that force is a satisfactory way to train a dog, although there are times it must be used. Dogs resist force mentally even when they submit physically and I view the use of force as evidence of something lacking in me. If you are skillful, your dog will obey you because he wants to please you but he must be shown what you wish of him. He can learn to obey a whisper but will respond only to loud tones if you yell at him. There are moments when he will drive you to the extremes of both yelling and force. If you realize you can't correct a transgression, pretend you didn't see it. Conversely, if you can appear omniscient when he doesn't think you see him, make the most of it. Anticipation is one of your best tools.

The two most important things to stress in a grouse and woodcock dog are pointing and quartering. Instinct to point must be bred-in but stanchness can be intensified; desire to find birds is hereditary but teaching to quarter can guide the dog in his quest and is your most effective control when he becomes too wide, which usually happens in his second season.

There are mechanical devices to make a dog work close. Hanging a heavy chain on his collar breaks his pace from loping to trotting but destroys the beauty of his motion and ceases to be effective when removed. A check cord turns the dog but doesn't teach him to quarter at the desired range. I have never resorted to the electric collar; there is danger of making the dog a "blinker" if he is on birds when the shock is applied, and I think it can destroy style. It is negative. It can, hopefully, train a dog to *not* do certain things but I doubt if it can make him *do* something. Some dogs have been satisfactorily corrected with it but others require the collar indefinitely, forcing the gunner to wear the transmitter while hunting, which leaves some doubt as to who won. An ad in an outdoor magazine under "Exchange" offering an electric shock collar for a young bird dog implies volumes. Calling in and whipping has little effect on wide rangers, for they usually take their punishment, uncertain if it is for coming to the whistle or for looking for birds—their reason for ranging wide. It sometimes helps to make the dog walk at heel for several minutes; it always helps to work the dog alone to avoid competitive ranging.

I have found that too much whistling only apprises the dog of your location and lets him merrily go on self-hunting. If you whistle once and move in a new direction—or even stand quietly—he will, unless he is a confirmed bolter, form the habit of looking you up. You are avoiding trouble if you teach the dog to quarter when he is young.

I started Bliss sight pointing at three and a half months. With a rod and line, I dragged a grouse wing in front of her (not a rabbit or squirrel hide, which might encourage interest in fur) and snapped it out of her reach each time she tried to catch it. Sight pointing is arrested stalking, and after a few unsuccessful pounces Bliss began sneaking up and drew into a point, becoming more intense as I stroked her and repeated, "Stay." After each point, I "flushed" the wing out of reach and repeated the procedure.

One day when I noticed her getting scent from the grouse wing, I sent her downwind and hid the wing above ground in a shrub. Running back with the wind in her face, she wheeled toward it and pointed. Any man with imagination could take it from there. I hid the wing in deep grass, still on a line but with no pole, and after each point snapped it in a pseudo flush and slipped it out of sight under my coat.

The next experiment was in actual grouse cover. With Bliss quartering in hemlocks and rhododendron I tossed the wing behind a log. She crossed, hit the scent from eight feet away and stiffened.

Education of a Grouse and Woodcock Dog

In a few weeks Bliss made a hundred such points in bird cover and on each I handled her as I would on live birds, always "flushing" the wing while I made her *stay* steady at flush. Scent pointing a wing should be done while the dog is young, for by seven months he is past such make-believe. Planting the wing strategically, you teach the puppy to search the birdy-looking places; by occasionally hiding it above ground you encourage his working with a high head. It is a fine pre-bird introduction to pointing in summer before bird work is possible.

I discovered I am not the first man to train a dog on scent pointing without live birds. Richard Blome's 1686 edition of *The Gentleman's Recreation* described training land spaniels to "couch" and lie close to the ground, remaining still while a net was dragged over them, and to associate the crouching position with the scent of partridge, which it was suggested could be duplicated "by boiled bullock's liver."

Bliss's quartering lessons began about the same time as wing pointing, when she was developed enough to run well. An older dog will teach a pup more about ranging than you can but control must be taught by you. If worked alone he may be timid at first. Work him in open fields where you can see each other, and limit early sessions to fifteen minutes to keep him eager. If he's bred right, he'll soon be out there hunting, although he may not know for exactly what.

This period, when he is not yet absorbed in birds, is the time to teach whistle signals. To some men a whistle is for calling a dog in; to the knowledgeable dog man the whistle is his means of communicating. Ideally, he works his dog the way a skillful dry-fly man works the fly—far enough ahead so the quarry doesn't see the man, who enters the picture only after the bird is pinned. Until you learn this, you will not get the utmost from your dog.

After Bliss acquired keenness for her runs, I made her *stay* each time we started out. With upraised hand, I walked a few steps in front and stopped, my hand still aloft. Holding her a few seconds, I sent her on with *all right, go on* and a wave of my hand accompanied by two blasts on the whistle. Two blasts mean *go on*, one blast means *come here*. At first, I used them only when she was doing the appropriate thing—calling her to me in the field and giving one blast as she was running toward me; sending her out verbally and blowing two blasts as she was going away. I always start my dogs, training or hunting, with the *stay* and *go on* drill and the two-blast whistle. If you're consistent you can bring your dog to you or send him farther with whistle signals alone. An additional way to teach the *come here* whistle is to make the dog *stay*, then walk about ten yards from him and put his food down, keeping him in place until you blow one blast to bring him to you, at first accompanying it with *come here*. This one-blast whistle is valuable in early retrieving lessons to bring the dog to you with the bird.

The young dog must learn a third, the turning signal, which is a variation of the one-blast. While he is running, blow a long blast whipped up at the end and, as he looks toward you, wave him in the direction you want him to go and take a few steps in that direction. Your dog sees you from a distance as a silhouette, so you must wave your arm above your head or at one side.

When he has learned these signals—not before—take him to a narrow fenced field. Send him across and, as he goes, move in the opposite direction at a rapid pace. As he approaches the far fence, blow the turning signal and wave him across toward you. Repeat your maneuver as he is tacking toward your side, and by the time he reaches one side, you are on the other, turning and waving him across. The dog's course will fall naturally into a zigzag pattern down the field, with you walking down the middle. At first you may have to turn him with a long cord, but he will finally respond to the whistle and quartering will become habit, replacing wasted effort running straight out and back. This teaches the dog to turn at the end of his casts, something the bolter does not do. The average man has an average dog because he will not take the trouble to teach quartering.

You don't insist upon mechanical quartering in cover as long as the dog hunts efficiently—he should pass up unlikely areas and go directly to birdy spots—but quartering under control is the way to get him back in form when he becomes careless or moves too wide. Walk along a woods road and make him quarter to each side, keeping him within fifty yards to left and right but moving just as fast as if he were running wild ahead. Without basic training you have no way to make him do this. In cover, use the whistle sparingly, your voice even less. The dog learns to keep you located after each cast. As long as he checks with you, let him do the hunting. The desire to obey can be instilled when the dog is young. When you see a dog running wild, ignoring his owner's commands, you can be nearly certain he has had no early obedience lessons. Response of young dogs to obedience training is uniform; later, in pointing and field work, they respond individually according to their personalities.

We speak of grouse and woodcock dogs as if they were the same, the birds being found in overlapping terrain. Good grouse dogs will handle woodcock, although a few balk at retrieving them, but many competent youngsters able to pin 'cock will push a grouse out before they learn to point from a distance. In comparison with grouse, woodcock are naïve.

If I could prescribe a single thing to make a grouse dog it would be an abundance of grouse. Lacking that, we used to start our puppies on late-summer pheasants in the lowlands, but open fields encourage ranging too wide and pheasants condition a dog to their strong scent, which makes him try to get too close to grouse. I had consecrated Bliss to be a grouse dog and, since single quail make a good substitute for grouse, in September, when she was eight months old, I started her on training quail with a recall pen.

I flew out several quail in a plantation of young spruce with clearings grown to briars, then brought Bliss and let her run off her edge in an area away from the birds, finally casting her toward them. As she approached where one had landed I snapped a short check cord on her and let her work into the wind. She hit scent, wheeled and pointed. I began stroking her from her head to the tip of her tail, starting with the other hand before the first hand left her. Although I held the end of the cord, I needn't have. Bliss was in a trance.

With hot scent in her face, I lifted her by her tail and let her drop, setting her hind parts first to one side, then the other. I pushed against her haunches as if to shove her into the bird. This is important—dogs resist pressure with pressure in the opposite direction. Each time I increased my pressure, Bliss set back more firmly. All the while I soothed her with *stay* and stepped back, holding the slack cord while Kay flushed the quail. It buzzed out like a wild bird and Bliss came up against the check cord and got a stern *no*. I followed this with encouragement and patting—actually, I kissed her—and released her. Circling in frenzy, she ran into another quail without realizing what was happening, chasing it into adjoining

The Dogs

cover. Trying to stop her would have been useless. Instead of scolding her when she returned I took her to the site of the flush and made her *stay* until ordered on.

The youngster should be made to feel he is working birds on his own; the cord is only to prevent his diving in and catching the bird. The sooner he can be worked free, the better. Some trainers advise letting the young dog chase birds until he learns he can't catch them, suggesting he will then point as a natural response. I've seen eight-year-old dogs still trying to catch the bird.

There is middle ground between the uncontrolled dog and the dog that performs without initiative. If your dog points without spirit, you've probably been cautioning him too much. Repeated admonitions of *steady* as you walk in on a point make the dog uncertain and reveal your lack of confidence in him. When he moves up, instead of stopping him, drive him on with two blasts of the whistle, letting him decide when he is close enough. If he flushes, scold him as if he had bumped on his own. You'll soon see more fire in his points and have a stancher dog when he makes the decisions.

Talking distracts dogs while handling birds and the voice often flushes grouse—even some woodcock—far ahead. I give a whistle like the *kree* of a hawk to let my dog know I see him pointing, training him to hold for this *kree* signal by using it with *stay* at feeding time.

Preventing a break on point before it happens is better than trying to stop a young dog in the explosion of a flush. Walking in from the side or front will make the bird lie tighter and reassure the dog because he has you in view. Raise your hand and face him, actually willing him to *stay* without speaking the word. After Bliss began to hold her points well, I fired .32 or .38 blanks in the air as I flushed the bird.

The young dog must learn to honor the point of a brace mate. For this I worked Bliss with Dixie—youngsters have respect for seniority. When Dixie pointed I swung Bliss toward her and stood as if backing the point myself. When she stopped, I used no command other than one *kree* whistle or *stay*, then went to her and handled her as on point. If the youngster fails to stop on his own or at your subsequent command, lead him to the pointing dog and handle him.

The *stay* drill at meals demonstrates what can be achieved by regular work. The way to develop stanch pointing—productives or backpoints—is by more pointing, and training quail provide this. I release my birds in different types of grouse cover, the only limitation being that the birds can return to the recall pen.

I don't object if the young dog chases at flush during his first season, but if he breaks point to put the bird out he must be corrected. A stiff jerk on a check cord as he dives in might seem the direct treatment. However, the most effective cure is to handle him on point, lift him by the tail and scruff of the neck and drop him back into place, repeat and drop him one step closer to the quail. Continue until you drop him right onto the bird and you'll find he will hold his position even if the bird flushes in his face. This procedure not only makes the dog steady to wing but is one of the best ways to develop intensity and stanchness.

Some dogs move in and flush the bird before the gunner even reaches them. To correct this, lead the dog to a planted quail, handle on point, then back off, leaving him pointing. Approach again, handle him and back off. Each time you approach, press him forward. This will eventually make him set back as you approach, rather than move in. Convenient as it might seem, the dog should never be sent in to flush a bird for you.

Correcting weaknesses should be by positive measures like these, not negative punishment. Some solutions you will devise when you come to understand how your dog thinks; some you will never discover though you know how the dog should perform. When you hit this snag, rest him from the work in which the fault occurs and the place where it most often happens and concentrate on things he does well. Repeated punishment can establish the fault rather than erase it. When he is worked on the things he does well, the flaw frequently diminishes in a smooth functioning of the whole. This takes time and is one reason training should begin considerably before the shooting season. Training should continue without lag, keeping pace with the dog's developing capabilities, which must be channeled. These daily "events" bring you and your dog to a marvelously close understanding, and only then do the two of you function on a high level.

It is said that a dog's memory is short in some ways associated with training. I think he is more nearly single-minded than short on memory when he ignores a command and continues what he is doing. Our setters have shown amazing capacity to remember. When we recently took Dixie to a distant training ground we hadn't visited for six years she began pacing the station wagon and peering out when we were still a mile away. She also does this, whining eagerly, each year as we approach the Canaan Valley woodcock flats where she had her first shooting on 'cock twelve seasons ago. I once gave Shadows a lecture for moving too wide. My words conveyed meaning I didn't intend for he followed at heel the rest of the hunt. Worse, he could not be persuaded to hunt that covert for years, though he did well elsewhere, and I had to leave him in the station wagon when I gunned there.

Early in Bliss's first October we took her to the Canaan Valley for two days to train. After her work on quail I was prepared for a brilliant performance on woodcock. Instead, she ran wild, flushing and chasing. Back home I rested her a day, then resumed work on training quail, where she did as beautifully as ever. We returned to the woodcock coverts and again she ran wild when hunted solo. But when hunted in brace with Dixie she adapted to Dixie's nice range and made three productives and a backpoint. While I prefer to start a young dog alone, occasionally the example of a good older dog is better than anything you can do.

Woodcock provide good pre-grouse education; the dog's natural range on 'cock permits control, there is action on birds that don't play tricks, and the number of kills hastens his maturing. Woodcock, like quail, lie tight enough to permit you to handle your dog on point as grouse almost never do. Handling him on several points on wild birds will do more to make him stanch than dozens of points if he is allowed to break and put the bird up.

One drawback is the dog's tendency to work woodcock with a low head. The whitewash and the bird's manner of lying almost under the dog's nose tempts him to search with his head down, which leads to roading into birds and must be discouraged if it becomes extreme. Driving him on with the two-blast whistle, running at him with *go on!* and clapping, or even firing a shot in the air will get the dog's head up to look around. If he persists in ground-trailing, pull him off the scent and rush him ahead full gallop. If this causes him to flush, he will associate birds with your sending him on and will be more likely to reach to find scent ahead, rather than under him.

Education of a Grouse and Woodcock Dog

Excessive cautioning makes a dog potter, which is what ground-trailing amounts to. There is a difference between the dog that works woodcock running with head extended, drawing in the layer of scent just above the ground, and the dog that trails with his nose to the ground. The former is winding, the latter is roading and may not detect body scent in time to stop before flushing. If he continues to road and you hope to make a grouse dog of him, take him off woodcock before the habit becomes fixed.

I shot the first woodcock of the season over Bliss's point and another, that day, over a point by Dixie backed by Bliss. To encourage stanchness I passed up shots at any birds she bumped, no matter how accidentally, to convince her that results came only when she pointed and held. This is a sacrifice most men will not make for their dog's career, but on woodcock, with abundant chances for points, it's not hard to do and I have found it wonderfully effective.

I have known few pleasures greater than shooting 'cock over Dixie and her daughter Bliss, a handsome brace of snow beltons, each with her individually pitched bell. As lightly ticked as gyrfalcons, they were visible in dense cover on the dullest day, both infallibly stanch, both would backpoint loyally. Often I would be alerted by both bells going silent, push my way into cover, to see the backing dog first and by that means, which is the purpose of backpointing, locate the other dog pinning the 'cock for me to take the shot. If after all this I missed the bird, it mattered little, for I had bred them and generations before them and had seen them grow under my hands into this superb thing—a brace of finished woodcock dogs. Small wonder that, with them, I passed up all shots that weren't over points.

Bliss went on to achieve the ultimate. For every ten woodcock a young dog points, he may get not one chance to point a grouse—the grouse see to that—but Bliss became one of those rare grouse dogs who seem to create their opportunities. I hid the first few grouse I shot and let her find and point the dead birds, an important experience for a young dog. She had proved high-headed on 'cock, an asset that contributed to the number of productives she made on grouse her first season. To keep her stanch, I had omitted retrieving lessons, but late in the year after observing the other dogs she began retrieving grouse like a veteran.

The Dogs

As you bring your grouse and woodcock dog closer to the finished stage, you face new situations. Few grouse hunters want their dogs steady to shot, for reaching a fallen grouse quickly often means the difference between a retrieve and a lost cripple. Experience has led your dog to expect you to hit when you shoot. Accept his taking a few steps when the bird flushes as a compliment to your shooting even when you don't fire. His move may be a clue as to what direction the bird went when you haven't seen the flush. However, the dog must not be permitted to dash after the bird and chase. When he does, return him to where he should have stopped and make him hold with *stay*. Do the same any time he chases a bumped bird. This teaches him to stop at flush. Accidental bumps can happen with the best dogs but the dog should stop, regardless of the circumstance.

If breaking at wing and chasing becomes a problem, you can make a dog steadier after his second season by working him once more on training quail. During training, handlers often put up birds in front of a point with a flushing whip. The appearance and action of the whip exerts restraint on the dog and I consider it more effective than pulling him back at flush with a check cord. But don't expect perfection if you are going to require your gun dog to go to fallen birds promptly after the shot.

Dogs are more inclined to false-point when working ruffed grouse than on any other birds except pheasants. On pheasants it is caused by the bird's running ahead of the point; on grouse it is because of the delicate balance of judgment required. The dog wants to move from foot scent to body scent, yet knows that one step too far may flush the grouse. If you caution him when you see him start on after hitting scent, you may be encouraging his pointing foot scent. Learn to distinguish between your dog's true and false points by his intensity and tail action. If he is too relaxed or grinning or if the tail is flagging—even the tip—drive him on with the two-blast whistle, preferably before you approach. Some dogs false-point from a desire to show off, having been praised for pointing when they had no bird. If it looks real, you must move in and honor his effort no matter how improbable the place or how difficult the terrain, but insist that he point positively. Top grouse dogs occasionally point a rabbit out of eagerness not to pass up a grouse. The dog should be shamed but not punished for this.

Education of a Grouse and Woodcock Dog

Some men aspire to make doubles on grouse. For me, one grouse cleanly shot over a stunning point by my dog transcends any double. Style on point is something I value above everything, worth sacrificing a few shots in the dog's early stages. That glorious fire must be preserved, not by using force to make him stanch but by encouraging the dog to make the decisions when pointing.

In his second year the youngster becomes bolder and begins ranging out of control. Quail dogs can hold their birds two hundred yards ahead of a gunner on foot; a good pheasant dog will search nearly that wide, but keeping a shifty cock bird pinned until the gunner walks that far is difficult. Woodcock cover can swallow a dog at twenty-five yards, but to limit him to that range is to locate few birds you wouldn't walk up. The greatest difference of opinion as to range concerns the grouse dog, the commonest standard being "close." A uniformly close grouse dog is like a cylinder-bored gun—inadequate in big country. The young dog should work close enough for the gunner to prevent his establishing faults but the finished dog need not be under constant surveillance. Novices want their dogs within shooting range at all times, treating them as flushing dogs. Sophisticated gunners prefer a grouse dog that searches wide, the limit being that the dog be stanch and that his points may be reached comfortably. The gunner who owns such a dog, giving him shots at grouse a closer dog would not have found, glows with a glory few men know.

It is important to understand when a young dog is skillful enough to be permitted to move wide. This is not to be confused with racing for the horizon. In her second season Bliss increased her range, but when I put a bell on her I found she was only hidden by cover or the shoulder of a hill much of the time I had thought she was too far out. For this reason, a bell is as important on a grouse dog as on a woodcock dog. Most significantly, Bliss was pointing more grouse out ahead than close to me—birds that lay tighter than those pointed nearby.

Grouse often freeze before a dog alone when they would have flushed at the additional sight and sound of a man. With the gunner moving close behind the dog, the grouse has two threats to watch and becomes nervous. With no man in sight, the bird's attention is focused on the quartering dog, and though the point alerts it, the prolonged immobility of the dog deludes it into a sense of confidence in its concealment. Hypnotized by the dog, the bird reacts less to the gunner's subsequent approach than when dog and man come into view together.

Once I grasped this and let Bliss set her range, she gave me magnificent shooting. When I didn't hear her bell I would blow one blast on the whistle, knowing nothing would budge her if she was on point. If she didn't show, I'd go toward where I last heard her bell and nearly always find her pointing. Like Ruff, Bliss did more than find grouse; she presented me with shots. To me, Bliss, too beautiful for time to spoil, was everything her name implied.

And now there is Briar—double great-grandson of Ruff, fifth-generation Old Hemlock—with his extraordinary nose and style and pointing instinct and his special problems, each one a challenge. You are never through training a grouse dog. Some aspects of performance can always be honed to further refinement, and we who work with and love these prima donnas cannot, if we are honest, say we know all the answers. C. B. Whitford, who trained and handled Gladstone around 1880, had an axiom: "Anticipate a fault and don't let it happen." Bolting, ground-trailing, lack of stanchness, rough-mouthed retrieving, gun-shyness, blinking could usually have been averted by early basic training and close understanding between the dog and his man. Acquaintance during a brief hunting season, when for the remainder of the year the two see each other only through a kennel fence at feeding time, just isn't enough.

Grouse and woodcock dogs are not for every man. I've never been able to separate the composite aroma of a favorite shooting coat and determine whether it is blood and feathers, gun oil, or dog drool that makes it smell so good. Upland shooting is like that, its elements are inseparable. But, if one is more essential, for me it is the dogs.

PART SIX

Mixed Bag

❦ / To hear, "Hen left, hare right, cock over,"
at woodside, when the leaves are brown.

—John Masefield, *Reynard the Fox*

Shooting Flying

> ❦ / Look at but one, with both your eyes;
> Then, elevate the tube with care,
> Still gazing on the bird in air;
> Follow it not along the sky,
> To take a formal aim, but try
> To draw the trigger just as you
> At the gun's end the object view.
> Nine times in ten the gun is right
> At first, obeying well the sight;
> But if you look, and look again,
> And doubt, and waver, it is plain
> Your hand has ev'ry chance to be
> Betrayed by such uncertainty.
>
> —ALARIC ALEXANDER WATTS, *Shooting Flying*
> (1797–1864)

I THINK OLD ALARIC SHOT very much as I do—an instinctive mount-and-overtake after focusing on the bird, though I can't remember any day when my gun was right "nine times in ten." But that doesn't matter if I can be in woodcock and grouse coverts on autumn afternoons.

The unskilled shooter, by crippling, often kills more birds than the good shot without knowing it. This is not something to laugh off, like poor card sense or a tin ear for music. If you are going to shoot, you have a sporting responsibility to shoot well—not to kill more but to kill more cleanly.

The discouraging thing about shooting problems is that we often don't know the reason for them. In its simplest form, wing shooting consists of looking with your eyes, your brain and your gun, and doing it with such concentration you scarcely hear the gun go off. (All shooters know how loud the gun sounds when they miss.) Most of us have normal eyes, properly corrected, and normal

Mixed Bag

nervous systems. If you are doing the right things and still missing, it may be the gun that is at fault.

A young friend brought a new gun to show me and, with it, his troubles. Pattern sheets revealed that he was shooting seven inches high at sixteen yards. The prescription was to get a new gun or have this one restocked. Being a trader at heart, he chose the former. After several deals he got a gun that fit approximately, but a good trade was too tempting and he let it go. The trader is not likely to make a good shot because he thinks in terms of guns, not fit. This is also true of the collector unless all of his guns are fitted identically. With a gun that fits, the one-gun man will usually be the better shot.

Of the many characteristics of a gun—gauge, balance, choke—it is the stock that determines how your gun does your looking for you. Focus on a spot on the far wall and, without taking your eyes from it, mount your gun. You should be exactly on it and seeing the forward third of your gun rib. If you see more of the rib, the stock is too straight and you would shoot high; if less, the stock has too much drop and you would shoot low. If your gun is a double, cut a small triangle of thin paper and close the breech on it with the point up. When you mount, if the paper "rear sight" is not aligned with the bead and the target, you need cast-off or, less probably, cast-on.

A dozen pattern sheets with a one-inch bull's-eye shot at exactly sixteen yards from the shooter's eye, not the gun muzzle, will give an accurate diagnosis of gun fit. Mount and fire as on an eye-level straightaway bird. Consistent deviation off-center will magnify error in stock fit sixteen times. Examples:

$$4 \text{ inches below target: } 4/16 \text{ inch too much drop.}$$
$$4 \text{ inches above target: } 4/16 \text{ inch too little drop.}$$
$$4 \text{ inches left of target: need for } 4/16\text{-inch cast-off.}$$

This test is for a gun that shoots where you look, which is the way I want my guns. Some guns are made to shoot high, with built-in lead for rising birds and high incomers, requiring allowances for all other types of flushes.

Cast-off is lateral stock bend away from the shooter's face, cast-on is toward the face and rarely needed. Cast-off is common on English stocks but usually absent on American guns. A broad-shouldered man mounts his gun well out on his shoulder and, with

Shooting Flying

no cast-off, finds himself looking down the left side of the rib, throwing the pattern left of where he is pointing. Measured at the heel as deviation from the projected center line of the rib, cast-off should be worked into the stock until the shooter looks directly down the rib every time he mounts. Like minor alterations in drop, it can be achieved by a gunsmith using hot oil and pressure to bend the stock, or by dressing down the cheek surface of the stock.

Using this test, I obtained a splendid stock fit on my old Fox. Indicated alterations couldn't be worked into the existing stock without difficulty, so I had a Pennsylvania gunsmith custom-build a stock to my specifications. It is essential to know what you need, for even reputable gunsmiths tend to pigeonhole gunners too generally. At the "rough" tryout stage—an important step—I discovered that the stock had been made nearly $3/8$ inch shorter than I had ordered, on the principle that all men of a given height take gunstocks of a given length. Once this error was corrected, the finished stock—a lovely piece of Pennsylvania walnut—was perfection.

Before making any alterations, be sure that deviations in pattern placement are not caused by improper mounting. If the stock butt is seated on the arm instead of into the shoulder, the pattern will be thrown off laterally and possibly too high. If the head is held too erect, the stock will appear too straight; if the gun is cheeked too deeply the test will indicate too much drop. Shooting low can be caused by anticipating recoil and leaning into the shot, dipping the muzzle; or the gun may be muzzle-heavy. A well-balanced gun has its center of gravity near the breech between the hands. Shooting with the head too far back—common in boys and women from fear of recoil—will lower the position of the eye due to slant of comb toward the rear and indicate too much drop. For fast wing shooting in cover, the gun should come up to the shooter's eye with little ducking or compensating to the stock.

The stock length, measured from the forward trigger to the center of the butt, should not be so long that the butt catches on the clothing in mounting or so short that the thumb is jammed into the nose by recoil. General opinion is that it should be on the short for fast mounting but I think most men would shoot better with a longer stock. My stocks are $14 7/8$ inches, considered long.

Any idiosyncrasy that bolsters shooting confidence is worth trying, as long as it has no ill effects on accuracy of mounting. I once thought it helped to shoot with an almost straight left arm, grasping the barrels forward of the fore-end. Some men approach a pointing dog with gun held at "present-arms" or crosswise with arms extended.

A mount is faulty if it pulls the butt back into the shoulder with a jolt, jarring it off target or varying the position of the butt each time. The smoothest and most consistent mount is to start with the stock under the arm, pressed against the rib cage, "facing the shot" with the gun straight out in front. Slide the stock butt up to the shoulder, almost touching your coat, which seats it in the same place every time. This must be practiced until it becomes reflex.

Pointing a shotgun across the chest with one shoulder and foot advanced is a bad habit boys learn from rifle shooting. It allows a long swing in one direction only, locking the gunner up if he has to swing the other direction. In wing shooting it is important to face the shot, then mount.

Stock drop is interpreted both as drop at comb and drop at heel. The latter should put the butt comfortably into the shoulder with neither the heel nor the toe as point of contact. Drop at comb means little because no part of the shooter touches the forward end of the comb where the measurement is taken. The most neglected and most critical dimension of stock fit is drop at cheek point, which governs the relation of the master eye to the barrel. Cheek point is actually an area about two and a quarter inches along the comb, as you will discover if you smear your cheek with shaving cream and mount your gun. Mark the fore and aft extent of the imprint with rubber bands around the stock and repeat a few times to get an average. The relation of cheek to stock is so delicate that clenching the teeth will bulge the jaw and push the face away enough to throw the pattern off-target. My stocks are fitted for me to shoot with my mouth ajar—in part, compensating for my amazement at a grouse's flight.

To measure drop, lay the gun upside down on its rib on a flat surface with barrels resting on the bead to give an accurate line through the bead. Inserting tapered cardboards on edge between the stock and the table surface will show the drop at various points.

If you belong to the breed that feels nothing is a gun unless it is a double, the most gratifying solution to a gun problem may be to have a good old double altered to your specifications. A new stock is usually preferable, but moderate alterations in drop can be made

Shooting Flying

on the existing stock by working the wood down or by building it up with inlay. Shortening by amputation or lengthening by adding a filler and/or a recoil pad is simple, but pitch at heel should be considered here. When extreme, this dimension may cause the gun to shoot either high or low. Moderate variation in pitch isn't noticeable because the butt seldom makes complete contact with the shoulder. However, if you are duplicating the dimensions of a gun that fits you, the pitch should be kept the same.

With a gun made to fit you like prescription glasses, all you have to do is learn where you should look. Overconsciousness of lead has made more poor shots than any other factor next to improper gun fit. You certainly can't hit a moving target by shooting directly at it unless it is going straightaway, but say "lead" to a thoughtful man and he begins memorizing varying leads for varying angles—disastrous to shooting in thick cover.

Since I began in my early teens, I have learned to shoot about every way it is possible to shoot wrong. My father's rule to "lead a crossing quail about a gun-length" worked on birds that were kind enough to cross, but I found myself poking at a spot ahead of birds, hitting some and missing many more. Judging lead at varying angles is for computers. One day I shot a long way ahead of a duck taking off low and saw my pellets churn the water ten feet behind it. I doubled my lead on the second shot and dropped it. A long lead is well enough over open water but how do you manage it in thick cover? When I asked other gunners they answered, "I pull right on the bird and if I see it I hit it," or, "I pull as I swing past its head." The better shots shrugged and said, "I can't tell you how, it just happens."

My first intelligent step was to learn to shoot with both eyes open. If your master eye is on the wrong side, you have to close it and let the other eye take over, but shooting with one eye almost eliminates depth perception, necessary for judging range. The next step was to abandon the gun-length-ahead method. Shooting at a spot in front of the bird is called spot shooting when it is done from stationary barrels. I increased my hits by learning to hold on a sustained lead rather than shoot at the spot ahead. Bringing the gun up in front of a crossing bird, I kept the muzzle swinging at the same speed as the bird, which is called "pointing out." When I shot without slowing the barrels, I usually hit, but too frequently I stopped them. The sustained lead has the advantage of more accurate alignment with the bird's line of flight than the spot shot and does not require ten feet or more of space to lead the bird. But, like spot shooting, it calls for definite concepts of proper lead for different angles and I approached each day's shooting with memorized data, which drained from my brain in the excitement of a flush.

Then after twenty-seven years of shooting my old Fox, I tested it and discovered that it didn't fit me. With a new stock, the gun seemed to mount itself and become the part of me I looked with. When I checked it on clays I found I did best if I focused on the sailing target before I even started to mount, then mounted and overtook it, firing as I passed through. Catching up with the bird did something for my timing and I could forget about conscious lead. When I watch someone else do it, the cycle is completed so swiftly it appears to be a spot shot. But it has the advantage of aligning with the bird's flight in the overtake, requiring little or no lead.

That grouse season I made shots I had never before brought off successfully. I forced myself to forget about calculated lead and approached all shots as something to deal with as they came up, not as memorized solutions. Most important, I made myself see the bird clearly before I mounted the gun, and not take my eyes off it until I had overtaken and hit it. If I missed, it was usually because I had focused on my gun barrels. Some men doubt that you can point with your gun barrels and still not see them. I use a large white bead but I look through it, not at it, the way you look down at the floor without seeing your nose. If you shoot with one eye closed, the bead becomes solid and difficult to ignore.

Perfect shooting occurs only on the trap or skeet range, not on birds. In thick cover, some shots have to be taken quickly or not at all and this often accounts for misses. Snap shooting at the sound of a flush, aside from endangering a companion or a dog, is responsible for a lot of bad shooting. Instinctive shooting is not banging away at a blur. It is essential both to *see* the bird and to *think* the hit. Total concentration on the moving bird ties in with the responses of the brain the way concentration focuses the force of a blow in karate. Focusing can be as rapid as your optical response, although an extra split-second assures that you are seeing the bird clearly *before* mounting. Once the mount-and-overtake is begun,

Shooting Flying

it is done in one smooth rapid motion and the trigger pulled with no dwell or riding-out the bird. The gun muzzle is ahead of the bird by the time the gun discharges and the entire sequence from beginning of focus until you hit the bird is completed in 1½ or 2 seconds—no longer than it takes some men to stab at a bird and miss.

On quartering shots, by firing as you go through, the speed of the overtake accounts for the proper lead. On crossing birds, horizontal or rising, I find it effective to pull a little after I am through the bird but without estimating how much. Just being ahead seems to be enough, the speed of the bird affecting the swing. On slightly angling birds—what I call "away-left" or "away-right"—I fire on them with a sense of going *with* the bird and, as Alaric Watts put it: "draw the trigger just as you at the gun's end the object view." I have hit these by spot-shooting them, holding to one side, but I usually wing them on that side instead of centering. On truly straightaway birds I spot-shoot right on them. On rising going-away birds you can spot-shoot just above or swing up-through but the swing must be fast.

The important thing about swinging is to do it, not solely with the head and arms, but with the entire torso and hips as a unit with the head and gun, beginning at the ankles. (A common fault when swinging through a crossing bird is to "scoop out" or dip under the bird, shooting below it. Dry practice will correct this.) With the left thumb extended along the barrels as part of the pointing left arm, you mount, releasing the safety on the way up, and overtake the bird like swinging at a rolling polo ball. The trigger is pulled quickly and decisively, not squeezed. If you hesitate, the "ball will roll away from you" and you will shoot behind. Second-barrel shots can be taken in this way with the gun already at the shoulder, but they are normally a matter of correcting after a miss and are usually "pointed-out."

Making a fetish of lightweight bird guns is not always conducive to good wing shooting. For all a light gun's fast handling in cover, pointing it can be like pointing a walking stick—wobbly compared with the heavier gun. The heavier gun comes up solidly to the shoulder and stays there, and, once the swing is started, overtakes and follows through with a smoother sweep. The lightweight gun snaps rapidly into the shoulder but with a tendency to bounce, frequently swinging past the bird with a jerky motion. I don't recommend shooting birds with a trap gun but I hit grouse as well with my 7¾-pound Fox as with my just-under 6½-pound Purdey.

You hear about good shots with abnormally fast reactions. There would be more good shots if reactions were delayed until the bird was clearly seen before mounting, not snapped at as a sound of wings. Once the eyes are locked on the bird, the overtake-and-pull is properly a fast reflex in the sense of a disciplined response and done by feel, not calculation. Eye exercises stressing rapid change in focal depth and pointing with the extended left arm will improve your shooting, as will gun-mounting practice to develop muscle control and gun feel.

Probably nothing can destroy a man's ego more than trying to shoot grouse. In spite of this, I believe, with the exception of novices, every grouse gunner is secretly convinced he is a good shot, no matter what he may profess. At one time I hesitated to shoot any birds except grouse, feeling specialization would help my shooting, but when I began shooting woodcock and pheasants I found my shooting on grouse improved. Timing on these three birds is different but the focus-and-mount principle is the same. A woodcock is the most variable, sometimes floating, at other times taking off with the velocity of a grouse, especially on late, cloudy afternoons when 'cock are thought to see better. But even with its smaller size, my shooting averages indicate it is easier for me to focus on a woodcock than on a grouse.

Only occasionally does a woodcock climb gradually. Normally it either jump-flushes vertically and levels or it takes off low and horizontally, a difficult shot. In thick cover and in late afternoon it seems to get out of sight quickly and the gunner snatches at the bird too close for a decent pattern. As a result, woodcock are usually either hit too hard or missed too hard. Since a large number of shots at 'cock are taken at 12 to 15 yards or not at all, a "cylinder" 30 percent choke delivering a 26-inch killing circle at 15 yards (vs. the 20-inch circle of an "improved cylinder") would make an excellent woodcock gun and tear up fewer birds.

Any trouble I have with pheasants comes from having too much time to think. They appear to fly so slowly, look so damned big, and —worst of all—I feel down deep that I should never miss one. This isn't so, nor does it turn out that way. But if I can visualize a flying pheasant as a clay target sailing along—neither very fast nor very slow—I can, by concentrating on the bird and firing as I overtake and go through it, manage the desired result.

Never-miss grouse shooters are heard, not seen. Something implicit in the cover and in the flight of a grouse makes it impossible for a man to hit every time. Keeping shooting averages is not appealing to the majority of gunners, but those who do it learn about their shooting. To say you dropped two out of three birds shot at implies 66 percent shooting—true, if you used only three shells to do it. Dropping one bird with the second barrel, missing the next both barrels, and hitting the next with one shot is shooting two out of three birds shot at, but taking five shells for two hits—a good average on grouse but only 40 percent shooting.

High averages on only a few birds are not usually representative. Improbable shots that may feather birds should not be tried but, taking all sporting shots over a long season, a grouse shooter seldom averages in the top half. My grouse shooting averages since 1932 have been low at times, reflecting my trying too hard in years of grouse scarcity, in others just poor shooting. When they are 33 percent—one bird for three shells—I feel I am doing well; several 40 percent plus seasons have been above what I expect, and one average I'm not going to quote was something I'm still trying to account for. A factor was a large number of grouse that year, which improves anyone's shooting; another was my restocked Fox, which with 3 dram 1⅛ ounce No. 8 loads patterns an open improved cylinder in the right barrel, 70 percent in the left—a beautiful grouse gun in spite of its 28-inch barrels and 7¾-pound weight.

It is the beginner who thinks he has to have a stick of dynamite behind a load of coarse shot. Besides giving you flinch, in a lightweight gun a heavy load can jar your finger onto the rear trigger, causing a double discharge. Three drams with 1⅛ ounces of shot is a good grouse load and I used No. 8's for years. This is available for 12, 16 or 20 gauge. You don't need 461 pellets to kill a grouse but you often need almost that many to reach through dense cover, for all the shot doesn't arrive simultaneously. On several late-winter grouse that were not killed cleanly in spite of multiple pellet hits, the No. 8 shot was just beneath the skin or barely into the muscle—inadequate penetration through grouse plumage at its densest in

Mixed Bag

January and February. Changing to No. 7½ for normal grouse shooting and going to No. 6 in late December, I find the increased velocity of heavier shot more effective.

Too much No. 9 shot will mince a woodcock at close range. I use 1 ounce of No. 8's and still occasionally shred a 'cock. The classic bobwhite shot size is No. 8 or No. 9. There is difference of opinion as to pheasants, but I prefer No. 6.

More shot in front of a given load of powder will tighten the pattern in terms of percentages; less shot will spread wider. Pattern variation can be achieved by varying the load of powder behind a given load of shot—less powder tightens the pattern. Until you pattern your gun you can't know how it handles different loads, for no two guns with a label such as "improved cylinder" throw the same spread with the same shell. The accurate way to designate choke is by percentage. In all bores larger than the .410 (36-gauge), the percentage of pellets is measured in a 30-inch circle at 40 yards and the spread of shot is approximately the same for a given percentage, regardless of gauge. The notion that a 50 percent choke 20-gauge requires more skillful shooting than a 50 percent 12-gauge is nonsense; the pattern spread is the same except that the pattern is thinner with the standard 20-gauge loads, which can be overcome by using heavier loads.

My Purdey 12-gauge has two pairs of barrels, one originally bored 72%/76%, which I had opened for woodcock to pattern 50%/60% with 3 dram 1 ounce No. 8 without plastic sleeve. That "50 percent" barrel throws a plus 70 percent pattern with 3 dram 1⅛ ounce No. 8 *with* plastic sleeve. This is more extreme than most, but every gun throws a tighter pattern with plastic shot sleeves. Confronted with shells loaded almost exclusively with plastic sleeves, the gunner now finds himself shooting a gun with a pattern about 10 percent tighter than when he ordered it. This may be fine for trap and waterfowl gunners but it is disconcerting to the rest of us. The plastic sleeve is useful to tighten a "modified" choke to "full" for long shots but for right-barrel shots the grouse and woodcock gunner must either go to handloads without shot sleeves or have the choke opened.

The old-time southwest Pennsylvania grouse hunters I knew, weather-tanned and long of tooth, never considered an improved cylinder choke. Market hunters weren't above sawing all the choke off their barrels but the sportsmen invariably shot "modified and full," and 28-inch and 30-inch barrels were as much a part of them as canvas leggings. This was also true of the early grouse hunters in New England, as is shown in William Fosters's drawings in his *New England Grouse Shooting*. They valued a gun that would reach out, as did the men in my area. Charlie Seaton, a gentleman shooter who owned the old Wiggins Place, would, according to an uncle of mine, "give you the itch while he let a 'pheasant' top out over the trees before he shot it." With many more grouse, those men could pick their shots. Today, taking shots as they come, the fast skeet-field swing with a short improved cylinder barrel is the best way to shoot grouse.

Instead of the conventional "improved and modified," I consider the ideal grouse gun one that is choked 50 percent and 70 percent, handling close flushes with the right barrel and long over-the-tree flights with the left. I have this combination in my Fox and Purdey, but it required additional opening of one of the Purdey right barrels to deliver 50 percent patterns with plastic sleeve loads. The size of the killing circle at 20 and even 15 yards is far more important than percentage patterns at 40 yards. In my grouse barrels, the right delivers a 20-inch circle at 15 yards, 26 inches at 20 yards, but it requires particular loads to do this.

Testing my guns with various loads, I discovered that they threw tighter patterns at 40 yards with plastic sleeves but at 20 yards had a curious way of throwing as large or larger circles with plastic shot sleeve loads than with loads without shot sleeves. With each gun performing individually with different loads, it is important to learn your gun's eccentricities by patterning it—unless you are hitting beautifully, in which case don't do anything to break the spell.

The left barrel is seldom used in woodcock shooting, but in grouse and pheasant shooting learning to judge range and disciplining yourself to use a 70-percent left barrel selectively can produce gratifying results, not only for distant crossing shots but also for the bird that flushes going-away at 25 yards. The latter is soon out of range for an improved cylinder but shooters rarely think to take it as a left-barrel shot. No man can switch a selective single trigger in time, and for this reason I prefer two triggers on a double. The single trigger offers no advantage in speed and prevents selective use of the left barrel.

In spite of what you may be told, it is possible to lead a bird too much. This is true on crossing shots at 35 to 40 yards if you use the fast swing-through. Because a short movement of your gun barrel is magnified in terms of lead at greater distances, the time lag produced by firing just after you are past the bird may, if you swing exceptionally fast, throw your pattern too far in front. This can be overcome by being just a bit more aware of *sweeping through* the bird, but most certainly not by dwelling on it. Sometimes pointing-out these long left-barrel crossing or quartering shots works best.

Grouse shooting is made more difficult by the psychological factor. With shots so rare, you tighten up when you miss, knowing a chance to try that exact angle again may not come for several seasons. In low grouse years, you tend to try nearly impossible shots, missing and further undermining your confidence. Tension plays the devil with anything as finely honed as the mental/physical act of hitting grouse, and an adverse state of mind, even though unrelated to gunning, can destroy your shooting efficiency for the day.

We all shoot in two ways—the way we intend to and sometimes do, and the way we too often snatch at a bird with a fast snap when it goes up. Anyone who has shot doubles at skeet has done better on the second target because he gets his eyes on it and overtakes it with no dawdling or it's gone. Though this second shot is made with the gun already at the shoulder, this is the kind of swing that is effective on grouse. I suspect that gunners who say it is necessary to spot-shoot grouse and woodcock are moving their barrels without knowing it, not realizing that one inch of sidewise muzzle movement produces 2½ feet of lead at 30 yards. Some confusion also results from use of terms. It is called "spot shooting" (sometimes "snap shooting") when the gunner shoots directly at the bird or at a spot ahead of it with stationary barrels. By "snap shooting," some shooters mean pulling the trigger the moment the stock butt touches the shoulder, even though the gun is swinging. For clarity, I make this distinction between the two.

The bitterest miss in the spectrum of shooting—whether it be a clay target, bobwhite, woodcock, grouse, or pheasant—is the wide-open straightaway bird you know you are "on" and that still sails

Shooting Flying

away untouched. The experience can devastate you because, theoretically, a straightaway is the easiest shot you can get. Non-wing shooters can hit straightaways when they can't touch another bird, simply because they take time and deliberately *aim*, something a good wing shot wouldn't dream of doing. Perhaps in this lies the secret of missing straightaways—the dedicated wing shot gets himself fouled in principles.

There are other reasons why more straightaway birds are missed than any other shot: (1) the gunner, unaware that he needs cast-off, shoots to one side of where he looks; (2) faulty mounting jars the gun out of line, especially if the gun is lightweight; (3) the gunner flinches from anticipating heavy loads; (4) a slight change in line of flight throws a straightaway bird out of line of fire; (5) a straightaway grouse offers a mere 4-inch circle of silhouette with an edge view of wings, a woodcock about a 2-inch circle, and a pheasant presents an armor plate of pelvic bone; (6) a going-away bird is getting farther away by the split-second.

A further reason for such misses is that the bird may not actually be going straightaway. A bird that does not fly in a trajectory from your gun muzzle like a load of shot is not flying straightaway in terms of shooting. Some rise and level off in this line, but most are either coming up in relation to your line of pointing or coming down, even when they are flying parallel to the ground. The true straightaway can be centered by spot-shooting directly on it. The bird that is below eye level, even if it is not climbing, must be handled like a rising bird and you must come up through it or hold a bit above it. The bird above eye level, even if flying parallel to the ground, is coming down in your perspective and must be treated that way, for you are pointing up.

A good shot on driven Scotch grouse, in describing how to take low incomers, gave me an idea on handling straightaway birds. With the fore-end higher than the stock, he brings the left hand up until it covers the bird, then simply brings the stock up and fires as the butt touches his shoulder. If you will practice mounting on an imaginary straightaway bird, using a spot on the opposite wall, you will notice that much of the time your gun muzzle bounces off the spot as you come up. If this occurs in actual shooting, you miss, unless you re-align your barrels, which is not good wing shooting. If, instead, you try the Scotsman's mount—with gun inclined, bring the fore-end up and cover your "bird" with the left hand, then bring the stock to your shoulder—you will almost invariably be "on" the bird without bounce or wavering. I used this during the past 'cock and grouse season with success on straightaways or almost any shot that required spot-shooting with no chance to swing. On any but spot shots, my normal mount comes up smoothly without bounce because the gun is swinging onto the bird.

It is dangerous to shoot at low incomers for they may be flushing from your dog, which could be in line with it. High incomers against the sky are best taken quickly, rather than as going-away birds after passing. When to swing through and when to hold to one side, above or below, is best handled by feel. If there is relative motion across your field of vision, it is wise to swing through.

My weakest shot on grouse and pheasants is the overhead going-away. For some reason I have little trouble with this shot on woodcock. A grouse is more difficult because of its speed, a pheasant because of its apparent slowness, especially if it is angling. I have in mind a recent two-barrel miss on an overhead-away pheasant that made even the bird's face red. One day I watched a grouse come at me overhead, turned and missed it twice in the open. Next day I set my skeet trap on a second-story porch and had a friend throw targets over my head from behind, offering shots like the grouse. I broke them by shooting from stationary barrels held below the target, letting it come down to the gun and shooting when the amount of intervening daylight looked right—about the diameter of a bird. The shot is best taken further out with less variance in angle of shot and flight.

An important part of shooting is the way you handle yourself in the woods to be able to take a shot when it comes. Stance, as sometimes described, doesn't exist in grouse and woodcock shooting. You try to keep on two feet, you don't tarry in tangles where you couldn't shoot, and when a flush occurs, no matter what your position, you wait to mount until you get the bird in focus. Last November I somehow dropped a woodcock from a crouched kneebend in the middle of a hawthorn thicket.

A comfortable and safe way to carry your gun is by the grip with the butt resting on the pelvis or the front of the upper thigh, freeing the other hand to ward off brush or maintain balance. If you fall, the gun is held vertically and no discharge can reach you, your

Shooting Flying

dog, or a companion; above all, you never let go of the gun. Mounting from the vertical carry is done in a smooth motion, with the stock sliding up between the arm and ribs, the fore-end falling into the palm of the free hand in perfect balance. You can protect the stock to some extent with your arm, but a nice gunstock takes punishment in dense thorns.

Hitting with the first shot of the season works a charm—until the inevitable miss. Grouse seasons often open with a string of misses until you become convinced it is impossible to hit a bird. You carry the blame for this like a curse, but more often it is beyond your control—heavy foliage; dry, noisy woods; birds not yet using normal cover. But this is minor compared with the mid-season slump.

Anybody can hit when he is hitting; it takes guts to come out of a mid-season slump. Shooting *Angst* is on you before you realize what is happening. One day you miss a shot you shouldn't have missed—not too important in pheasant or woodcock shooting, where you know you'll soon have another chance. But when you miss an opportunity on grouse, you feel in your bones it was your one chance for the day—perhaps the week. You try shots you should never try, and miss, and soon you are eating your heart out and shooting more and more raggedly.

There was Black Friday in October of '64. Dixie made the first point and, instead of the grouse I was set for, a woodcock flushed vertically within inches of my left shoulder and I missed a foolish try at close range. Bliss made the next point in second-growth hardwoods and again it was a 'cock that floated behind some trees. You are not supposed to miss woodcock with both barrels but I did. In a hawthorn and crab thicket where woodcock should have been, a grouse skimmed out like a low jet, not too far for the left barrel but I used the right. My state of mind kept pace with my shooting, affecting the dogs, and when young Bliss bumped a 'cock I brought her in for correction. This flushed a second bird from the edge of a little run and I wheeled and shot so quickly it was not until I missed it that I recognized it as a grouse. I was still pouring salt in my wounds when a woodcock came at me and I used two more shells without hurting anything but my feelings. At last I dropped a crossing woodcock, and as a commemoration of the event we moved to another covert. There I changed to Shadows, missed two tries at a grouse, shot one 'cock and missed another twice. I had fired four shells at grouse and out of nine shells at 'cock had hit two. Kay, who is adept in the care and feeding of a psychotic, made an observation on the drive home: "Since no one hits every shot, isn't it logical that on certain days the misses should occur in strings—like the hits?" It was a nice try but that slump lasted more than a week.

Though I know it isn't true, I can best bring myself out of a slump by telling myself, "It really doesn't matter." If I can make myself believe that, relax my eyes and stop straining for the bird that isn't there, I loosen up. When at last I pull the trigger and see a grouse fall, the stinging bitterness of those misses fades in the burnt-hair after-smell of the shot, and my gall dissolves and I am whole again, probably because the hit establishes to my ego's satisfaction that I can do it.

A good proportion of misses are not the shooter's fault. Much depends upon how birds are coming up; a well-meaning cry of "Mark!" from a companion can throw you off when you are near enough to see the bird yourself. But if you can approach shooting as something to be enjoyed, not a frustrating obsession, it can enrich your life. Find the gun that is exactly right for you and stay with it; then be clear about what you are trying to do and have confidence you can do it. If faith is "believin' what you know ain't so," it still helps when you go into coverts with a gun to feel you can hit anything that flies. You just might be right.

The Pleasures of a Shooting Diary

❧ / *The strongest memory is weaker than the palest ink.*

—*Chinese proverb*

7/22/1893
Chestnut Hill, Pa. 11 birds (1 grass plover) Doves in plenty.

THOSE NOTES WERE WRITTEN by seventeen-year-old Charles Norris, the first entry in a gun diary that recorded sixty-six years of shooting—days like these:

1/8/1898
Huntley, Md. 1 goose, 2 dippers Bay frozen in first fine day.
1 Blk. duck, 9 quail   With W. B. Cadwalader.
5 Jack Snipe

10/26/1938
Yarmouth, Nova Scotia. 8 'cock, 1 grouse Total 4 guns: 14 'cock.
1 'cock missed   4 grouse
10 shells used   1 snipe

11/10/59
Amwell, N.J.   0   11:30-1:00 Ideal autumn day. Charm 2 pt.
Nellie 1. One cripple lost. Dogs good work.
3 hard single barrel chances. Felt sick.

That last was Dr. Norris's final day with his gun. In his papers I found a separate game book tabulating the number of each species of game and fish he had taken.

A gun diary is possibly the most revealing view of a shooting man anyone will have. I wish my father and my grandfather had kept them. My shooting notes began in 1932 as a log of hits and misses and the number of birds moved, with mention of weather. I tried to capture experiences that make a day special and added sketches, especially of birds shot at, indicating where I had pulled or should have pulled. I felt the need to credit productive points and retrieves of each dog, to distinguish between the number of separate birds moved and the number of flushes. In '52 I started noting the sex of each grouse, its markings, crop contents and whether the bird was adult or juvenile. Recently I have been recording age and sex of woodcock shot.

My notes are on loose pages in wooden boxes, grouped by years. Going over them is like taking a wonderful journey again. Not all the memories are happy—there are empty places after each dog has gone—but in those pages are more than a thousand days lived with those dogs and I know they asked no more. There is that first season after the war, back home in our mountains and the glory of October. In '51, a note: "Old Blue slept this season by the hearth, confining his record to birds-sniffed-at-the-door." There is a sketch of the fox trap that caught Feathers, beaten into a knot when I got through with it; Ruff pointing stanchly in the middle of a trout stream; a thumbnail sketch, "Stones Under a Tree," of a pine with ancient tombstones lost in a woods; Dixie as a puppy wading downstream to keep even with a drink.

Beyond experiences kept alive, a gun diary can be a valuable record of shooting averages, loads used, a dog's performance, the number of days you have hunted, how certain coverts have produced. It is important only if these are more than mere statistics. To make them cold science is to defeat the purpose of a personal gun diary. My entries are in this form:

Saturday 11 November '67	Sugar Run
Warm, 60° partly cloudy, breezy.	Moved 1 grouse—4 flushes.
2:30 to 5:30	3 shots—1 hit.
Yearling cock: interrupted tail band.	Bliss: 1 productive
	1 kill
Crop: few grapes, cinquefoil, rubus.	1 retrieve.

I follow this with description of the action. For the man who doesn't have the time or desire to keep more than data, a simple log will do, with the covert, date, birds moved, flushes, birds shot, and the number of shots and hits, in this manner:

The Pleasures of a Shooting Diary

Piney Mountain: Oct. 14, 4-9-0, 1 shot—no hit.
　　　　　　　　Nov. 6, 9(5)-10-1, 2 shots—1 hit.

The figure in parentheses in the second entry indicates new birds, discounting four of the nine as the birds moved on the October 14th visit. A log kept in this form tells at a glance how many times you gunned a covert, how many separate birds it contained, how many you took, and offers comparison of the covert in different years.

At the end of each season's notes, I do a page summarizing the shooting:

1966

56 days hunted　　　36 coverts　　　6.44 bird/covert ratio.
Grouse: 60 shots—18 hits, 30%.　232 birds moved—444 flushes.
Woodcock: 34 shots—20 hits, 58.8%

Bliss: *Grouse*　　　　　　　　　　*Woodcock*
　　　56 days hunted.
　　　77 productives, 1 backpoint.　27 productives, 4 backpoints.
　　　18 kills (6 over points).　　20 kills (over points).
　　　16 retrieves.　　　　　　　　13 retrieves.

　　　Lifetime '64 through '66:　167 days hunted.
　　　　　(grouse only)　　　　　159 productives, 4 backpoints.
　　　　　　　　　　　　　　　　　57 kills.
　　　　　　　　　　　　　　　　　35 retrieves.

There are similar entries for each dog, with lifetime records on grouse. To analyze my grouse shots I keep a page with a column on the left describing the angle of the shot, with entries of hits (vertical marks) and misses (horizontal) for each season:

		1965	1966	1967
Quartering left, normal		≡ ‖	— |	‖
"	" low	≡ ‖	— |	— ‖
"	" rising	‖‖	≡ |	
"	" rising acutely	—		—
"	" leveling		—	
"	" high	—	—	
"	" overhead			
"	" from tree	— |	|	

There are groups for quartering right, crossing left, crossing right, away-left, away-right, incoming, incoming-left, incoming-right—altogether eighty variations, and still there are shots difficult to classify. Comparisons for each season offer a quick survey of my shooting. For example, in the quartering-left angle I seemed to be doing better with rising shots in '65 than in '66; poorly on rising acutely and high shots; not badly on normal and low shots; rather well, for me, on out-of-tree shots; and overall 48.5 percent, which is above average for me on grouse. This can be revealing when compared with loads used in a certain gun.

A gun diary will show fluctuations of game populations as personal experience. To appy limited samplings to broad areas can magnify error. Game biologists' counts contain flaws intrinsic in almost any method. The flush-per-hour count is not accurate, for with a good dog I may find and reflush the same grouse five times in an hour, giving me five flushes per hour; if I shoot that bird on the first flush I have a one flush-per-hour count—both counts possible with the same single bird. This is equally true with pheasants and woodcock. Several men in a party usually flush birds more times than one man, without putting more birds in the covert. Quail populations can be reflected in covey counts, provided someone doesn't count them over again the next day—a flaw in any statewide hunter report on game.

Because a male grouse may drum on several sites, drumming counts can be inflated and, like woodcock singing counts, indicate only male birds, unless you think optimistically that there is a girl for every boy. In 1967, 75 percent of the grouse I shot were adult males. If this ratio was typical, drumming counts the previous spring would have been unrealistic. That spring I saw more grouse broods than normally and had corroborating reports. Yet, by October young grouse were extremely scarce and I shot only one adult hen, suggesting a high mortality of brood hens during the summer. If this occurred while the chicks were dependent upon the hens it could account for the decimation of what had appeared to be plentiful broods. Too frequently, summer brood counts have no relation to fall population.

Population counts based on kill reports are unrealistic. High kills may only reflect more men hunting, and whether a group of men are good or poor shots does not assess the number of birds

The Pleasures of a Shooting Diary

present. If expert shots work one or two coverts to the bone, a high kill report may indicate that there are few, if any, birds left—no base for determining the population for the following season. At the other extreme, there are men who could be in a bird population explosion and fail to hit one.

Acknowledging that any bird-count method has shortcomings, a gun diary can show the gunner what he has been encountering in game numbers; it is more accurate than relying on memory, which may fog-over some seasons that were not extremes, and consistent in that it is one man making the observations without the variable of confusing viewpoints. Over the seasons my notes have revealed a ratio that closely reflects grouse populations. Gunning a large number of coverts, each from one to four times per season, I keep a conservative count of separate grouse moved. In 1948 I moved 150 separate grouse in 23 coverts. The number of visits to a covert does not affect the result, for birds moved on former visits are discounted on later visits. The number of grouse moved, divided by the number of coverts, gives a bird/covert ratio of 6.52 for 1948. The following season I again shot in 23 coverts, many of them the same as in '48, but I moved 207 separate grouse, giving a bird/covert ratio of 9.0 for 1949. Any season averaging 6.0 birds per covert has been a fair year for grouse. There have been years when the ratio was as low as 3.0, others as high as 11.38. It is rare that all my coverts average more than ten grouse.

The bird/covert ratio has an obvious weakness. It is possible to gun a covert only once and not move all the birds it holds, just as it is possible to hunt only in a few coverts that hold abnormally high numbers of birds. Since my shooting includes a comparable number of one-visit hunts every season, the ratio is fairly well balanced.

A twenty-season sample from my shooting diary shows how I have found grouse populations. In this list I have omitted all the coverts I gunned that were not under the effects of the same temperatures and rainfall, in order to make comparisons between the critical brood-season weather—May 15 through June 30—and the grouse population the following autumn.

No experienced gunner doubts that ruffed-grouse populations fluctuate, but dividing the years into cycles of ten will not forecast his chances for a given season. My records show that grouse populations in the wide scope of coverts I gun in the Alleghenies have not followed a pattern. The same is true of localized areas such as the Blackwater-Canaan. In this sample, the only uniform ten-year cycle —'51 through '60—contained nine good years, eight of them exceptional. Seven of the next ten were below normal, with two twenty-year lows.

Most of us have believed that cold wet weather following the hatching causes high mortality among grouse chicks, resulting in a low population for the subsequent shooting season. A number of conspicuous exceptions to this rule prompted me to check rainfall and average temperature. In twenty years there was no consistent relation between the size of fall populations and wet or dry weather during the critical brood period.

TWENTY-YEAR GROUSE POPULATION FLUCTUATIONS

YEAR	BIRDS MOVED	COVERTS	BIRD/COVERT RATIO	TOTAL RAINFALL	AVERAGE TEMPERATURE
				(Brood period, May 15—June 30)	
'51	234	27	8.66	10.92"	64.8°
'52	181	19	9.53	8.17"	65.1°
'53	206	23	8.96	2.45"	66.1°
'54	296	26	11.38	5.29"	62.9°
'55	285	29	9.83	6.18"	59.6°
'56	279	27	10.33	11.68"	60.9°
'57	221	25	8.84	5.75"	64.9°
'58	209	21	9.95	7.83"	60.4°
'59	140	18	7.78	3.37"	54.8°
'60	131	28	4.68	4.37"	62.4°
'61	97	15	6.47	9.44"	58.3°
'62	89	19	4.68	3.31"	66.1°
'63	58	15	3.83	8.41"	61.1°
'64	99	22	4.5	7.16"	62.1°
'65	205	29	7.07	2.88"	63.2°
'66	214	27	7.93	2.25"	62.7°
'67	92	25	3.68	4.24"	61.9°
'68	131	30	4.37	12.49"	61.7°
'69	142	27	5.26	2.68"	62.9°
'70	140	29	4.83	5.70"	63.9°

Exceptionally high rainfalls occurred in the brood periods of '51 and '56—excellent grouse years. Twelve were good grouse years (five with above-normal rainfall, seven with below-normal). Eight were poor years (three with above-normal rainfall, five with below-normal).

Average temperature for the twenty spring brood periods varied only slightly, and the three lowest averages were followed by good fall grouse populations. The U.S. Climatological Reports I studied showed extreme short-term concentrations of rain during the brood periods in only one of the poor grouse years—1968.

It would be so easy if everything could be divided into tens and into wet and dry springs, and if, after each grouse low—and they do happen—the birds would come back, as Riley Worden used to say, "Thick as ever." But my experience shows that each time grouse recover, they do not seem to regain their former high levels.

Records and conclusions can comprise a gun diary, but even more than facts about the birds I shoot and about the dogs I shoot them over, certain days glow like a sifting of golden maple leaves in an old lane in October, moments uncovered as I turn a page spotted with gun oil: a Hunter's Moon viewed through bare branches after a day's shooting; a feathered form laid in my hand and setter eyes that seemed to say, "George, did I do it right?" Mention of a sun disappearing behind a purple ridge as I climbed that last hill to the station wagon with an empty game pocket, bone-tired but immeasurably happy. For as long as I have these pages, many of them yellowed and beginning to smell of time, my setters will range the fall and winter woods. And, for just as long, I'll be there.

Bird and Bottle

❦ / *Bon appétit*

A DEVOUT CHRISTIAN ONCE said to me, "Religion is something you believe. If you stop to think, it doesn't make sense." Shooting men feel that way about the preparation and serving of the game they shoot. If they didn't, I wouldn't consider them true believers.

Occasionally the other man's creed is difficult to go along with, such as serving woodcock complete with head tucked under wing and the 'trails left in the body cavity, but there was a time when the English shootin' man frowned upon any other way. The Scots' red grouse may improve with hanging until the feathers drop but I don't feel the need for that with our ruffed grouse. In his *The Physiology of Taste*, Brillat-Savarin (1755–1826) went a few steps further than I care to go to get the most out of—or into—a pheasant roasted on a spit:

> The pheasant is an enigma which is savored at its best only by initiates. Each edible substance has its peak of flavor. Some reach it when they begin to spoil, such as the woodcock and, especially, the pheasant. The latter, eaten within three days after its demise, is nothing exceptional. It is not as delicate as a fat pullet, or as pleasing to the sense of smell as a quail. At its peak the aroma of the bird is enhanced by an oily exudation which ferments slightly, like the oil from coffee obtained by roasting the beans. At this time there is a change in the color of the breast. At this stage the bird is plucked and larded. It should not be plucked too soon for birds kept feathered retain more flavor.

Bird and Bottle

Take two *becasse* (woodcock), bone them and draw the entrails and livers. Make two heaps; one of the meat and one of the entrails and livers. Make a stuffing of the meat by chopping it up with beef marrow (steam-cooked), a little grated bacon, pepper, salt, fine herbs, and whatever quantity of excellent truffles is needed to fill the interior of the pheasant. Take a long and wide slice of bread (extending at least two inches beyond the pheasant in front and rear). Then take the entrails and livers of the woodcock and mash them into a paste with two large truffles, an anchovy, a little grated bacon, and a suitable portion of fresh butter. Spread this paste on the bread which is then placed under the pheasant so it will receive all the drippings from the bird.

When the pheasant is done, serve it resting on the bread, surround it with "bitter oranges," and you will be well content. This dish should be accompanied by a vintage Burgundy, as I learned by calculations more involved than a table of logarithms. A pheasant so prepared is worthy of being served to angels.

We would deprive no one of his beliefs, but Kay and I have savored game for enough years to have the conviction of our tastes and to indulge in a few agnostic excursions. Eating wild game began before man was civilized but it has become one of his most civilized pleasures. As such, it should be possible to discuss it, not without emotion but without violence where differences of opinion occur.

The first of our differences concerns the practice of laying bacon or salt pork on a game bird, or cooking it with, of all things, carrots or onions "to give it flavor." The flavor of a game bird is not something to conceal or lose.

One of Dr. Charles Norris's precepts was that water should never touch the inside of a bird, but that the body cavity should be merely wiped with a damp cloth after drawing. That this was not taken literally in his kitchen Kay discovered when she went there to obtain the recipe for bread sauce. "You should see the blood and feathers inside those pheasants," his cook confided. "How would I get rid of that without water?"

The problem of shot and wadded feathers raises the touchy question of whether to pluck or to skin a bird. It is surprising how few of the great number of pellets in a load of shot reach even a well-centered bird, but usually some of them will have gone deep. En-

MIXED BAG

countering an occasional No. 8 at table, characteristically flattened on one side, is part of eating game. I had one perplexing experience when I found not only the No. 8's I expected but two No. 6's and one No. 4 in a grouse. The bird had not been carrying old wounds and I can only guess that the manufacturer had put a mixed batch in the shell. Regardless of the colorful aspect of coming on one or two pellets, to be served a plucked bird with shot and feathers beneath the skin detracts from the joy of eating it. Kay and I speak out in favor of skinning birds. Beyond being unable to clean a bird thoroughly with the skin left on, it has been our experience that the tender skin of any game bird is usually torn in several places when plucked, permitting the skin to draw away from the flesh in cooking, leaving the surface of the meat white and unbrowned. A delicious sticky golden finish can be achieved when the skin has been removed and the meat itself basted and browned. A common objection to skinning is that the bird becomes dry in cooking, but this offers no problem to a skillful cook.

Woodcock lose something when frozen with the skin on but are still delicious after a year in the freezer if skinned when dressed. It is especially desirable to skin woodcock to remove the fat deposits underneath. This fat, along with organs, is where residual pesticides accumulate.

Hanging game birds has several things to recommend it. There is the opportunity to admire your game longer; it gives it time to cool thoroughly; and hanging seems to enhance the flavor in most cases, though I prefer to hang birds only a few days—a week at the most. A bird must not be allowed to freeze while hanging. A coat or blanket should be wrapped around the bird if the temperature threatens to fall into the twenties. I used to hang my birds by the neck but I now prefer to hang them by the feet. Drawing or dismembering a bird in the field permits the entrance of bacteria. Unless a bird is so badly shot that the viscera are exposed it should not be drawn, but should be hung intact until dressed. If game must be drawn in the field the entrails should be buried. Beyond spoiling a young bird dog, eating the entrails can make any dog ill if decomposition has set in, and you owe consideration for the next man's dog.

An exception to the rule of hanging game applies to a grouse

Bird and Bottle

prepared and served the day after it has been shot, when it has a special juicy, crisp quality. If not served then, it should hang for several days. I think any game bird is slightly better when eaten without having been in the freezer, but all upland game birds keep well in a freezer for a year or longer if properly handled. Our birds are labeled as to covert, date shot and which dog pointed and/or retrieved. It seems unrealistic to impose the restriction of possession limits, which in most cases is twice the daily quota, on birds in the freezer. It makes no sense to say a gunner may, with no season limit, kill five times as many birds as he is allowed to have in his freezer, provided he gobbles them up or gives them away.

Since personal tastes should be indulged where game is concerned, I will begin at what I consider the top. In the manner of old game recipes, I shall say, "Take a fine grape-fed cock grouse you have shot yourself—" No bird tastes quite so good if someone else has shot it; if any grouse can be better than another, the large cocks are usually more tender than the hens; and nothing I have put in my mouth has been quite so delicious as a grouse that has fed on grapes —and next to that, on beechnuts.

Kay prepares grouse in two ways. The objective in cooking all game birds is to make them tender and juicily brown. Braising does this. A tightly covered heavy skillet is essential. If, when the bird is cleaned, the inner breast muscle is partially separated from the outer (which is often necessary to remove shot, wads of feathers and blood clots) the breast can be flattened, making it easier to brown.

GROUSE IN BUTTERMILK GRAVY: Flour lightly the breast, legs and upper back with inner joint of wings attached, liver and heart. Brown in corn oil. After turning, cover with a tight lid and cook on low heat for an hour or more. Salt and turn occasionally and add a small amount of water, replacing lid, until golden brown and tender. Remove to a heated serving dish. Make gravy with flour and water in the browned residue in the skillet, thicker than desired. In the last minute or two, thin with buttermilk—about ¼ cup to a grouse. Serve around the grouse.

GROUSE IN SHERRY SAUCE: Brown as above. Add a medium-dry sherry, pouring over grouse a little at a time while cooking over low heat in covered pan. When grouse is removed to heated serving dish, make a pan gravy, adding water and more sherry if necessary, scraping and stirring up browned particles. Pour over the grouse.

A grouse should be devoured almost alone as the sole feature and not smothered with a salad or side dishes. Why wild rice should be so exactly right with grouse remains one of those delightful enigmas. Next to wild rice or a mix of wild and white rice, we like white rice with herbs and mushrooms. One year when our garden was spared by frosts and the grouse season opened early, we discovered that grouse was exceptionally compatible with tiny limas so young they had the delicate flavor of oysters.

To us, it is important that grouse be accompanied by a good Cabernet Sauvignon or Moulin-à-Vent in crystal and eaten with reverence before a log fire or, if the evening is too warm, by candlelight. And, if anything could be better than that, with a background of a Mahler symphony—No. 2 or No. 5. One more word. It is a privilege to introduce friends to the experience of game, but serve grouse only to someone you can be certain will appreciate it with full attention and with a minimum of conversation.

The two of us share one grouse, served always in a certain silver dish. After dinner, the setter who made the retrieve gets the serving dish, the dinner plates going to the others for a ritual of polishing with paint-brush strokes of pink tongues.

If grouse should be eaten to Mahler, woodcock deserve Debussy. Perhaps because woodcock has a special quality—breast meat dark, leg meat white—it is the one upland game bird that insists upon a dry white wine. Hemingway acknowledged this in *A Farewell to Arms*, when he described woodcock with a bottle of Pouilly-Fuissé. And, while Hemingway's *becasse* was not our American woodcock, you can't do better than to drink his wine with our 'cock, though a well-chilled good Rhine wine or a Moselle will do a woodcock pleasure. Blackberry flummery is a fine dessert after woodcock or grouse. The sauce for our woodcock was suggested by Dr. Norris.

WOODCOCK WITH ORANGE AND SHERRY SAUCE: Lightly flour and braise woodcock breasts and the legs joined by the lower back in oil in covered pan. It will cook tender in less time than grouse, but the slow and juicy browning takes time with any bird, so allow at least forty-five minutes. Along with a little water, add sherry while cooking; salt, of course. When ready to serve, make a pan gravy with water, sherry and a tablespoon of frozen concentrated orange juice for each four 'cock. Serve with wild rice. Dip the bite-size legs in the orange-sherry liquor and eat with your fingers. Save a last bite of breast meat and eat in its sauce with a spoon.

A pheasant seems more frivolous than other game birds and I've even seen pheasant served with a white wine, but I like a Burgundy. We first tasted bread sauce with pheasant but it goes equally well with grouse, partridge or quail. Pheasant makes an ideal dinner for entertaining—it is deliciously game-bird but safely so for any guest who may not have the sophisticated taste for woodcock or the discernment to appreciate grouse. One cock ringneck will serve three generously and one of the big Reeves cocks will make four people happy. A preserve pheasant requires no more time than grouse to cook tender. A wild pheasant might best be prepared with tenderizer, and with a handsome big old wild cock you can only hope.

PHEASANT IN SOUR CREAM: After floured pheasant parts are well browned in oil, they are turned breast, outer leg and back parts up, salted; freshly soured cream is poured around them, they are tightly covered and cooked for an hour over low heat. The cream may have to be stirred smooth, thinned or even thickened carefully with a little cornstarch, before being served around the bird.

BREAD SAUCE: Basically this is dried bread (crusts removed) rolled to fine crumbs, stirred into scalded milk and seasoned. Add salt, oil and minced onion. We like to add rosemary (brewed and strained), thyme, and, just before serving, a tablespoon of sherry. Serve hot, the consistency of whipped potatoes, and persuade guests not to cover it with gravy.

The only partridge I have shot is the chukar, which we think is best prepared with sherry as in the second recipe for grouse. They turn out to be surprisingly large on the table, with legs meatier than those of a grouse—one bird makes a nice meal for two. I hope someday to try a Rhone Valley wine named Chante Perdrix (Partridge

Song) with this bird, but until that time, a Cabernet Sauvignon with chukar partridge makes music enough for me.

Nash Buckingham said that only a fool would fry quail. When I was very young I ate quail soaked overnight in salt water, then parboiled and browned in butter—enough to ruin any bird, but they were still good. Since I've stopped shooting bobwhites we no longer eat them at home—a sacrifice to a principle—but my moral fiber is not above a relapse when I'm a dinner guest. One memorable evening, guests of Meade and Betty Foster, we had quail charcoal-broiled with oil and sherry on the canyon brink above the Blackwater, "where the rapids rip and roar." With a chilled bottle and eaten with our fingers, they were superb.

All the small preferences we accumulate as we experience the good life are properly to be cherished, particularly in anything so rare and fine as game. It is a special blessing with which shooting men are endowed. In whatever way he prefers it—skinned or plucked, roasted on a spit or braised—each man's taste in game deserves respect, whether or not you concur. Like your own, his are the pleasures of the shooting life as he pursues it. He knows best when he does his game honor, both when he shoots it and, once more, when it is on his table.

A Gun to Remember

> ❧ / *And I left my gun,*
> *Forever standing lonely in the hall.*
>
> —ARCHIBALD RUTLEDGE, *Exile*

IT WAS A DROOLY AFTERNOON in June and, as we swung into the lane, rain pasted a leaf against the windshield, where it clung a moment and was snapped off by the wipers. We wound up the hill, out the level stretch and, at the end, there was Fairhill brooding under its dripping ivy. As I pressed the bell button it was as though we had come to see for ourselves to prove that it was so.

Inside, in what I always thought of as the "great hall," we listened for Charm's and Nellie's nails to come clicking over the floor to greet us. This time it was a lovely collie, not a gun dog. And then a figure was coming down the dim stairs, as that other figure had come the first time.

We had met Mr. William Norris and his son, but there was a constraint among us as though we were waiting for one more to complete the group. In the drawing room it was better. There were the volumes on songbirds on the table beside the opera glasses he had used instead of binoculars and, beyond the windows, the feeding station and a rain-soaked cardinal. Kay sat at one side of the unlit fireplace and Mr. Norris sat in that other chair. My chair was too wide where Nellie's unyielding plumpness used to make a tight fit for the two of us in the afterglow of a day's gunning. We talked in the quiet of the house the way you talk of someone who is dead, telling each other things each already knows. Seeing me glance at my watch, Mr. Norris rose.

"His secretary has gathered his manuscript together. It's upstairs in the study if you care to go up now. The guns are up there, too. You are to have your choice."

The guns in their English trunk cases were still in his bedroom, bringing back the evening Dr. Norris had shown them to me. I had followed him and Nellie and Charm into the faintly lit room. Two chaises longues flanked the fireplace in the right wall—one for Nellie, one for Charm, and those two ladies promptly took their ease. Dr. Norris and I carried the three cases, heavy as anvils, to a bedside desk topped with leather as old and dark as the gun cases.

One of the Purdeys had been built for Dr. Norris in 1929, a 12-bore with 27-inch barrels. He assembled and handed it to me. "I had this gun built for woodcock shooting. It's really too open for pheasants."

I had on shooting gloves so I could handle the guns freely. The stock was extremely straight, with the checkered wood butt of a standard London best.

"The little Purdey and the Churchill here," Dr. Norris laid his hand on the other two cases, "were left to me by an old friend, Lynford Biddle. He was a splendid shot, the only man I ever knew who was equally good at shooting and fishing as well as games. Lynford shot on the U.S. team against the British and had this Purdey built in 1915. One pair of barrels is a tight improved cylinder and choke. The second pair is tight in both barrels, bored for pigeons."

I had assembled the second Purdey. Like the other, it was dripping oil and I shuddered for the wood, which was very dark.

"I believe in using enough," he said. "Oil never harmed metal."

The Churchill was also a 12-bore, had two pairs of barrels and, like the Purdeys, had a straight grip. "I don't know what possessed Lynford to order that Churchill with a box lock instead of sidelocks."

"They're beautiful," I said. "All three."

Nellie had climbed on his bed and was snoring with her head on his pillow. That evening with Dr. Norris, having those guns in my hands, is one I'll not forget.

Mr. William Norris and I carried the guns over to Dr. Norris's study, where Kay was waiting. There we opened the cases and admired them.

I selected the lovely "little" Purdey with the two pairs of barrels.

A Gun to Remember

His unfinished manuscript was boxed and waiting on the floor beside the overflowing desk. Through rain-spattered windows, light was fading and memories, too recent not to hurt, were pressing in. All the way down the wide oak stairs no one spoke.

Outside, the rain was diminishing. As we drove away, neither Kay nor I could look back.

I've dreamed elaborate dreams about shooting, but that I would someday own and shoot a Purdey was not one of them. I had shot my Fox for thirty-four years, and while no love affair lasts that long without a crisis, after the restocking job we were closer than ever and I had intended to continue shooting it as long as the two of us lasted. Now I possessed one of the finest guns made. Its brass-cornered, leather-covered oak case—twenty-six pounds without the gun—is lined with red billiard cloth and compartmented for both pairs of barrels, fore-end, and stock so accurately that a gun with the slightest variation in dimensions would not fit. There are compartments for fittings—one, a spanner for installing the spare striker pins and springs that are in a horn container. There are nickel-plated dummy cartridges with hard rubber centers for dry-firing or testing trigger pull. Mounted on the underside of the lid are two cards—one with data regarding loads used in patterning the gun, length of cartridge chambers and bore, the other an engraved Purdey letterhead like a formal invitation to use this magnificent gun, and I almost expected *R.S.V.P.* in one corner.

The gun is a 12-gauge weighing 6 pounds 7 ounces. It has an extra pair of 26-inch barrels, the No. 1 pair bored 72 percent and 76 percent, the No. 2 pair 54 percent and 71 percent. It appears exactly like an 1886 Purdey I saw illustrated in a woodcut, with the same Purdey rose-pattern engraving on the sidelocks and action. It is identical in appearance with the standard Purdey today. There are side wings at the breech and an extra locking member above the ejectors—what Purdeys call "third grip and clips to action." It has a beautifully figured French walnut stock with a straight grip, checkered twenty-four lines to the inch.

I was taller than either Dr. Norris or Lynford Biddle and have a longer neck, longer arms, wider shoulders, requiring more drop, more length and more cast-off. I made these changes myself. Normally, a gunsmith could have achieved the additional drop and cast-off by bending the stock under pressure with hot oil, but the walnut in Purdey stocks is at least eleven years old when the stock is made, and the age of this stock made it too risky to try bending.

Beginning with coarse sandpaper and finishing with fine, I worked the comb down to the drop I wanted. The stock had ample thickness to achieve the cast-off by working down the face side. Additional length was gained by adding a recoil pad. When the stock tested to my satisfaction I finished it with twenty-two coats of GB Linspeed oil, rubbing it down between each coat with Behr-Manning 400A Speed-Wet Durite Paper and water, bringing the old wood to glowing life.

This Purdey had been chambered for $2\frac{5}{8}$-inch shells, the standard 12-gauge shell in the U.S. when it was built. Rather than have the chambers altered, Dr. Norris ordered short shells in case lots. I shoot different loads for woodcock, grouse and pheasants and lengthening the shell chambers to $2\frac{3}{4}$ inches seemed more practical. After some searching, I located a gunsmith equipped to do the job.

The British gunner likes his gun to throw its patterns high for rising birds or driven incomers. This was achieved with a rib that pitched low to the muzzle, with a small metal bead set below the tops of the barrels. The line of the barrels, or line of fire, was on a rising angle compared with the line of vision from the shooter's eye through the bead, throwing the pattern 10 or 12 inches high at 40 yards.

There are men who insist that a bead on a shot gun is superfluous. I find a large white bead helpful in pointing, even though I am focused on the bird and merely feel the bead subconsciously. With a mock-up bead of modeling clay, I determined how high the bead should be to make my line of vision coincide with the line of fire. My gunsmith made the alterations on both pairs of barrels, installing an $\frac{11}{64}$-inch white bead on a metal platform, which gives the illusion of a bead on a normal rib when the gun is mounted. There is an advantage to this when shooting in rain or snow, for the raised bead is above accumulations of snow or water.

During the summer of these changes I was in correspondence with Purdeys. One of their letters began by corroborating my gun's number, when it was built, bore, barrel lengths, length of chambers and weight. It continued:

A Gun to Remember

As you rightly say we build only one quality so, therefore, there is no need for us to put a Grade name such as "Royal" or "Crown" etc.

Our gun in its standard state is finished with our fine rose pattern engraving but, of course, we do finish some of our guns with special engraving such as large scroll, game scenes, or deeply carved with gold inlays etc. for which we naturally charge extra, but the actual gun itself is of one standard quality.

In the latter part of the last century we did for a short time build two or three qualities which were marked "B," "C" and "D" quality; very few were made for it was quickly found to be a bad policy and was stopped.

Regarding the marks on the lower surface of the left barrel, the W. H. were the initials of the barrel filer, William Hill, for it has always been a policy of this Company that each individual craftsman should have the right to put his initials on the part of the gun he made and this is still carried out today. You should, if you examine your gun carefully, find the initials of the man who made the action, the ejector etc., but you would have to strip the gun to find some of these. The letter "S" is no longer stamped on the barrels for this mark was introduced when steel barrels first came into use, to define them in the manufacturing stage from the Damascus Iron, and though we gave up using Damascus tubes in the 1880's, this mark was kept until approximately 1920—customs die hard!!

The numbers 50047-48-49-50 are the actual numbers of each individual tube, for it enables us to check each tube back to any particular batch of steel and forging, for we keep perfect records of every tube used, and for which gun.

Thanking you, and assuring you of my personal attention at all times.

Yours sincerely,
Harry Lawrence
Managing Director

Purdey stocks are cut from the finest walnut, which comes in rough unshaped blocks previously seasoned for six years, then seasoned for at least another five years in the Purdey Factory. The stock is worked, hollowed and weighted according to the weight and balance of the gun being made.

At the completion of each stage in the building of the gun, the

Mixed Bag

work is "viewed" by the factory manager. Finished and assembled, the gun is again viewed, tested and shot at the shooting grounds. The final examination is at Audley House, where it is examined by the managing director before being passed for delivery to the customer.

The barrels of my Purdey have a display of proof marks on the flats that look like a page of heraldic symbols. These are London Proof House marks, differing from those of the Birmingham Proof House.

The Provisional Proof mark is the letters GP with lion rampant, stamped on the barrels after the first test in the rough stage. The barrel is proved without the action by inserting a charge via a plug screwed into the breech end and discharged through a "touch hole" like a cannon. The Definitive Proof mark is the letters GP surmounted by a crown, stamped on the finished barrels.

My barrels carry a Nitro Proof mark—the letters NP surmounted by an arm dexter, embowed, holding a scimitar—also the words NITRO PROOF and the numeral $1\frac{1}{8}$, indicating the maximum charge of shot to be used.

The View Proof mark—the letter V surmounted by a crown—appears on the barrels and action. I suspect it is the appearance of a crown in the proof marks that gives rise to the myth about a "Crown Grade" Purdey.

The numeral 12 indicates that the inside diameter of the barrel taken nine inches from the breech end is between .720 and .729 of an inch. If this mark had been $\frac{12}{1}$ it would have indicated a bore between .730 and .740, rather on the "wide" side. The nominal gauge of the cartridge is indicated by $\frac{12}{C}$ within a diamond. The length of the cartridge is now usually included. The word CHOKE is stamped on each barrel to indicate that some degree of choke has been bored in each.

The first season I shot the Purdey the 54%/71% pair of barrels proved effective on grouse but rough on woodcock—one 'cock disintegrated like a clay target—and I decided to have the tight 72%/76%pair opened to 50%/60%. My gunsmith did this in seven stages with me making pattern sheets between each step. These "woodcock barrels" pattern well with 3 dram 1 ounce No. 8 in both barrels. When I expect grouse in woodcock cover I carry 3 dram $1\frac{1}{8}$ ounce No. 8 in the left barrel, tightening it to 70 percent for a

A Gun to Remember

long shot over the alder tops. I later had the right barrel of the No. 2 pair opened to 50 percent using grouse loads with plastic sleeves.

Purdey guns are spring-loaded so that they are "self-opening" when broken. This does not mean they should be allowed to swing open on their own, jolting the mechanism, nor should they be slammed closed, letting the breech lever snap home. As the stock is brought up to the barrels, the lever should be stopped with the thumb and let gently into place. Handled intelligently, a Purdey almost never wears out.

James Purdey—the second James Purdey gunmaker—was building guns of this quality when George III was king. He had been apprenticed to the gun trade with Joseph Manton, and left Manton to become manager of the Forsyth Gun Company. In 1814 he started business on his own in Leicester Square. Twelve years later he took over Joseph Manton's premises in Oxford Street. His son James was apprenticed to him in 1843, the third James Purdey to be a gunmaker. When the father died in 1863, James "the younger" carried on. To accommodate the expanding firm, Audley House at 57–58 South Audley Street, W.1. was built in 1881, the present home of Purdeys.

The Long Room at Audley House, with its red brocade walls, heavy furniture and globe lighting fixtures, serves as a boardroom as well as showroom. To hedge against the possibility that gunmaking might be less than successful, the Long Room was originally designed so it could be converted into an art gallery. In a sense, it is a sort of gallery now. Besides portraits of the Purdeys—James Purdey, Athol Stuart Purdey, Captain James Purdey and his brother Tom Purdey (all now dead)—its walls are nearly covered with prints and photographs of Purdey customers, including an elderly gunner who "died shooting in the heather." On one side of the room, a leather upholstered rail before a Victorian mantelpiece invites pausing where more than one shootin' man has warmed his back while talking guns.

One exhibit is a miniature working model of a Purdey hammer shotgun seven and three-eighths inches overall, a duplicate of a pair presented to H. M. King George V on his Silver Jubilee in 1935—small-scale copies of the Purdeys he used, capable of firing tiny cartridges made for them.

A red-draped table with silver furnishings dominates the Long

Room. On the walls there are shields of members of the firm who have held the position of Master of the Worshipful Company of Gunmakers. And in wall cabinets, the real works of art—the Purdey guns.

The reaction of most people upon seeing a Purdey is expressed in terms of price. Purdey shotguns and extras are listed under two prices, Export and Home Price. Today my gun, with extra barrels, third grip and clips to action, and trunk case, would, with the 14½ percent U.S. customs duty on British shotguns, run well toward halfway between three and four thousand.

My Purdey is beyond price to me because Dr. Norris wanted me to have it, knowing what it would mean to me, knowing I would coddle and cherish it like a thing alive. He would have been unable to sleep if he had gone to bed with the Purdey left uncleaned, whether it had been fired or not. I'm certain he knew, once it was mine, it never would be.

When you come by a fine gun you become a little bit of the man who loved it, for a shooter lives on in proportion to the manner in which his gun is used and enjoyed after he is gone—a nice way to be remembered.

A Box of Shells

❦ / *3 drams Opportunity 1⅛ ounces Luck*

You wouldn't expect a box of twenty-five shells to last for more than fifty years, but this box was exceptional. For one thing, they were mixed loads, not even all one gauge, from paper shells with the load indicated on the disc at the crimped end to the later ones of the age of plastics. I can still feel the recoil from some, and smell the compelling scent of discharged powder. Many proved nothing, if a shot at a flying bird over a dog in a lovely setting can be called nothing; others did things for my soul. Here is my box of hits and misses.

1. I have the empty shell in front of me, a yellow 20-gauge Winchester "Repeater" impressively inscribed *1st. shot-gun shell shot by Geo. Evans in his 20 gauge gun. July 4, 1919.* This can be important when you're twelve and I had waited since Christmas. On that hot July day with my father, I carried my new Fox Sterlingworth into the woods behind Johnny Wiggins's house at Chalk Hill and we tacked up a newspaper. I carefully stepped back, loaded the right barrel and *aimed*. When I pulled the trigger I got a jab that made my cheek tingle all the way back to the car. Those original Fox stocks gave a wicked kick. That night when I undressed, my right biceps bore a yellowish-purple bruise I hoped wouldn't go away too soon, for I sensed that this episode was significant. I had fired my first shell.

2. The second shell, another 20-gauge from that Fox, dropped my

first grouse in November of '25. I had shot rabbits (running only) and had graduated to quail with moderate success, but none of them remain as clear as that grouse—a high right-crosser far out—and I saw it tumble with an incredulity that appeared corroborated when my father and I failed to find it. Disconsolately we gave up but on the way back to the car hours later, by what seemed to me a miracle, two-year-old Speck found the trail of the wing-broken bird to where it was hiding beneath an undercut bank. That day I was "blooded" as a grouse hunter for life.

3. Old Speck was nine when this shell was fired in 1932 and Kay was blooded as an upland gunner's wife. The Depression respite from a New York career was giving us an odd dividend of full-time shooting, and on this opening day of Pennsylvania woodcock season —Kay's first experience—I warned her not to expect to see a shot in woodcock cover, even if I got one. I've heard her describe this first glimpse of shooting and dog work until I recall it more from her viewpoint than from mine. Speck and I were working the alders with Kay above us on the edge of a field. Looking down as on a stage, she saw Speck draw to a point, saw me walk in, saw the woodcock flush and reach the peak of its arc, then drop at the shot, saw Speck move in and "point dead." If I had planned it, I couldn't have staged it that way. Speck and I did more than put on a show that day; we made a total proselyte of Kay. Falconers have a saying: *One falcon, one wife; two falcons, no wife.* Nearly forty years after her first taste I think I can say: No dogs and no shooting, no Kay. In any case, I'd hesitate to risk it.

4. This was a Super X with No. 6's, years after I had changed to my 12-gauge Fox. I had finished a sandwich sitting on a log beside a woods road and had taken a few steps when Blue showed interest in scent on the slope above. Leaves had been stirred up in a large area, apparently by a group of grouse, and I followed the scratchings up the hillside only to see a flock of robins take wing. Disappointed, I swung Blue along a rhododendron ravine and soon found him on point. Fifty yards ahead, forms like charred stumps became turkeys, motionless, watching Blue. There were five in front and at least twice as many among the trees. No one had reported turkeys in that area for a generation and I considered the possibility of domestic birds, but something about the position of the rigid

A Box of Shells

heads, red and bluish-bald, told me I was seeing my first flock of wild turkeys.

They were beginning to talk and I couldn't hope for a wing shot at that distance. Turkey hunters say you don't wait for turkeys to fly, so with a long-range load in my left barrel I held on the head of the largest bird in front and fired. At the shot it rolled over and the rest of the flock spread with a flapping of wings. When I ran up, my turkey lay thrashing on the ground and I could see chestnut tail tips and tail coverts and burnished red legs. Once it became quiet I was aware of a strange thing. Instead of melting away as in stories, one of the turkeys was watching me from a sapling and there were more among the tree trunks, "frozen" like frightened does. I laid my gun down and flushed the turkey from the branch but it only flapped clumsily to another tree. When I rushed at the birds on the ground, they ran a few yards and stopped and I remembered old hunters proudly telling how they had shot several from one flock. Feeling deprived of the afternoon's grouse shooting, I gathered up my fourteen pounds of bird and started toward the station wagon with Blue, puzzled, following at heel. On the way I saw several of the turkeys near the log road; one was limping from a pellet in its foot.

I suppose every man wants to shoot his first wild turkey as much as I had. Calling them and shooting under some conditions must be exciting, and the flesh, pink from wild grapes, is a gourmet experience. But I don't think I'll shoot another one—certainly not unless it is flying, and then it will have to be on an impulse I don't harbor now.

5. It was Christmas week in 1944. This was the only time I have shot without a dog but this was wartime and I was far from Old Blue. With a one-day leave, Kay and I hoped to celebrate my thirty-eighth birthday shooting, and on Navy Aerology's promise of a high, we had rushed out of Washington in time to try a half hour's gunning beyond Winchester, Virginia, before dusk. The ice storm caught us as we stepped into the woods and within minutes we were glazed. Our shooting coats crackled when we bent our arms and I had to clean ice from the inside of my barrels with switches and wads of Kleenex. It required chains to reach Winchester. At Thornhill, built by Hessian prisoners after the Revolution, our hostess, Mrs. Sandy Baker, thawed us out with eggnog followed with dinner

MIXED BAG

by candlelight. Nothing sets a more gracious mood for shooting than an old house like Thornhill during the holidays. In our enormous bedroom we found a copy of *Eneas Africanus*, a favorite from Kay's girlhood, and she read it to me in bed, after which I dreamed I was shooting quail in an ice storm in Georgia.

As if it were a special birthday gift, we looked out in the morning to see blue sky and sunshine on frozen snow. After breakfast of fried apples, cornbread and sausage we drove to the foothill country we had tried to hunt the day before, a chocolate-drop formation with mountain laurel, Virginia pine and scrubby oaks. The landowner had told me there were a few grouse but this morning he reiterated, "You're welcome to hunt if you'll promise you won't shoot my birds. There's one covey I've been feeding."

"Birds" in our mountains means grouse, but in Virginia "birds" are bobwhites and in those days I would have loved to shoot a brace, even without a dog. But I gave him my word and we started behind his house, walking on a sheet of ice. I was sidling along a hill when I saw a covey fan out from under a laurel bush and explode. The thought occurred that if we flushed a grouse further on I might hold my fire, mistaking it for one of these bobwhites. Just then a straggler rose from the site of the covey flush. Something about it whipped me into action as it quartered left and I swung through and fired, losing sight of it after the trigger pull. I heard Kay's cry, "I saw it fall!" and slithered down the slope, wishing for Blue. The grouse lay on its back with its fan spread, its wings throbbing in ever shorter beats. A fallen grouse on snow is lovely and this one, coming as it had among the quail, seemed an unbelievable chance that made that birthday memorable. After sandwiches over a small fire we returned to the car and drove back to the Navy and a uniform.

6. This shell concerned my father's last grouse. Though he had done no gunning for years, he still kept a couple of setters, still took out his license, but each season found him not quite up to going out. One fall when he was feeling a little stronger we decided to shoot one of my gentler coverts, and to make it specially his day, we gunned over his favorite setter Grouse. The terrain lent itself as well as any grouse country can—an old logging railroad trace winding around the shoulder of a mountain—and keeping him on the

A Box of Shells

grade, I worked the sides. Everything was delightful, except the birds; they either flushed wild or near me.

At last I was pleased to hear Father shoot. When I got to him he was standing on the tramroad, his spent shell on the ground. He had walked into three grouse in some grapevines and had tried for one with no success. I could appreciate his disappointment, considering how long it had been since he had seen a grouse, but I gathered it had been a slim chance, well out over the treetops.

I returned to my position below and soon walked into a single in a ledge of rocks. It was a close shot and the grouse went down in a cloud of feathers. I started to call that I'd got the bird, then checked myself as an idea bloomed. Searching frantically among the rocks, I looked up to see Grouse proudly holding the bird, waiting for my praise. I snatched it from him feeling heartless, and stuffed it into my game pocket just as Father peered over the cliff.

"Did you get it?" he asked.

"No," I said, hoping he wouldn't see the down still floating in the air. "Let's go back. I know about where it went."

After a fake cast I said the bird must have reflushed, and then steered us to where he had missed his bird. Keeping him on the slope below me, I began to play on that old deceiver, Hope, eternal in a shooting man.

"That grouse you shot at—are you sure there isn't a chance you hit it?"

"It was too far out. I shouldn't have tried."

"Sometimes they carry shot a long way and then fall," I reminded him. When we were a logical distance, I checked to make certain he didn't see me and, pulling my bird from my coat, tossed it to Grouse. Grouse gave me a resentful look and started to walk away. Still hoping to bring it off, I grabbed him by the collar, picked up the bird and called, "Look what Grouse is bringing in."

Father came scrambling up the hill, much too fast. "I felt I was on that bird," he gasped. He took his grouse, blinking as he smoothed its feathers. "It seemed to flinch as I shot but then I thought I must have imagined it. Now that just goes to show you. What would you do without a good retriever?" With his other hand he was stroking Grouse.

"You're right," I said. "Let's sit down and have a sandwich."

Mixed Bag

Though Father lived some years longer, that was the last time he fired his gun. A few days later when Kay and I visited him he greeted us with a description of his grouse when dressed. (It had taken my right barrel at fifteen yards.)

"That bird of mine," he went on, "was plastered. It just shows they're never as far out as they seem."

I said he was certainly right, and scratched Grouse's ears.

7. On Thanksgiving Day in '52, Kay and Ruff and I were bumping down a steep mountain road over rocks scraped white by some foolhardy driver in the past. The drop-off on the left was draped with vines blue with grapes, but there was no place to park the station wagon and Kay let us out and arranged to meet us at the bottom of the ridge. Ruff was five—in his prime—and as I watched him quarter the cover above the road he went on point, his legs spread, clinging to the slope. Before I could reach him, two grouse were sailing down the mountain through pole-size timber—one into hemlocks along a trout stream at the bottom.

Joining Kay, we followed the bird and Ruff pointed, his fore parts buried in rhododendron on the bank of the stream. I reached up and tugged a grapevine like a bell pull and the grouse streaked downstream, a dark form banking left, then right among rhododendron. We crossed, Kay taking a tramroad while I hunted along the stream with Ruff. On its third flush, the grouse went out wild and continued down the stream like a salmon running for the sea.

At the mouth of a tributary flowing off the mountain, Ruff plunged in ahead of me and went on point, standing in fast-running

A Box of Shells

water. I waded to a position below, with Ruff immobile except to twist his nostrils right, then left, trying to pinpoint the bird in the heavy rhododendron. I pushed into the tangle on the far bank and waited, my pulse almost obliterating the chuckle of the water. Two more steps brought the grouse boiling up into a piece of sky where, at my shot, it hung spinning, then dropped back the way it had come, falling on Ruff. For a wild moment Ruff and the grouse rolled until he pinned it with his paw, its wings still thrashing. He delivered it, sitting, to put the last touch to three productives on four flushes of one grouse. My gun diary mentions that we came home to a hunter's Thanksgiving dinner of *crêpes Appalachian* (buckwheat cakes with maple syrup) and thanks for a certain dog and a shooting life.

8, 9. When Feathers was three, I took him to a covert that held grouse when I discovered it in '39 and does today. It was cold with occasional sun and grouse were moving. Hunting down the mountain in late afternoon, Feathers flash-pointed our eighth bird but it pitched before I could shoot. Rounding a shoulder, he worked into grapevines and briars and, as I stepped after him, there was a flush and I saw the grouse crossing above me. I was shooting the newly restocked Fox and everything about that gun was right. Feathers saw the bird fold and in seconds was coming through blackberry canes taking the punishment full in his face, carrying a big red-bronze cock that matched his orange-roan color. In the fullness of the moment, I told him I hoped the last grouse I would ever shoot could be just such a bird.

Before turning back, I hunted to the next hollow, and as we approached I saw a grouse flush from rhododendron along the run. For years I've set myself a restriction not to try for a second grouse near where I've shot a bird unless I'm into a group or it is over a point, and I didn't mount my gun. As I stood, another bird flushed from the same spot, following the first one out the ridge. Still I didn't shoot but the idea began to form that if there was another—it came off the hillside in a wide left-quartering flight low to the ground. I swung past and saw it go down, a long right-barrel shot. Feathers made one circle and picked up the grouse and delivered it, as large as the first. I laid the two on a mossy rock and compared them. Both were red-bronze adult cocks, both had semi-interrupted tail bands, both

MIXED BAG

had empty crops (I later discovered that both had small seeds in the gizzard). They were too beautiful and unruffled to put in my game pocket and I carried them to the car, gripped by the legs. On the way, I remembered my hope expressed to Feathers that the last grouse I should ever shoot would be exactly like the first of these identical grouse in my hand. The cold breath on my neck was, I am certain, only wind off the mountain but I stepped a little faster.

10. One afternoon of her first season, I was hunting Dixie solo on an old farm that had surrendered to strip mining. Above me I could hear, without seeing, Canada geese, their voices like a pack of children, growing softer in the south. We crossed a stream and, hunting with sun in my eyes, I walked into a flush from some grapevines where Dixie had disappeared. There was a piping sound and the bird came directly toward me against the sun. Blinded, I swung up through and pulled, and with blue-green discs on each retina glimpsed an odd-looking tail as the bird somersaulted over my head and out of view. I turned to see it, still tumbling head-over-tail, hang itself by the neck in the fork of a sapling where it dangled—a hen pheasant that had no earthly business in this grouse country. When I examined the soft mottled plumage I found the neck broken by the fall, the crop full of grapes and acorns. There are scarcely any wild pheasants in West Virginia, the state's only recognition of the species being mention of a two-bird season limit. An occasional pheasant will stray from a shooting preserve but in those days there was no preserve within miles of where I made this shot. There are times I think I must have shot a ghost.

11. I see two woodcock flying against a golden sky with the distant wall of Canaan Mountain so purple as to be nearly black, and I can smell the damp chill that creeps into that country as the sun slides toward the mountain. I had stopped in for a half hour's shooting after an empty day in grouse coverts and even here my luck held poor, with points but no chance to shoot. Now I could hear both dogs' bells in the alders in their last effort to make the day productive. The tinkling stopped and then there were two 'cock hurtling left to right above the alders like a Schaldach etching, one several yards ahead. I remembered an old-timer's words: "Take the front bird, so if you don't lead enough you'll drop the next one"—as unacceptable to me as shooting into a covey rise and hoping for what

A Box of Shells

you may hit. I swung through the rear bird—against that light it was impossible not to have it focused—pulled and saw it fold. The lead bird was right-quartering now, with my barrels overtaking it still in easy range. Making a double sometimes seems important but one of the pleasures of shooting is the choice to spare a certain bird, and I wanted that 'cock to go on flying. I lowered my gun and watched it shrink to a tiny dot and disappear. Something moved at my side and I looked down to see Dixie with my bird. I accepted it from her easy mouth, soft and limp like so many she has brought me. Of these two, the one I most remember isn't the one that fell to this shell, but that other 'cock still winging over those alders in a sunset that doesn't fade.

12. It was very cold and grouse were lying in snowy rhododendron along the creek. Ruff and I had moved three, with a productive point on one, and were following it to the top of a steep ridge. In a slashing with brush piles and several small hemlocks, I saw the bulk of what appeared to be a squirrel nest in one of the hemlocks, so much like a grouse it could have been mistaken for one. Then I saw the long neck and raised crest. The bird thought it was so well concealed I had to move close under it before it would flush, and by that time we had gazed into each other's eyes so long I couldn't bring myself to shoot as it sailed away.

Once more along the stream rushing dark green between ice-covered boulders, I moved two grouse, missing a crowded shot at one. Clotted snow clouds were shutting out the light and I hurriedly finished my sandwich, leaning against an oak, and started back downstream. Keeping to the trace of a log road, I heard a wild flush as I was squirming between loose rusty barbed wires. Then, fifty yards ahead of me Ruff drew to a point into rhododendron that choked the old path. I got to him, and while he held, solid as the big rock beside him, I plunged through the rhododendron in a burst of snow and came out the far side, quickly running my hand along my barrel rib to clear it. Three seconds later the grouse went out below me without giving me a chance. As I relaxed, a second grouse exploded like a powder keg in front of me, climbing right-crossing over the path, and at my shot tumbled in a spill of feathers. Ruff was on it, fumbling for a grip in a flapping of wings, then he was trotting to me in the snowy dusk, the grouse's head in limp rhythm with his

MIXED BAG

step, completing the beautiful sequence. How many times I've seen him do it. The setting sun broke through the clouds and the far side of the valley caught fire, burned slowly to the top and went out.

13. An honest point well done and a shot made or missed is what life is about to a gun dog and her man. One mid-November day in '59 I was hunting on Canaan Mountain with a friend, using Ruff and his daughter Dixie, not yet two. There was a sifting of snow on the rocks, and the spruce, black in the 15° temperature, made a setting for my orange and blue belton brace ranging ahead. We flushed a grouse and followed it up a hillside, where it gave Dud a surprise shot, which he missed. Estimating its new line of flight, we came to a scattering of hemlocks on top of the ridge. Dixie was ahead of Ruff and I saw her change directions so abruptly she appeared to have been lifted by the neck and tail and dropped into a point at right angles. She was in profile to me and I could see her straining scent out of the bitter wind, her little lightly speckled face dead-earnest. The grouse bored out straight over Dixie and I waited until it was safely behind her and took it as a low right-crosser. Dixie had it within seconds and retrieved it on the double—a young cock.

My companion probably admired her point, but to many men a point is what a bird dog does. In '67 when Dixie lay so nearly dead we had literally to infuse life into her, that point, gay and proud, kept coming back to me. Now that she's well and hunting, three years after that, it is still that point that is the picture of Dixie I see most clearly against my brain.

14. Two days before Christmas, when Dixie was very young and Shadows was only five, I tried a change of pace from grouse. I had heard stories of a few ringnecks seen for the past seven years in the Big Glade. No one could say how they got there but, unlike most of our mountains, the swampy flats had evidently proved compatible and some must have reproduced.

The weather was cold with imminent rain and there was an inch of old snow among the alders. Crossing a frozen beaver pond I broke through and went in over my boot tops and learned, to my pleasure, that insulated boots will keep your feet warm even when wet. Coming out on a large field, I saw posted land beyond and had to work the dogs downwind to avoid flushing birds out of bounds. As a result, they bumped two pheasants from a strip of woods—a grand

A Box of Shells

big cock that sailed cackling defiantly over the NO HUNTING notices and another that crossed out of range back into the swamp. In the swamp I soon found the long-stride tracks running like a deer's through alders and tangled vines until I lost them in a blow-down. Pinning a wild pheasant in such cover is nearly impossible, and since the soft snow had given me a discouraging census of birds in this pheasant island, I decided to give up, for I had a long drive ahead of me and it had begun to rain.

Near where I'd entered the glade I came on fresh tracks. With a choice between the cover and an open field on the outside, I stayed inside with the dogs, who were out of view ahead. I heard that beautiful sound of a cock bird kukking, saw it climb above the trees and —glorious feeling—saw it head my way, its long tail spread and streaming behind. I waited, the way you ought to wait, and with icy rain in my face took it incoming and overhead, firing almost over my right shoulder. It faltered, folded and rolled out of my field of vision behind me. Knowing it would run, I wheeled and called the dogs. There were neither feathers nor tracks but I kept Dixie searching close and let Shadows hunt it in his own way. He was gone a long time and I had small hope he was finding it, then I saw him coming back with the cock in his mouth, straddling the long tail to keep from stepping on it as it dragged between his front legs—a vision in a drizzling cold rain.

It was the largest ringneck I've shot and it had been feeding on grapes. We saved it for New Year's dinner. Served with a good Burgundy and certain nice accompaniments, it was so tough we couldn't chew it, though the setters managed. I'm convinced that that cock bird had been flying and running for the full seven years pheasants had been seen in the Big Glade.

15,16. I remember these shots always as "Confusion at St. Peter's." Kay and I were hunting with Art Thomas, who is a fox hunter, not a grouse hunter; we were hunting at St. Peter's, which is a church, not the pearly gates, though it stands high on the mountain below Heaven Hump. We had moved two single grouse from a scrub thicket—one coasting down past Art, who couldn't find the safety on his gun, the other flying around the hill. Art stayed below to follow his bird while Kay and I worked Dixie higher up. In a clump of hawthorns at a spring seep, Dixie pointed and I walked up for the shot. The grouse flushed back in a flight below eye level that is poison to me and I missed it, both barrels. As I stood with my gun open, another grouse flushed from the same clump—and another—and another—until five more had boiled out in single flights as wide open as skeet targets. With the air full of grouse like a hatch of mayflies, I jammed a shell into my gun and tried for the last one, achieving a gentle click as I pulled the wrong trigger. If I remember this as Confusion, Art heard it, far below, more nearly as Benediction, for my words were straight out of church as I called on all Three to witness the Misery of Man.

17. Certainly there is no nicer way to celebrate Christmas afternoon than by gunning, regardless of weather. It had been raining in the morning and fog smothered the ridge tops, but in spite of dripping brush we were out shooting—and moving grouse. In a favorite greenbrier corner I came to Shadows pointing, bulge-eyed, on the upper side of a path with Dixie pointing solidly at his side. I stepped toward him, trying to guess which of three ways the grouse would take. It took none of them but came at me a few feet off the ground. I waited for it to clear cover, then missed twice, my left pattern lodging entire in a cherry trunk.

On the Fourth Day of Christmas, which is my birthday, we returned to this covert, once more driving through fog. This time we found the hemlocks iced and frozen drops on every sapling twig. Again, we hunted paths, moving birds but with no shots. In the same greenbrier tangle, Shadows pointed and again Dixie backed him. When I walked in and nothing happened, I ordered Shadows on but he refused to move, and Dixie continued to stare hypnotically at her feet. My next step brought a grouse wriggling out of the vines in a short run before it became air-borne. Kay dropped to give me the shot and I turned and took it away-left. Shadows was the first to reach the fallen bird and retrieved it, sitting to deliver. The double point had been six yards from where Shadows and Dixie made their double point three days before; it could have been the same grouse; my ejected shell fell within feet of my two empties still lying there, but this is the shell that mattered and this time, like Shadows, I was grinning.

18. It was October 24 in '66 and we had found one of our favorite

A Box of Shells

Canaan coverts pre-empted by five woodcock hunters. To add to the joy, a hard rain had set in. The rain did let up and we had an afternoon in another covert, with a point on grouse by Bliss and one wild woodcock flush but no shots. Returning to our first area, we were delighted to find the other gunners gone (I wonder how often, by departing, I have made somebody happy) and, with an hour's hunting ahead of us, set out with new enthusiasm. There was plenty of whitewash but the birds were so wild after their more-shots-than-hits workout they wouldn't lie for points. I managed to get one bird over a point by the time we got back to the station wagon, where Shadows, under heavy medication after a severe nervous attack the week before, roused to greet us. He was so pathetically eager I took him, mostly as a gesture, for one last turn with Dixie and Bliss while Kay started a fire for our cookout.

In spite of his condition, he pushed into the alders rather than stay on the path with me. On our return, we moved a woodcock from some aspen, the flush carrying it toward Kay and the station wagon. I had almost reached Kay when I saw Bliss pointing, with Dixie backing. Shadows, who couldn't see the point, went on to Kay. I walked up the 'cock but undershot it and saw it flutter on across the alders with a leg dangling, one of the rare woodcock I have seen carry shot. Calling the dogs, I hurried along the edge and was aware that Shadows was running after me. At the far end, all three plunged in and began scouring the swamp. I was uneasy Shadows would become overstimulated as he plowed through deep mud, running blindly into brush, but he went on searching loyally. At last, Dixie gave up and came to heel but neither Bliss nor Shadows would quit. Deciding it was hopeless, I turned to call them and saw Shadows wheel toward a clump of swamp grass beyond where we'd been looking. Appearing to hit scent, he nosed into the grass and picked up the dead woodcock, carrying it with his head held so high shivers ran up and down my neck. He brought it to me, his old eyes glittering, and at my word, sat and delivered it to hand. I doubt if there have been any just like Shadows.

After a tailgate supper, we sat on, looking at big Cabin Mountain dimly luminous in misty moonlight filtering through clouds, and all the while, with the two girls dozing on the station-wagon floor behind us, Shadows sat erect with his ears cocked, seeing with eyes that didn't need to see.

MIXED BAG

19, 20. The sorcery of woodcock—dropping almost out of nowhere into remote coverts, bringing them alive for a few days, then vanishing—working their spell each autumn in places many times unseen by men, is a wonder I can never take for granted. We were shooting over Bliss, exploring a new grouse covert in high flat country. It was classic hardwood-hemlock cover with rhododendron and a small run with an unexpected stretch of alders. Bliss's bell went silent the moment she reached them and I found her pointing what, from her manner, was going to be a woodcock. When I moved past her the 'cock rose steeply and a bit close. I saw it level a split-second after my shot, then heard the twitter-up of a second bird, wheeled and missed it clean as it banked for an opening. With my face tingling from two misses, I pushed on and came to Bliss on another point across the run, her head turned toward a mossy log. Telling myself to relax, I walked in, tight as a harp string, adjusting my cap—a foolish thing I do when I'm tense. Still nothing happened, then I saw it lying breast-up to one side of Bliss's entranced stare. With my attention drawn to the second flush, the first 'cock had, instead of leveling, been falling dead.

21. This shell was not fired so expertly as to demand mention, yet I see the sequence in curious detail, probably because it broke a long spell without shots at grouse. It was in November '67, a wonderful year for 'cock. Kay, Dixie, Bliss and I were gunning a big expanse of hawthorns and I had shot two woodcock over double points. On the return we hunted just within a good grouse woods beyond the thorns and I changed to heavier loads. Two single grouse flushed without giving me a chance, doing nothing for my composure. At the end of the woods I changed to woodcock loads before stepping back into the hawthorns. Turning to speak to Kay, with my gun still broken open, I heard a flush behind me in the thorns and wheeled to see a big grouse coming out high. I often don't, but this time I had the sense to snap the gun shut and try it nearly straight up and left-crossing. The pattern centered and the grouse came down counter-clockwise, falling on a big maple log and bouncing to the far side. Bliss found it and came with it through an opening under the log, to deliver a large jet-ruffed cock with a tan tail fan. Kay tells me I kept repeating, "What a shot! *Boy*, what a shot!" The big grouse and my two woodcock made a pleasing feel in my

A Box of Shells

game pocket on the way out and, as Brillat-Savarin so nicely put it, I was well content.

22. It was a lovely December day in '68, warm with snow melting on the ground—a day that soon turned into a series of frustrations. In spite of damp quiet in the woods, several grouse had gone out wild; we moved one flush of five young birds and, as often happens, had got a poor chance at those, one of which I'd missed. I marked and followed one, and within yards of where I expected it, Bliss skidded to a point, frozen in a crouch. Gesturing to Kay, I moved into the greenbriers and the bird went out, giving me no shot, and Kay's movie camera jammed. Again, I pinpointed the bird's flight to a woods edge but it flushed before the dogs and I could reach it. It was getting late and I was for giving up, but Kay insisted that she go for the station wagon while I follow the grouse with the dogs.

Keeping on the knob in old fields, I came to a thin stand of locusts and dead goldenrod and swung the dogs toward a ravine below me. Bliss came around and hit scent, working it up the slope and drawing into a stretched-out point with Dixie backing, like an engraving on an old sidelock. Even in these mountains, the cover said *ringneck*. I walked in above Bliss and from the reedy goldenrod there was a fluttering right-quarter rise—glory be, a grouse—and I caught it leveling. Bliss was on it when it fell and retrieved it nicely, but just as she reached me the bird struggled free. Running down the slope, it darted into a hole in the roots of a wild cherry as if it lived there. Bliss was close behind and began nosing into the hole, but rather than risk the bird's getting beyond her grasp, I brought it out and dispatched it—an adult hen. I carried the grouse to the old road where Kay had sounded the horn, and held it high for Kay to see above the low haze forming on the melting snow—the last grouse I was to shoot over Bliss's splendid points.

23. It was the second week of Briar's first season and we were gunning the high mountains in the first-burning of golden birch and maple leaves. To escape a biting 40° wind, we moved to a lower covert and hunted alders in the basin of a cove. Briar gave us a point on a woodcock I didn't get to shoot—just as well, for he made two more points on it before it left the country, an obliging bird. Later, we ate lunch in a setting I'll never forget, in a shower of yellow

Mixed Bag

beech leaves on a log that was the curliest of bird's-eye maple, its whorled grain showing in knobs all over it.

Back in the alders where I was expecting 'cock, a grouse flushed close, rising steeply, and I shot a half second too soon at about five yards. The bird pitched over, righted itself and went on with both legs dangling, leaving a float of feathers coming down in front of me. I saw the grouse reach the shoulder of the basin, turn acutely right, and watched it keep on going, a silhouette against backlighted yellow leaves. Swinging Briar up the slope, I tried to intercept the line of flight where I thought it might go down. Almost at the spot, Briar went on point. The ground pack was disturbed but the point proved empty. I was searching in a circle when I heard Kay call, "Briar's pointing over here." This time I saw the dead grouse on the leaves in front of him. After holding the point a few moments longer, he saw it and picked it up. Standing, uncertain what to do, he started to carry the bird, paused again—a beautiful pose for Kay's movie—and at my words retrieved it to me—his first grouse.

24. This shell, fired on New Year's Day of '62 when Ruff was nearly fifteen, is not in proper sequence. But in my memory it keeps getting out of place.

Where the path drops to the Wildcat Rocks, I found Ruff solidly on point. The years had silvered his orange-roan muzzle and had taken the loftiness out of his magnificent points—his head was lower, his tail a little harder for him to hold up—but nothing could tarnish his integrity. There he stood, immobile except for a quivering muscle in his left thigh, his soul in his face and in his nose. I think I whispered a supplication that I could shoot the bird for him as I stepped past him into deep snow. Young Dixie was circling above and as she came from in front I heard the flush and saw the grouse, low, but couldn't tell if it was going away or coming head-on until it appeared to grow larger. It swerved to my right, still sailing low, and at my shot it rolled in a cloud of feathers and snow. Dixie got to it before Ruff and made the retrieve, a large adult cock so hard hit it felt boneless when I accepted it.

It was the last grouse I shot over Ruff in his fifteen full seasons dedicated to the bird. From his first point as a half-grown youngster with an unruly cowlick of hair on the small of his back until this,

his 547th productive on grouse, each shell I fired over him—and there were many—seemed to come from a charmed box.

25. The last shell of this special box is still lying loose in the bottom, unfired. It was long ago when I opened this box with the shells laid neatly, heads to tails, and even then I knew that each was a wonderful moment to be lived. Like some men who collect shells, I might be wise to keep this one so I could say I had not fired my last shell. But the shells I collect are spent shells, making certain each autumn when these trees envelop me in fairyland that I don't leave any living undone.

No shooting man wants to be aware of when he has shot that final shell, but when he does, let it be in the gun he most loves, at the bird he loves most. For me, I want it to be over an Old Hemlock setter on the kind of pulse-pounding point they have given me, with Kay there making it fine and beautiful. I'll be happy if it is in October, nor could it be more nearly perfect than in November; and if it should be in late winter I'll have had that much more of the shooting life well lived. I needn't say I want to fire that shell at a grouse.

If my shooting average hasn't changed, there are two chances to one I'll miss it, and if I do I think I'll be glad, for I want there always to be grouse. Years ago I gave my heart to these mountains and with each shooting season I succumb anew to their gold and scarlet and hemlocks needle-sharp against a sunset, to their immense quiet and their smells. I want there to be woodcock forever flying over in October, and solitude, and Hunter's Moons. But most, I want there always to be grouse—of all wild things, the wildest—in these endless mountains we call home.

INDEX

INDEX

abandoned farms, 23, 27, 84, 132
Addison (Pa.), 181
Allam, Dr. Mark, 210
Allegheny Front, 25, 37–8, 104
Allegheny Mt. (W.Va.), 34, 83, 85, 99, 181
Allegheny Mts., 18, 25, 84, 87, 97, 110, 119, 267
Allegheny Plateau, 25, 37
Allen, Arthur A., 122
American Field, The, 214
American Game Bird Shooting (Grinnell), 5, 219
American Game Birds (Edminster), 20, 126, 135, 147
American Wildfowlers, 182
American Woodcock, The Book of the (Sheldon), 72
Ames, Hobart, 183
Ames Plantation (Grand Junction, Tenn.), 182, 184
Amwell Preserve (N.J.), 9, 59, 155–60, 263
Anthony Creek (W.Va.), 34
Antioch (Va.), 140
Appalachian Mts., 15, 25, 175
Appalachians grouse range, 25–6
Au Sable River (Mich.), 31–3
Audley House (London), 283
Avent, Jim, 183

B. & O. Railroad, 29
Babcock Grade, 43
Backbone Mt. (Md. & W.Va.), 26, 29, 43, 47
Bailey, John, 183
Bailey, Wayne, 89, 202
Balling, M. T., Jr., 201
Bath County (Va.), 34, 203
Bayard (W.Va.), 43
Beaver Creek (W.Va.), 43
beaver ponds, 36, 38, 40
Beech Mt. (W.Va.), 199

Biddle, Lynford, 208, 278–9
biologists, wildlife, 9, 17–18, 42, 51, 58, 70, 81, 89, 125, 128, 137–8, 147, 202, 266
Black Moshannon (Pa.), 13
Black Mt. (W.Va.), 35
Blackwater Chronicle, The (Kennedy), 41
Blackwater Falls State Park (W.Va.), 43, 64, 80
Blackwater River (W.Va.), 26, 36, 39–40, 42, 59, 82, 276
Blackwater-Canaan (W.Va.), 26, 35–44, 55, 81, 83, 100, 108, 179, 268
Blogg, Percy, 13, 213
Blome, Richard, 235
bobwhite quail: age, 138, 142; age ratio, 143; bevy, 138; chicks, 142; and cold, 137; *Colinus virginianus floridanus*, 137; *C. v. texanus*, 137; *C. v. virginianus*, 136; coverts, 135 40, 143; covey continuity, 138; covey habits, 138; covey thinning, 137; eggs, 142; flight and behavior, 140–1; kills, 138; law of inversity, 137; management, 138; nest, 142; pheasants vs. quail, 135; populations, 137, 143, 266; predators, 137; preserves, 143, 152, 154; range, early, 135; range, present, 136; refuge, 143; scent, holding, 141, 228; sex, 142; sex ratio, 143; shooting, 135–43, 186; singles, 137; Southern plantations, 138–9, 186; stocking, 138; for training, 137, 141, *and see also* dogs, training; voice, 137, 141; weather, effect, 137, 143
bogs, 23, 29, 35–6, 38–40, 82, 107
bow hunting, 8, 33, 179

[*iii*]

INDEX

Breda o-and-u shotgun: *see photo insert*
Briery Mts. (W.Va.), 58
Brillat-Savarin, 270, 299
Browning, Meshach, 29, 175
Browning shotgun, automatic, o-and-u: *see photo insert*
Buckingham, Irma Jones, 182–4
Buckingham, Nash, 139, 182–4, 276
Bump, Gardiner, 80; see also *Ruffed Grouse, The*
By-Paths in the Mountains (Davis), 42

Cabin Mt. (W.Va.), 13, 26, 37, 43–4, 104, 178, 297
Cadwalader, Dr. Williams Biddle, 208, 263
Caius, Johannes, 219–20, 230
Cal Price State Forest (W.Va.), 34
Cameron, Angus, 5
Canaan Mt. (W.Va.), 26, 35–6, 40–1, 64, 83, 123, 129, 292, 294
Canaan Valley (W.Va.), 15, 26, 36–9, 43, 59, 62, 82, 240, 296
Canada goose, 198–9, 292; *see also* shooting *and* wildfowl
Canadian flora, W.Va., 35–6, 38
Carman, Bliss, 2, 23
Carson, Rachel, 52
Chapman, Dan, 197
Cheat River (W.Va.), 26, 28, 134
Cherry River (W.Va.), 35
Chestnut Ridge (Pa., W.Va.), 21, 25
chukar partridge, 152, 154, 169
Churchill, Robert, 145
Churchill shotgun, 278
coal, W.Va., 26; strip mines, 26–7
Conaway, Obie, 185, 197
Connett, Eugene V., 129
Continental breeds, gun dogs, 230
cover: alder, 16, 23, 29, 36, 39, 59, 62; aspen, 17, 23–5, 31, 36, 39, 59, 62; balsam, 23; beech, 23, 28, 39, 104; birch, black, 13, 39; birch, white, 23, 31; birch, yellow, 39; blackberry, 27–8, 100; blueberry, 29, 37, 83; bracken, 82; cedar, white, 23, 31; cherry, black, 28; chestnut, 28; conifers, 17; crab apple, 17, 29, 85; dogwood, gray, 33; fir, 25; grape, wild, 27–8; greenbrier, 27–9, 296; hardwoods, 17, 23, 27; hawthorn, 17, 23, 29, 67; hemlock, 23, 26–7, 36, 104; laurel, 37, 89; maples, 23, 31, 39; mountain ash, 37; mountain holly, 37; oaks, 28, 34; pine, jack, 31; pine, white, 23, 29, 31, 34; raisin, wild, 56; regrowth, 24, 27–8, 36, 42; rhododendron, 26–7, 34, 37, 40, 89–90, 104, 108, 290–1, 293; serviceberry ("sarvice"), 28–9, 37; sphagnum, 36, 38, 82; spirea ("hardhack"), 60, 62; spruce, 23, 25, 36–41, 104; tamarack, 23, 31
coverts, 13–14; bobwhite, 135–40; grouse, 23–44, 104; pheasant, 18–22; woodcock, 15–17
Covington, Carl, 139
Cranberry Glades (W.Va.), 35
Cranberry Mt. (W.Va.), 35
Cranesville Swamp (Md., W.Va.), 29
Crissey, Walter F., 80; see also *Ruffed Grouse, The*
Crowl, Less, 31, 39, 94, 144, 150, 185, 198
Cry of the Hillborn (Carman), 23
Culpeper County (Va.), 139
Currier & Ives, 215

Darrow, Robert W., 80; see also *Ruffed Grouse, The*
Davis (W.Va.), 4, 35, 41, 43, 58, 62, 82, 176, 178
Davis, Henry P., 183
Davis, Rebecca Harding, 42
DDT: *see* pesticides
Deep Creek (Md.), 29
Deer Park (Md.), 30
Derrydale Press, 129
Deward (Mich.), 31
dogs, gun: aging, 132, 165, 167, 217–18; backpointing, 65, 67, 97, 150, 166, 238, 241, 297–9; bell, hunting, 65, 180, 201, 243–4, 292; bobwhites, covey dog, 139; bobwhites, work on, 201, 243; brace work, 56–7, 65, 67, 89, 97, 99, 103, 115, 150, 158–9, 240–1, 294, 297–8; breeds, *see specific breeds*; colored collar,

iv]

Index

dogs, gun (*cont.*)
streamers, 96; companionship, 3, 213; dock-tailed, 161–4; field trial, 216, 226; flush, manner at, 106; grouse, bird sense on, 75, 225, 227, 242; grouse retrieving, 78, 82, 88, 96, 112–14, 119, 134, 242, 289, 291, 293–4, 296, 298–300; grouse, work on, 76–8, 101, 133, 223, 225, 236, 242–3, 290, 293–4, 296, 299, 300; grouse dog, ideal, 215–16, 223–4, 244; grouse dog, relation to gunner, 75–8, 112, 131, 134, 216, 230–1, 239, 244; handling on points, *see* dogs, training; medication effect, 229; pheasants, retrieving, 150–1, 158–9, 165–6, 168–9, 295; pheasants, work on, 148, 158, 226–7; points, first, 65, 160, 237; points, style on, 226, 241–4, *and see also* dogs, training; prairie grouse, work on, 200; preserve birds, work on, 153–72, 226; preserve dogs, 153; scent, 57, 88–92, 96, 105, 107, 213, 225–9; selecting a puppy, 217; snow, effect, 93, 96–7, 227–8; temperature, effect, 87, 92, 227–8; weather, effect, 87–94, 227–8; woodcock, retrieving, 53, 60, 64, 66, 68–9, 232, 293, 297; woodcock, work on, 53, 56, 64, 202, 237, 240–3, 297–8

dogs, training, 214, 226, 230–44; blinking, 232, 234, 244; bolting, 234, 236, 244; check cord, 232–3, 237, 239; correcting weaknesses, 239; electronic collar, 190, 234; flushing whip, 242; force, 232–3, 239; ground-trailing, 227, 240, 244; grouse, 242; gun-shyness, 232, 244; handling on point, 233–4, 237, 239–40; initiative, 238; mechanical devices, 233; memory, 239; obedience, yard training, 232–3, 237; pheasants, 237; pointing, 233; pointing, back, 238; pointing, false, 242; positive points, 238, 242; preserves, on, 153; quartering, 233–5; range control, 233, 238, 240, 243; retrieving, 232, 236; retrieving, dummy, 232; retrieving, gentle mouth, 232, 244; scent-pointing wing, 234; shooting only over points, 241; sight pointing, 234; stanchness, 233, 238, 240, 244; steadiness, 238–9, 242; training quail, 237–40, 242; when to start, 231; whistle signals, 234–5, 238; woodcock, 64–5, 69, 240

Dolly Sods (W.Va.), 13, 26, 37–8
dove, 138, 175, 183, 194
duck boats, 195
ducks: *see* wildfowl
Dugan, Frank, 203
Dundee (Mich.), 150
Dunn, Duncan, 155–6

earthworm, 17
Eastern Upland Shooting (Norris), 4, 206, 208, 210
Edminster, Frank C., 20, 137; see also *American Game Birds* and *Ruffed Grouse, The*
Ellsworth (Me.), 208
Englishe Dogges, Of (Caius), 219–20
Evans, Kay, 3, 4, 7, 62, 66, 71, 82, 92, 170, 179, 186, 189, 213, 237, 262, 273, 277, 286–8, 296–301

Fairhill (Bryn Mawr, Pa.), 156–7, 194, 205–10, 277
Far Away and Long Ago (Hudson), 6
Farewell to Arms, A (Hemingway), 274
farming, effect: bobwhites, 135–7, grouse, 136, pheasants, 18–21, 150, woodcock, 16
farming, Intermediate Ridges, 27; *see also* abandoned farms
Field & Stream, 182
Field Dog Stud Book, 214–15
field trials, 182, 210, 215–16; *see also* dogs, gun
fire, 36, 39, 41–2, 139, 199
Fitzgerald, Scott, 3
Flatrock Plains (W.Va.), 39
fog, 38–9, 48

INDEX

food, game—
  bobwhite: greens, 136, 139
  grouse, 78–87; acorns, 29, 35, 79, 81, 110; apple, 84; beechnut, 81; blackberry, 28; blueberry, 29, 33, 37, 83; buds, 33, 82, 84; catkins, 84; cherry, black, 28, 83; cinquefoil, 80, 181; crab apple, 85; cranberry, 35, 38, 82; dogwood berry, 82; ferns, 80; grape, wild, 35, 79, 181; grass, 80; greenbrier berry, 29, 79; greens, 33, 35, 37, 78, 80, 84; haw, 35, 81; maple seeds, 83; mountain holly, 37, 82; mountain laurel, 80; rhododendron bud, 84; rubus, 80–1; seeds, 35, 84; serviceberry, 28, 37; sheep sorrel, 80; sumac, 83; teaberry, 35, 80; wild raisin, 83
  pheasant: corn, 19, 21; wild fruits, 19
  woodcock: earthworms, 17
Ford, Corey, 216
Foster, Meade, 141, 200, 276
Foster, William Harnden, 257
four-wheel-drives, 43, 190
fox: *see* grouse, predators, *and* pheasant, predators
Fox shotgun, 5, 50, 132, 140, 158, 168, 199, 252, 254–57, 279, 285, 291: *see also photo insert*
Francotte shotgun: *see photo insert*

gadgets, hunting, 190–1
game: attitude toward, 7–10, 58, 74–5, 111, 130, 186, 188–90, 209; hogs, 9; on the table, 270–6; management, 9, 27, 122, 139
Gates, Jack, 139
Gentleman's Recreation, The (Blome), 235
George Washington National Forest (Va., W.Va.), 34
glacier, 18, 20, 85
Goudy, William, 33, 63
Grayling (Mich.), 31
Greenbrier River (W.Va.), 34
Greener shotgun, 198
Greenfell, W., shotgun, 196
Griffith, George A., 33
Grinnell, George Bird, 5, 219

grouse, prairie (pinnated & sharp-tailed), 199–200
grouse, red Scotch, 43, 85, 153, 259, 270
grouse, ruffed: age, 123–6; Allegheny, 79, 119, 129; and autos, 98, 122; barometer, 90-1; bird/covert ratio, 265, 267–8; *Bonasa umbellus affinis*, 25; *B. u. brunnescens*, 25; *B. u. castanea*, 25; *B. u. incana*, 25; *B. u. monticola*, 25, 129; *B. u. phaia*, 25; *B. u. sabini*, 25; *B. u. togata*, 23–4, 29, 33, 84, 110, 129; *B. u. umbelloides*, 23–5; *B. u. umbellus*, 25; *B. u. yukonensis*, 25; broods, 95, 100–1, 110, 266, 268; Canadian, 23, 98; color phase, 128–9; counts, flushing, 131, 264, 266; counts, kill, 266; counts, separate bird, 131, 264; coverts, 23–44, 86, 129, *and see also* cover; crop contents, 78–87, 264; diet, effect on flavor, 79, 82, 84; drumming, 123, 266; ecology, 122; "feathered," 117–19; flight and behavior, 76, 97–110, 113–14, 127, 243; flight length, 107–8; flight speed, 105; flushes, second, 106, 108, 124, 131; flushes, time of day, 105, 124; gizzard, 85; gravel, grit, 85; hippoboscid fly ("louse fly," *Lynchia americana*), 122; human voice, effect, 131; mad moon, "crazy flight," 109–10; management, 122; "missed" birds found dead, 117; moult, 125; names, local, 33, 75, 127, 130, 175; pheasants vs. grouse, 148; plumage, late-winter, 255; plumage, marking, 127–9; poisoning from eating, 80; population, 42; population fluctuations, 266–9; predators, 119–22; range, 23–5; red-ruff, 128–9, 291; roosts, 100–1; ruff, 128; sex, 124–8, 266; shooting, 73–134, *and see also* shooting; size, 124, 127; snow, 85, 93–6, 288, 293; soil type, 85; sunshine, 92; tail, 124–5, 127–9, 291; temperature, effect, 87, 100–1, 268–9; towering, 115–16; water,

vi]

Index

grouse, ruffed (*cont.*)
85; weather, effect, 87–97, 268–9; wind, effect, 91; wing, 125; wing-broken, 112–14, 118; wounded, 82, 111–19, 228, 255, 286, 300
guides, 32, 179
gun: *see* shotgun
gun diary, 5, 78, 127, 210, 263–9
gun pressure, 17, 18, 49, 124, 138, 150, 155, 186

hare, varying, snowshoe, 38
hawk: *see* grouse, predators, *and* pheasant, predators
heath, *re* grouse, 43, 85; crossleaf (*Erica tetralix*), 43
Heath, Melvin, 62, 178–9
heather, Scotch (*Calluna vulgaris*), 43
Hemingway, Ernest, 274
Herring Hall (Va.), 139
Holland, Dan, 84
Horseshoe Lake goose sanctuary (Ill.), 198
Huckleberry Plains (W.Va.), 37–8, 83
Hudson, W. H., 6
Hunt, Mrs. C. P.: *see* setter, English
Huntley (Md.), 263

Intermediate Ridges, 26–9, 83, 85, 129, 132
Italy, shooting, 197
Ithaca shotgun, double-barrel, pump: *see photo insert*

jeep: *see* four-wheel-drives
Johnson, Samuel, 104

Kennedy, Philip Pendleton, 41
Kennison Mt. (W.Va.), 35
Kinsey, Harold, 198
Kotchek, Dr. Leo, 223

L. C. Smith shotgun: *see photo insert*
Labrador, 23, 206
Labrador retriever, 159, 160, 230
Lake States Forests grouse range, 24
Lambert, John, 175
Lambertville (N.J.), 155
Land-Rover: *see* four-wheel-drives

lark shooting: *see* Italy, shooting
Laverack, Edward: *see* setter, English
Lawrence, Harry (Purdeys), 281
Lesser, Walt, 58–61, 196
Llewellin, R. Purcell: *see* setter, English
Loop Road, Twenty-two Mile Grade (W.Va.), 13, 41
lumber camps, 82, 178
lumber railroad grades: *see* tramroads
lumbering: *see* timbering

mallard: *see* wildfowl
Manistee River (Mich.), 32–3
Manton, Joseph, 283; shotgun, 216
market hunting, 30, 32, 257
Martha Washington Inn (Abingdon, Va.), 139
Martin, Dutch, 160–5
Martin, Emmet, 201
Maryland, coverts, 101; *see also* Tableland
Masefield, John, 144, 205, 225, 245
Mason-Dixon Line, 213; *re* pheasants, 18, 20; *re* woodcock, 71
men, shooting, 175–210; fantasies, 130–1, 191–2; gadgeteer, 190–1; lone shooter, 187–8, 192; long-shot addict, 189; novice, 73, 191; old-timers, 176–84; older shot, 155, 157, 159, 205–10; purist, 192–3; reporter, 191–2; shooting companions, 185–7, 194
Menzie, Calvin M., 53
Michigan grouse shooting, 31–3
Middleburg (Va.), 140
Migratory Bird Populations Station (Laurel, Md.): *see* Patuxent Wildlife Research Center
Monongahela National Forest (W.Va.), 34, 37
Monongahela River (W.Va.), 21, 25
Moriarity, Gene, 201–2
Morton, Clyde, 183
Mose, 161
movies, 4, 48, 55, 62, 82, 145, 156, 158, 162, 166, 169, 186, 189, 209, 300

National Field Trial Champions (Brown and Buckingham), 182

INDEX

National Field Trial Championship, 180, 182, 214
Nebraska: *see* prairie grouse
Negro Mt. (Md.), 181
Nemacolin Trail Hunting Reserves (Pa.), 155, 166–72
New Brunswick, 23, 48, 52, 206
New England, 23, 84, 175
New England Grouse Shooting (Foster), 257
New York Conservation Dept., 105, 123; see also *Ruffed Grouse, The*
Norris, Dr. Charles C., 4, 48, 115, 144–5, 148, 155–60, 185, 194, 205–10, 263, 271, 274, 278–84; *see also photo insert*
Norris, William Pepper, 277–8
Northeastern Forest grouse range, 23
Nova Scotia, 23, 48, 206

Oakland (Md.), 29
Of Englishe Dogges: see *Englishe Dogges, Of*
Old Hemlock (Bruceton Mills, W.Va.), 5, 213, 215; bobwhites on, 136; woodcock on, 69
Old Hemlock setters, 3, 165, 213, 219, 301; Bliss, 3, 40, 48, 57, 65–91, 101–3, 171, 223, 231–44, 261, 264–5, 297–9; Blue, 3, 112–13, 117, 126, 217, 221, 264, 286; Briar, 3, 223, 229, 244, 299–300; Dawn, 217; Dixie, 3, 53–62, 64–9, 82, 96, 101–3, 108, 114–15, 159, 168, 170–2, 213, 222, 231, 240–1, 261, 264, 292–300; Feathers, 3, 82, 94, 156–9, 165–6, 213, 221, 264, 291–2; Ruff, 3, 41, 59–60, 94–9, 114–15, 131–4, 150, 156–9, 165–8, 217–23, 244, 264, 290–3, 300; Shadows, 3, 51, 56, 60, 65, 82, 96, 99, 101, 111, 118, 150, 158–9, 165, 168, 170–2, 213, 221–2, 240; Wilda, 97, 158, 220, 223; *see also* setters, English
Osthaus, Edmund H., 4, 56, 150, 180, 216
owl: *see* grouse, predators *and* pheasant, predators

Parker shotgun, 5, 181–2, 195; *see also photo insert*
partridge, 197; *see also* chukar partridge
Patuxent Wildlife Research Center (Laurel, Md.), 52, 63
Pelee Island (Lake Erie), 147
Pennsylvania, University of: Medical School, 206; Veterinary School, 210
Pennsylvania coverts: bobwhite, 135; grouse, 28, 99, 126; pheasant, 20–1; turkey, 202; *see also* Intermediate Ridges
pesticides, 18; DDT, heptachlor, levels in woodcock, 52–3
pheasant: age, 146; Alleghenies, 18–19, 294; broods, nides, 147; coverts, 18–22, 150, 161; flight and behavior, 148–50; flight length, 150; flight speed, 105; flushes, second, 150; glaciated soil, 18, 20, 85; gun pressure, 147, 150–1; gunning tactics, 148–9; hens, shooting, 147, 148, 153, 158–9; human population, effect, 18, 155; human voice, 149; kill, 148; melanistic, 164; pen-reared, 148, 152; population, 146, 266; predators, 147, 153, 164; preserves, 146–7, 152–72; range, 18; road hunting, 150; runners, 148, 150, 170, 172, 228, 242; shooting, 144–72, 197, *and see also* shooting; spurs, 146; stocking, 18, 147–8, 153; strains, Caucasian, Chinese, Iranian, Japanese, and Korean, 19; strain, Reeves, 167–9; survival, 146–7; temperature, effect, 19–20; training dogs, 21–2, *and see also* dogs, training; voice, 149; vs. grouse, 148; vs. quail, 135; weather, effect, 18–20, 159; wounded, 147, 150, 153, 228; yearling ratio, 146
Pheasant Mt. (W.Va.), 14
Physiology of Taste, The (Brillat-Savarin), 270
Pinebloom Plantation (Ga.), 139, 167
pipelines, gas and oil, 27
Piper, Frank, 202
Pocahontas County (W.Va.), 34, 88

viii]

Index

Pocomoonshine Lake (Me.), 201
pointer, English, 10, 140, 231; Ariel, 183; Luminary, 183; Saturn, 183; *see also* dogs, gun
pointer, German shorthair, 160, 166, 230; *see also* dogs, gun
pollution, 26, 183
Porte Crayon: *see* Strother, David Hunter
Porte Crayon, Mt. (W.Va.), 39
Potomac River, North Branch (Md., W.Va.), 29, 41
Pottsville conglomerate, 85
power lines, 27, 86, 101
power plants, 36
Prairie Lane Preserve (Ohio), 155, 160–6
preserves: fees, 154; shooting, 143, 147, 152–72, 189
Purdey, James, & Sons Ltd., 281–4
Purdey shotgun, 10, 50, 56, 64, 156, 210, 216, 222, 254–7, 277–84; *see also photo insert*

quail, 197; *see also* bobwhite quail

Red Creek Plains (W.Va.), 39
refuge, 17, 143
Remington pump shotgun: *see photo insert*
Reynard the Fox (Masefield), 144, 225, 245
Ridge-and-Valley Province, 25
Rinell, Kermit T., 125
road hunting, 32, 41, 150
Roaring Plains (W.Va.), 39
Rockwell, Willard F., Jr., 139, 166–7
Rocky Mountain–Pacific Coast Forests grouse range, 24
Ruffed Grouse, The (Bump, Darrow, Edminster, and Crissey), 80, 85, 105, 119, 126, 129
Rutledge, Archibald, 173, 277
Ryman, George, 216; *see also* setters, English

Sage, A. G. C., 183
sand hills (Neb.), 19, 199–200
Scala, Luch, 196
scent: *see* bobwhite quail; dogs, gun; *and* woodcock
Schaldach, William, 292

Seaton, Charlie, 257
Seaton's Lake (Pa.), 214
Service, Robert W., 11, 40, 44
Seton, Ernest Thompson, 109
setter, English: belton, 65, 82, 205, 216–20, 241; bench-bred, 220; breeding, 215–20, 224; breeding, line-, 218–20; color, 219; Count Noble, 214, 216; early setter, 217, 219, 235; early setter, strains, American Natives (Campbells, Davidsons, Ethan Allens, Gildersleeves, and Morfords), Beaudesert, Duke of Gordon, Duke-Rhoebe, and Edmund Castle, 215; Eugene's Ghost, 184; Gladstone, 182, 216, 244; Hunt setter ("Pinewild"), 216; Laverack setter, 215, 219, 222; Llewellin setter, 182, 214–16, 222; Mohawk, 217; Nugym, 216; Old Hemlock setter, 216–24, *and see also* Old Hemlock setters; Prince Rodney, 217; puppies, 217, 221, 223; registration, 215; Ryman setter, 214, 216, 222; Sir Roger de Coverly, 214; Sport's Peerless, 214, 222; Sport's Peerless Pride, 214; Statter, Field & Armstrong, 215; Tony's Gale, 180; Twombley, Earl, 216; Victor Okaw, 4; *see also* dogs, gun
setter, Gordon, 215–16, 230; *see also* dogs, gun
setter, Irish, 216, 230; *see also* dogs, gun
Sharp, Ward, 42, 199
Shay locomotive, 43, 178
Sheaffer, Walter, II, 198
Sheldon, William G., 72
shells, loads, 255–6, 286; for grouse, 255–6, 280, 282; for pheasant, 146, 256, 280; for quail, 140, 256, 280; shot, 50, 56, 140, 146, 196, 200, 255–6; shot penetration, 255–6; shot sleeve, plastic, 256; for woodcock, 50, 56, 196, 256, 280, 282
shooting: aiming, 259; averages, 255, 264–6; bobwhite, 139–41, 197–8, 200–1; clay targets, 252, 254, 256, 258, 260; doubles, one-two

INDEX

shooting (*cont.*)
flushes, 113, 140–1, 192, 258; dove, 194, 263; duck, 195–6, 256, 263; eye, 254; eye, master, 251; flinching, 189, 259; focus, 145, 247, 252–4; goose, 198–9, 263; grouse, prairie, 199–200; grouse, ruffed, 73–8, 82–3, 102–4, 113–14, 132, 181, 209, 252, 255–62, 264–5, 287–96, 298–300; gun carry, 260; instinctive, 252; Italy, 197; lead, estimating, 250–1, 258; long shots, 145, 257–8; manners, 49, 185; mount-and-overtake, 145–6, 247, 252–5, 258; m-and-o, movie sequence of, 145; m-and-o, time of, 253; mounting, 50, 249–50, 253, 259–61; over points, 67–8, 102, 140, 192, 238; pheasants, 144–6, 149–50, 156–60, 162–3, 172, 254, 260, 263, 292, 295; pre-1900, 30, 41–2, 135, 175, 207–8, 263; psychological factor, 258, 261–2; slump, 258, 261–2; snap shooting, 252, 258; spot shooting, 251, 253, 258–60; stance, 103, 260; sustained lead, pointing out, 251, 253, 258; swing, 253, 257, 260; swing, fast, *see* mount-and-overtake; turkey, 199, 202–4, 286–7; women, 188–9; woodcock, 50–1, 55–6, 60, 64, 201–2, 254, 258, 292–3, 296–9

Shooting Flying (Watts), 247

shotgun: action, box lock, 278; action, sidelock, 278–9; balance, 249; barrels, Damascus, 179, 281; barrels, rifled, 191; bead, 252, 280; chambers, 280; choke, 50, 56, 254–7, 278–9, 282; drilling, 190; English trunk case, 278–9; fit, 50, 248–51; fit, test for, 248–9, *and see also* shotgun stock; gauge, 50, 140, 189, 256, 278–9, 282; grouse gun, 248, 255, 257, 282; muzzle loader, 165, 191, 196; pattern, 248, 256–7; pattern, killing circle, 254, 257; proof marks, 282; quail gun, 140; range, 189; trigger, double, 258; trigger, single, 258; trigger, weight, 189, 253–5, 279, 281; women's, 189; woodcock gun, 50, 56, 254, 278, 282

shotgun stock: alteration, 249, 250, 280; butt, 249, 251, 278; cast-off, 248, 259; cheek point, 250; comb, 250; drop, 248, 250; heel, 250; pitch at, 251; length, 249; oil finish, 280; restocking, 158, 249, 279

shots, types of: crossing, 253, 257; going-away, 145, 253, 257; incoming, 259–60, 280; overhead, 260; quartering, 253; rising, 253; 259, 280; straightaway, 145, 253, 258–9

Silent Spring (Carson), 52

Somerfield (Pa.), 180

spaniel, Brittany, 160, 164, 200, 230; *see also* dogs, gun

spaniel, English springer, 230; *see also* dogs, gun

Springer, Cliff, 179–82; *see also photo insert*

Springer, Frank Wright, 179–80

stock: *see* shotgun stock

Stoner, Robert G., 184

Stony River (W.Va.), 43, 99, 176

Strother, David Hunter (Porte Crayon), 41

succession forest, 24, 36, 43

Susquehanna River (Pa.), 195

swamp, 29, 31, 38, 40; *see also* bog

Tableland (Md.), 26, 29–31

There Are No Dull Dark Days (Blogg), 13, 213

Thomas, Art, 117, 185, 295–6

Thoreau, Henry David, 193

Thornhill (Winchester, Va.), 139, 287

timbering, 23, 27, 36, 42; clear-cutting, 27; pulpwood, 23, 27

Tower's Mountain House (W.Va.), 41

tramroads, 82, 99, 288, 290

turkey, 42–3, 126, 175, 181, 199, 202–4, 287

Twenty-two Mile Grade: *see* Loop Road

U.S. Fish & Wildlife Service, 53, 199

Index

U.S. Food & Drug Administration, 52–3
U.S. Forest Service, 38, 41, 197

Viering, Fred, 178
Virginia bobwhite coverts, 139–41
Virginia Canaan, The (Porte Crayon), 41
Vizslas, 230

Waddington, Richard, 153
Watoga State Park (W.Va.), 33–5
Watts, Alaric Alexander, 247, 253
weather: *see* bobwhite quail *and* grouse *and* pheasant *and* woodcock
Webley, James, shotgun, 179
Weimaraner, 160, 162, 230; *see also* dogs, gun
West Virginia bobwhite, 197; chukar, 169; grouse, 26–9, 33–44; pheasant, 19; woodcock, 15, 47–72
Westerman, Charles, 199
Whitford, C. B., 244
Whyel, Tom, 201
Wild Animals I Have Known (Seton), 109
wilderness, 36–7, 99, 129, 187
wildfowl, 152, 155, 159, 182, 195–6, 197, 251
wildfowlers, 181–2
Wilson, Lew, 150
Winchester (Va.), 41, 139, 287
Winchester Model 12 shotgun, 198
Winchester Model 21 shotgun, 197; *see also photo insert*
wing shooting: *see* shooting
Wingard, Bob, 195
women, shooting: *see* shooting, women
women shooters, 188–9

woodcock: age, 63; autumn ratio, 63; banding, 16, 51, 72; breeding, 15–16, 71–2; cattle, effect, 50, 59; courtship, sky dance, 69–72; coverts, 15–17, *and see also* cover; drought, effect, 48; egg, 71–2; flight and behavior, 54–5, 57, 64, 68; "flight birds," 16, 64; flights, migratory, 16–17, 48, 62–3, 71; ground, on, 57, 102; light level, effect, 57, 64, 70; moonlight, effect, 50, 71; moult, 63; "native birds," locals, 16, 64; nesting, 52, 71; pesticides, effect, *see* pesticides; *Philohela minor*, 50; population, 266; rain, 57, 61; range, 15; scent, repellent to dog, 54, 60; sex, 62; ratio in flight birds, 16, 72; shooting, 47–69; shooting, early season, effect, 72, *and see also* shooting; singing counts, 71–2; temperature, effect, 50; trapping, 51; voice, 69–72; weather, effect, 48, 57–9, 61, 70; whitewash, 17, 49, 59, 68; wing study, 52; wintering, 15, 52; moon, 47, 69; wounded, 53
Woodcock Hill (Pa.), 14
Worden, Riley, 43, 176–8, 269
Worden's Hotel, The (Davis, W.Va.), 43, 58, 176–8
Wright, Dr. A. E., 201

Yarmouth (Nova Scotia), 263
Yellow Creek (W.Va.), 82
Youghiogheny Dam (Pa.), 180
Youghiogheny House (Somerfield, Pa.), 180
Youghiogheny River (Md., Pa.), 25, 28–9, 181

A NOTE ON THE AUTHOR

The constant in George Evans's life has been upland shooting over English setters. Born in Uniontown, Pennsylvania, in 1906, educated at Carnegie Tech and the Chicago Art Institute, the author considered the years he had to spend in New York as a magazine illustrator as an exile from his favorite haunt, the grouse coverts of the Alleghenies. Mr. Evans and his wife, Kay, now live in the mountains of West Virginia where a setter and a fine old shotgun are always present. For a number of years they collaborated as a husband-and-wife team on mystery novels and other fiction. Mr. Evans, who has been doing freelance writing since shortly after his stint in the Navy in World War II, continues to write for the outdoor magazines, particularly *Field & Stream*, *Pennsylvania Game News*, and *The American Sportsman*.

A NOTE ON THE TYPE

The text of this book is set in Monticello, a Linotype revival of the original Binny & Ronaldson Roman No. 1, cut by Archibald Binny and cast in 1796 by that Philadelphia type foundry. The face was named Monticello in honor of its use in the monumental fifty-volume *Papers of Thomas Jefferson*, published by Princeton University Press. Monticello is a transitional type design, embodying certain features of Bulmer and Baskerville, but it is a distinguished face in its own right.

The book was composed, printed, and bound by The Haddon Craftsmen, Inc., Scranton, Pennsylvania.

Typography and binding design by
GUY FLEMING.